CheMystery

To: L $\boxed{O}$ $\boxed{Ga}$ $\boxed{N}$

C. A. Bruce

Science,
s!

'17

CheMystery

Written by C. A. PREECE
Illustrated by JOSH REYNOLDS

ThunderStone Books
Las Vegas, Nevada

Editing by Hannah Krieger
Lab reports design and layout by Kyle Preece and Brandi Ellebruck
Coloring by Rachel Clarke and Josh Reynolds
Published by ThunderStone Books

978-1-63411-008-2 (ISBN 13)

I want to dedicate this work to my late grandpa and uncle Jim; without their love, guidance and life lessons I would merely be the subject of chemistry instead of being able to subject it onto you.

- C. A. Preece

Dedicated to grandpa Andy. Had he not passed down his interests in science, comics, and nerdy pursuits, I could possibly be doing something really boring, like baseball.

- Josh Reynolds

Chapter 1

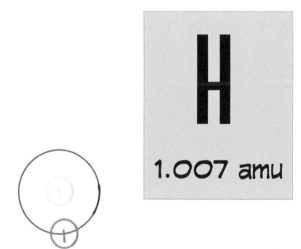

H

1.007 amu

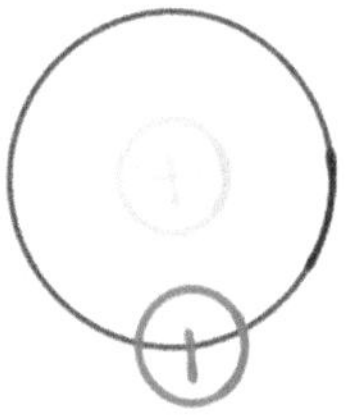

Hydrogen is an element but in nature exists as H_2: a compound.

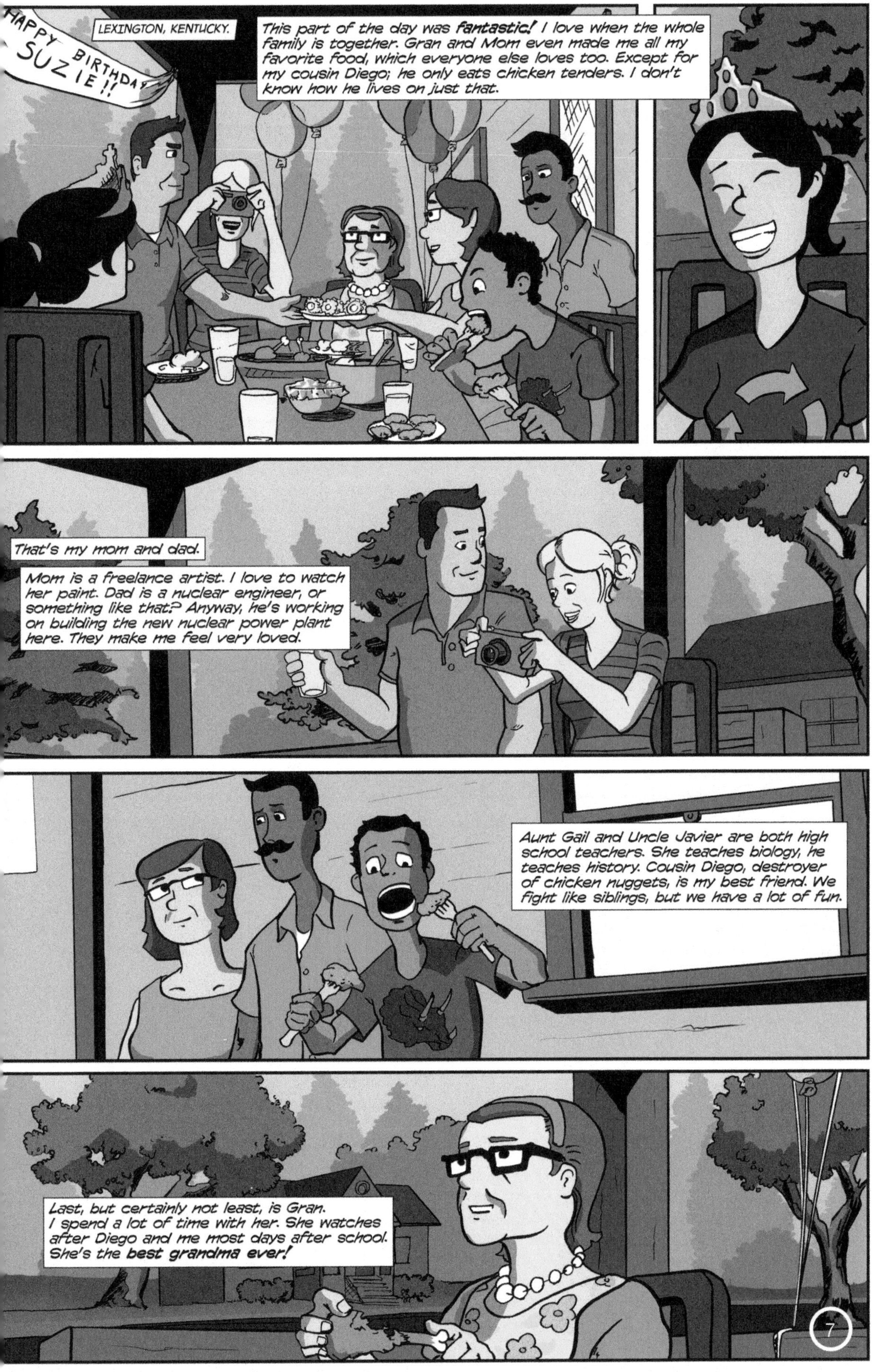

HAPPY BIRTHDAY SUZIE!!
LEXINGTON, KENTUCKY.
This part of the day was **fantastic!** I love when the whole family is together. Gran and Mom even made me all my favorite food, which everyone else loves too. Except for my cousin Diego; he only eats chicken tenders. I don't know how he lives on just that.
That's my mom and dad.
Mom is a freelance artist. I love to watch her paint. Dad is a nuclear engineer, or something like that? Anyway, he's working on building the new nuclear power plant here. They make me feel very loved.
Aunt Gail and Uncle Javier are both high school teachers. She teaches biology, he teaches history. Cousin Diego, destroyer of chicken nuggets, is my best friend. We fight like siblings, but we have a lot of fun.
Last, but certainly not least, is Gran. I spend a lot of time with her. She watches after Diego and me most days after school. She's the **best grandma ever!**

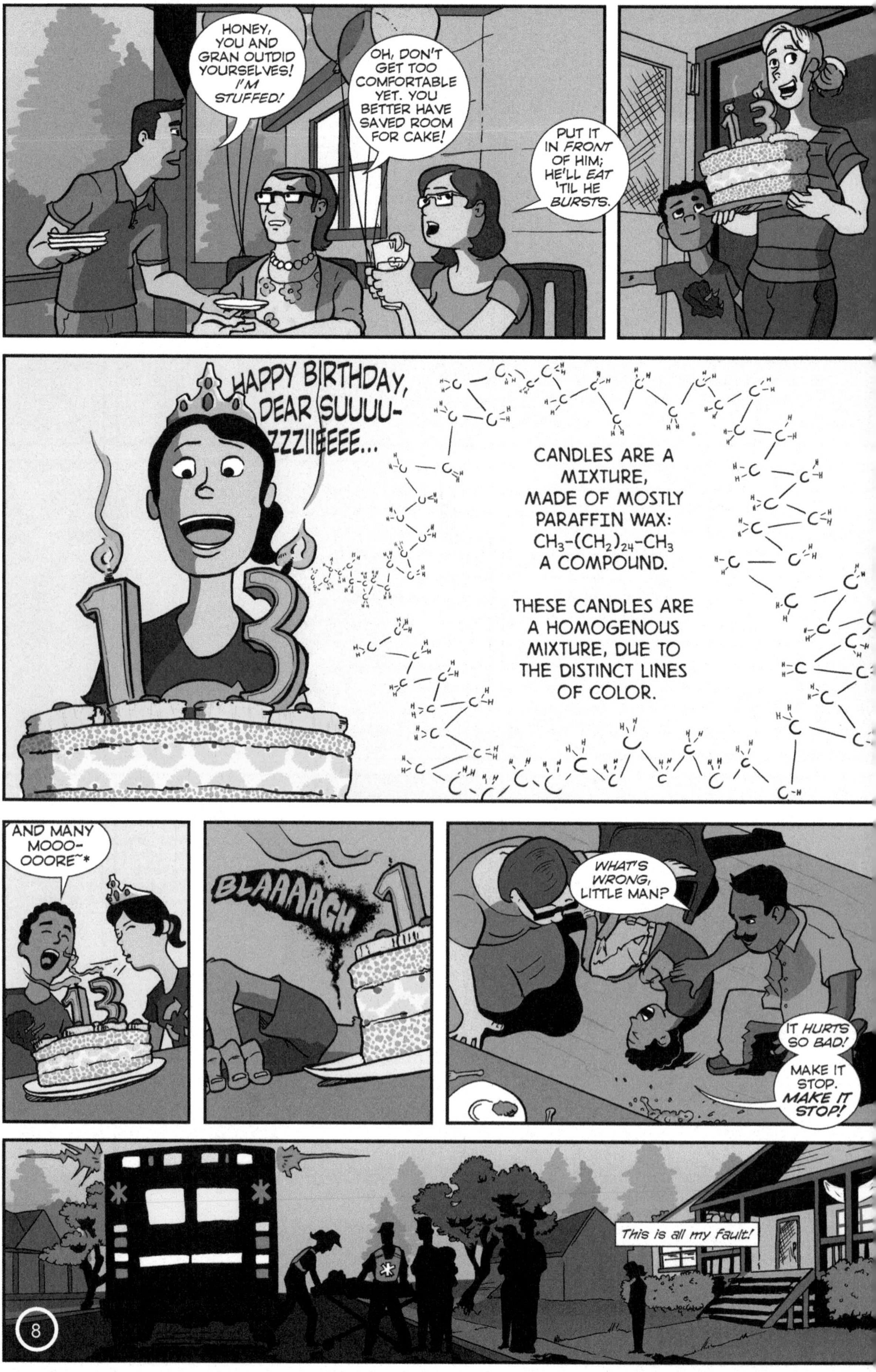
HONEY, YOU AND GRAN OUTDID YOURSELVES! I'M STUFFED!
OH, DON'T GET TOO COMFORTABLE YET. YOU BETTER HAVE SAVED ROOM FOR CAKE!
PUT IT IN FRONT OF HIM; HE'LL EAT 'TIL HE BURSTS.
HAPPY BIRTHDAY, DEAR SUUUU-ZZZIIEEEE...
CANDLES ARE A MIXTURE, MADE OF MOSTLY PARAFFIN WAX: $CH_3-(CH_2)_{24}-CH_3$ A COMPOUND.
THESE CANDLES ARE A HOMOGENOUS MIXTURE, DUE TO THE DISTINCT LINES OF COLOR.
AND MANY MOOO-OOORE~*
BLAAAAGH
WHAT'S WRONG, LITTLE MAN?
IT HURTS SO BAD!
MAKE IT STOP. MAKE IT STOP!
This is all my fault!

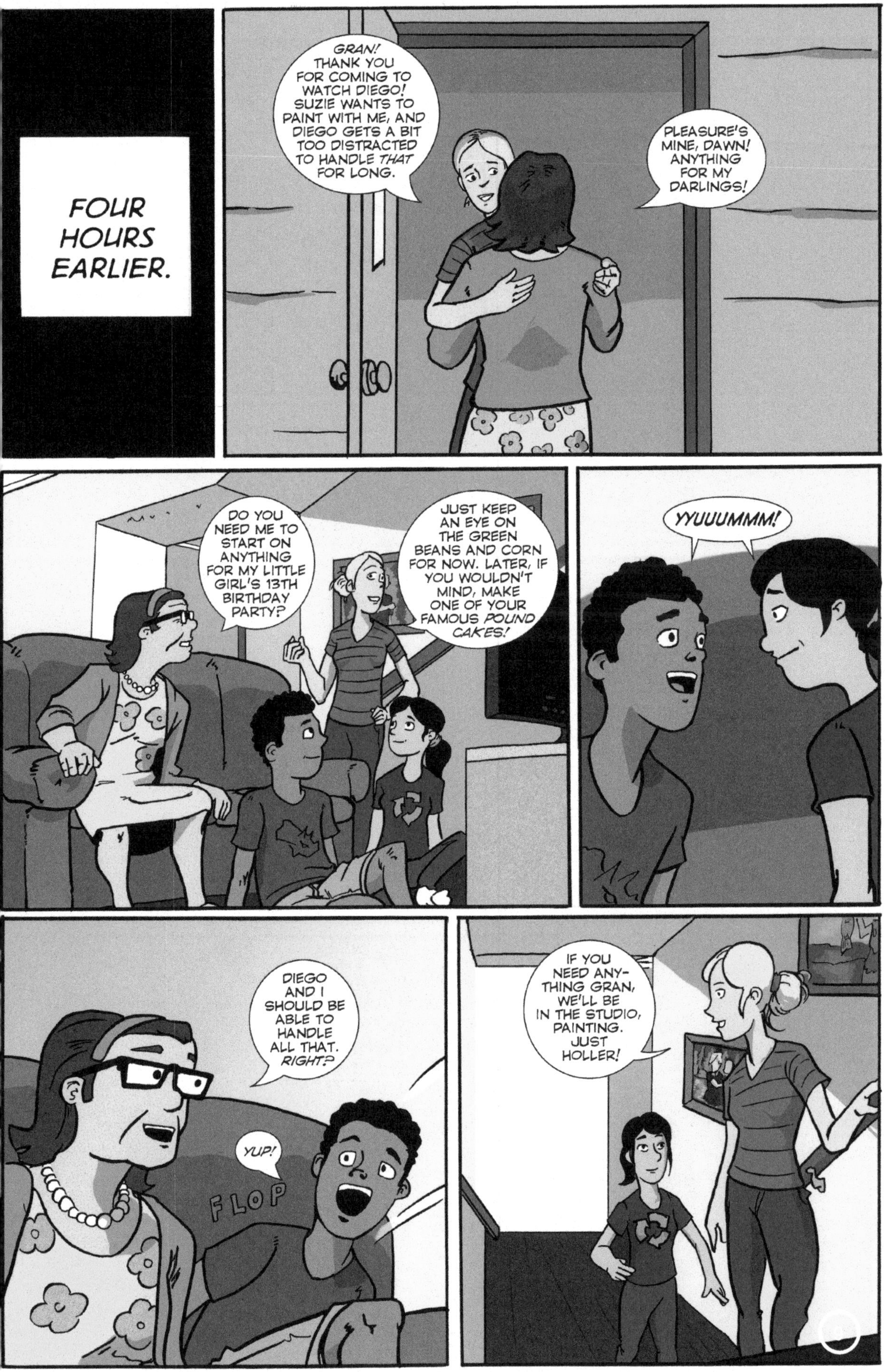
FOUR HOURS EARLIER.
GRAN! THANK YOU FOR COMING TO WATCH DIEGO! SUZIE WANTS TO PAINT WITH ME, AND DIEGO GETS A BIT TOO DISTRACTED TO HANDLE *THAT* FOR LONG.
PLEASURE'S MINE, DAWN! ANYTHING FOR MY DARLINGS!
DO YOU NEED ME TO START ON ANYTHING FOR MY LITTLE GIRL'S 13TH BIRTHDAY PARTY?
JUST KEEP AN EYE ON THE GREEN BEANS AND CORN FOR NOW. LATER, IF YOU WOULDN'T MIND, MAKE ONE OF YOUR FAMOUS *POUND CAKES!*
YYUUUMMM!
DIEGO AND I SHOULD BE ABLE TO HANDLE ALL THAT. *RIGHT?*
YUP!
FLOP
IF YOU NEED ANY-THING GRAN, WE'LL BE IN THE STUDIO, PAINTING. JUST HOLLER!

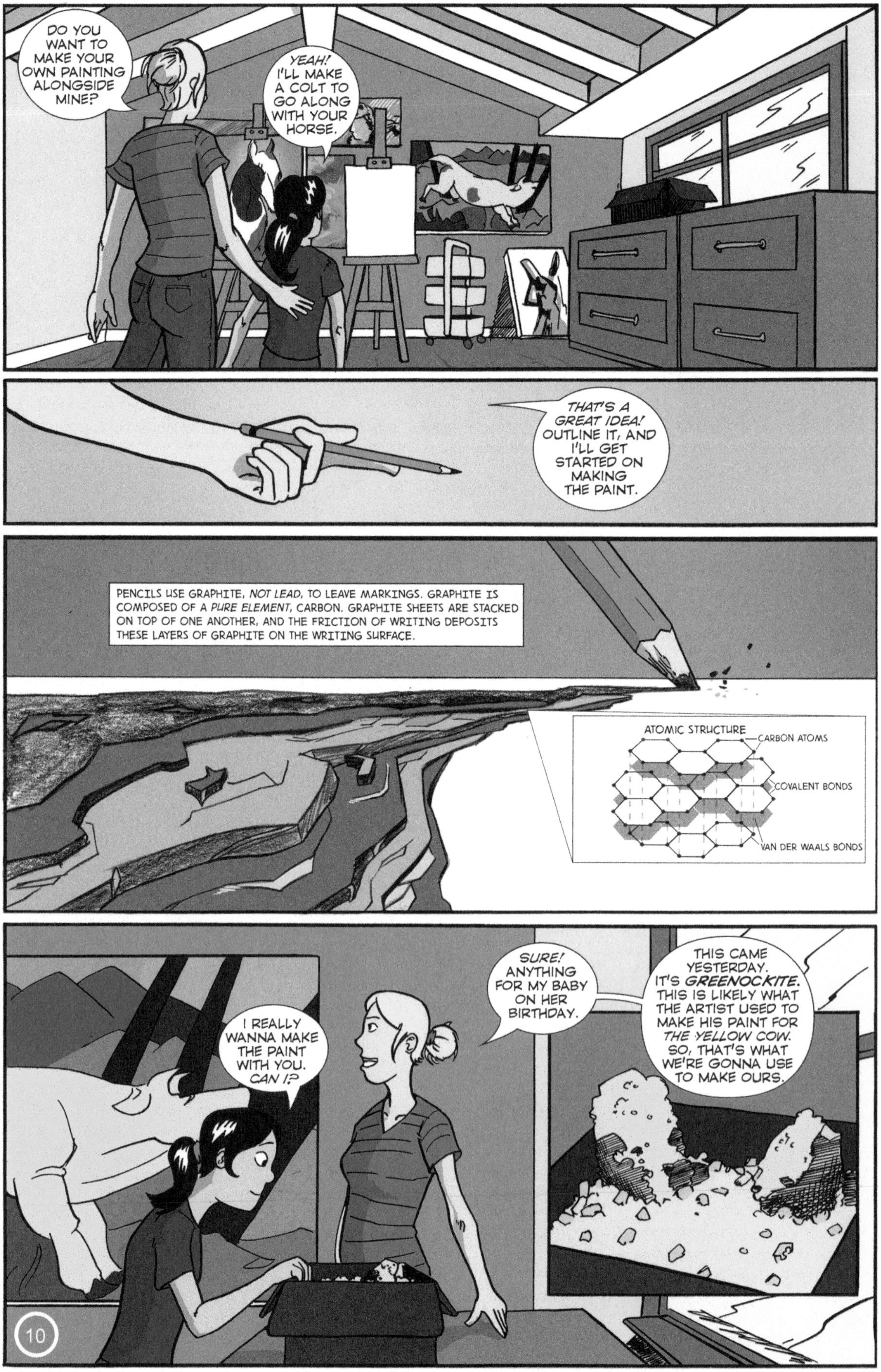
DO YOU WANT TO MAKE YOUR OWN PAINTING ALONGSIDE MINE?
YEAH! I'LL MAKE A COLT TO GO ALONG WITH YOUR HORSE.
THAT'S A GREAT IDEA! OUTLINE IT, AND I'LL GET STARTED ON MAKING THE PAINT.
PENCILS USE GRAPHITE, *NOT LEAD*, TO LEAVE MARKINGS. GRAPHITE IS COMPOSED OF A *PURE ELEMENT*, CARBON. GRAPHITE SHEETS ARE STACKED ON TOP OF ONE ANOTHER, AND THE FRICTION OF WRITING DEPOSITS THESE LAYERS OF GRAPHITE ON THE WRITING SURFACE.
ATOMIC STRUCTURE
CARBON ATOMS
COVALENT BONDS
VAN DER WAALS BONDS
I REALLY WANNA MAKE THE PAINT WITH YOU. *CAN I?*
SURE! ANYTHING FOR MY BABY ON HER BIRTHDAY.
THIS CAME YESTERDAY. IT'S ***GREENOCKITE.*** THIS IS LIKELY WHAT THE ARTIST USED TO MAKE HIS PAINT FOR *THE YELLOW COW*. SO, THAT'S WHAT WE'RE GONNA USE TO MAKE OURS.

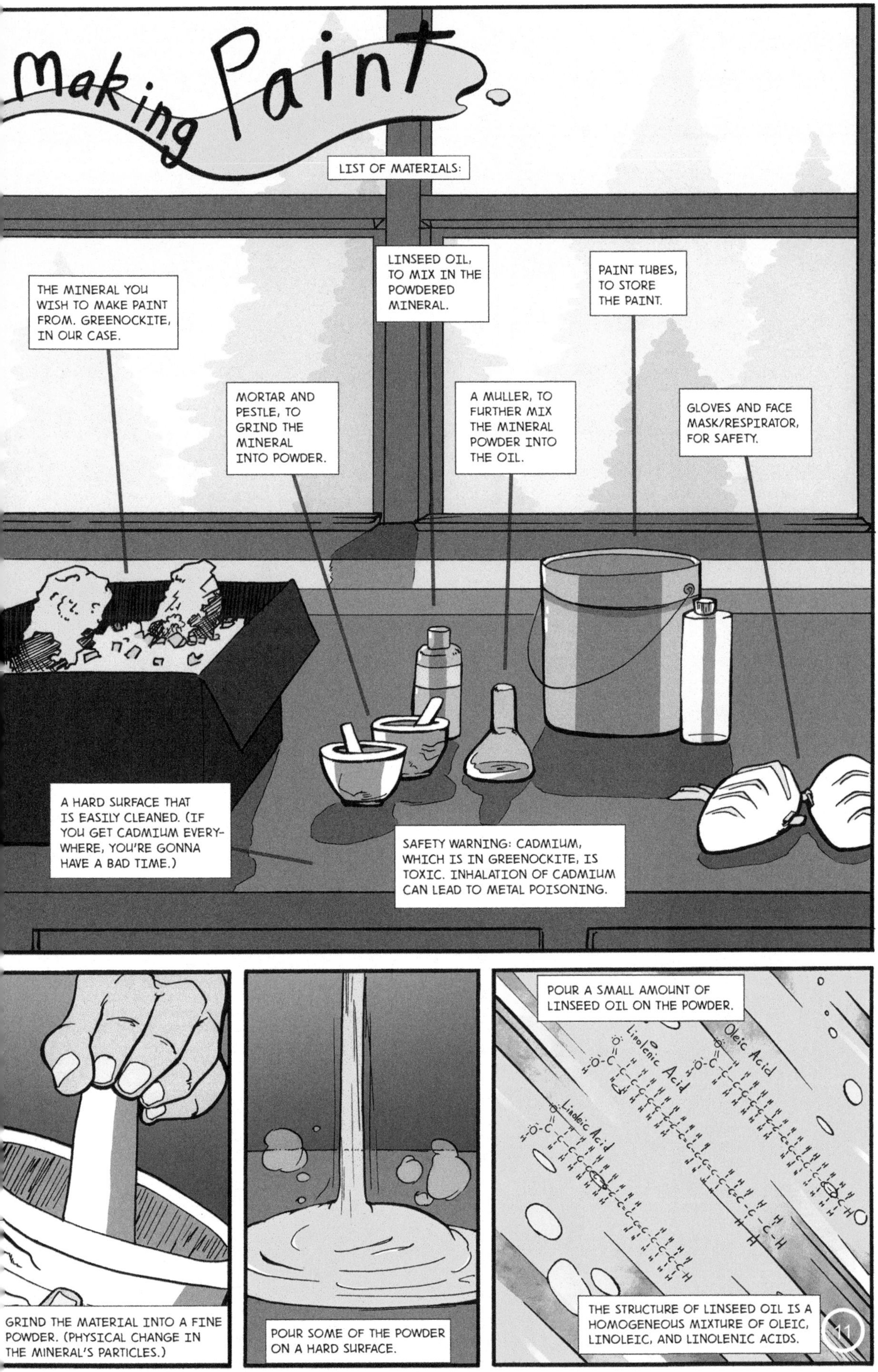
Making Paint
LIST OF MATERIALS:
THE MINERAL YOU WISH TO MAKE PAINT FROM. GREENOCKITE, IN OUR CASE.
MORTAR AND PESTLE, TO GRIND THE MINERAL INTO POWDER.
LINSEED OIL, TO MIX IN THE POWDERED MINERAL.
A MULLER, TO FURTHER MIX THE MINERAL POWDER INTO THE OIL.
PAINT TUBES, TO STORE THE PAINT.
GLOVES AND FACE MASK/RESPIRATOR, FOR SAFETY.
A HARD SURFACE THAT IS EASILY CLEANED. (IF YOU GET CADMIUM EVERY-WHERE, YOU'RE GONNA HAVE A BAD TIME.)
SAFETY WARNING: CADMIUM, WHICH IS IN GREENOCKITE, IS TOXIC. INHALATION OF CADMIUM CAN LEAD TO METAL POISONING.
GRIND THE MATERIAL INTO A FINE POWDER. (PHYSICAL CHANGE IN THE MINERAL'S PARTICLES.)
POUR SOME OF THE POWDER ON A HARD SURFACE.
POUR A SMALL AMOUNT OF LINSEED OIL ON THE POWDER.
Linolenic Acid
Oleic Acid
Linoleic Acid
THE STRUCTURE OF LINSEED OIL IS A HOMOGENEOUS MIXTURE OF OLEIC, LINOLEIC, AND LINOLENIC ACIDS.
11

USE A PALETTE KNIFE TO MIX THE OIL AND MINERAL

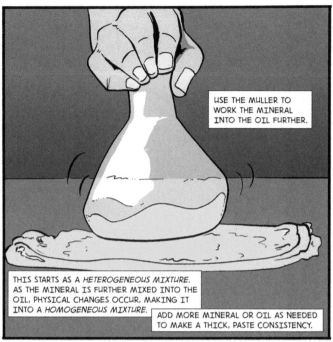

USE THE MULLER TO WORK THE MINERAL INTO THE OIL FURTHER.

THIS STARTS AS A *HETEROGENEOUS MIXTURE*. AS THE MINERAL IS FURTHER MIXED INTO THE OIL, PHYSICAL CHANGES OCCUR, MAKING IT INTO A *HOMOGENEOUS MIXTURE*.

ADD MORE MINERAL OR OIL AS NEEDED TO MAKE A THICK, PASTE CONSISTENCY.

STORE THE PAINT.

CLEANUP!

Paint SCIENCE

PAINTS ARE *HOMOGENEOUS MIXTURES*. IF THEY SET TOO LONG THEY WILL SEPARATE AND BECOME *HETEROGENEOUS* MIXTURES.

OIL PAINTS, AS THEY DRY, UNDERGO *A CHEMICAL CHANGE*. AS THEY ARE EXPOSED TO AIR THEY *POLYMERIZE*.

POLYMERIZATION IS WHEN COMPOUNDS START BONDING AND FORMING LONG CHAINS OF MOLECULES. THEY ARE NO LONGER THEIR ORIGINAL COMPOUND, BUT A *NEW ONE* WITH NEW PHYSICAL AND CHEMICAL PROPERTIES.

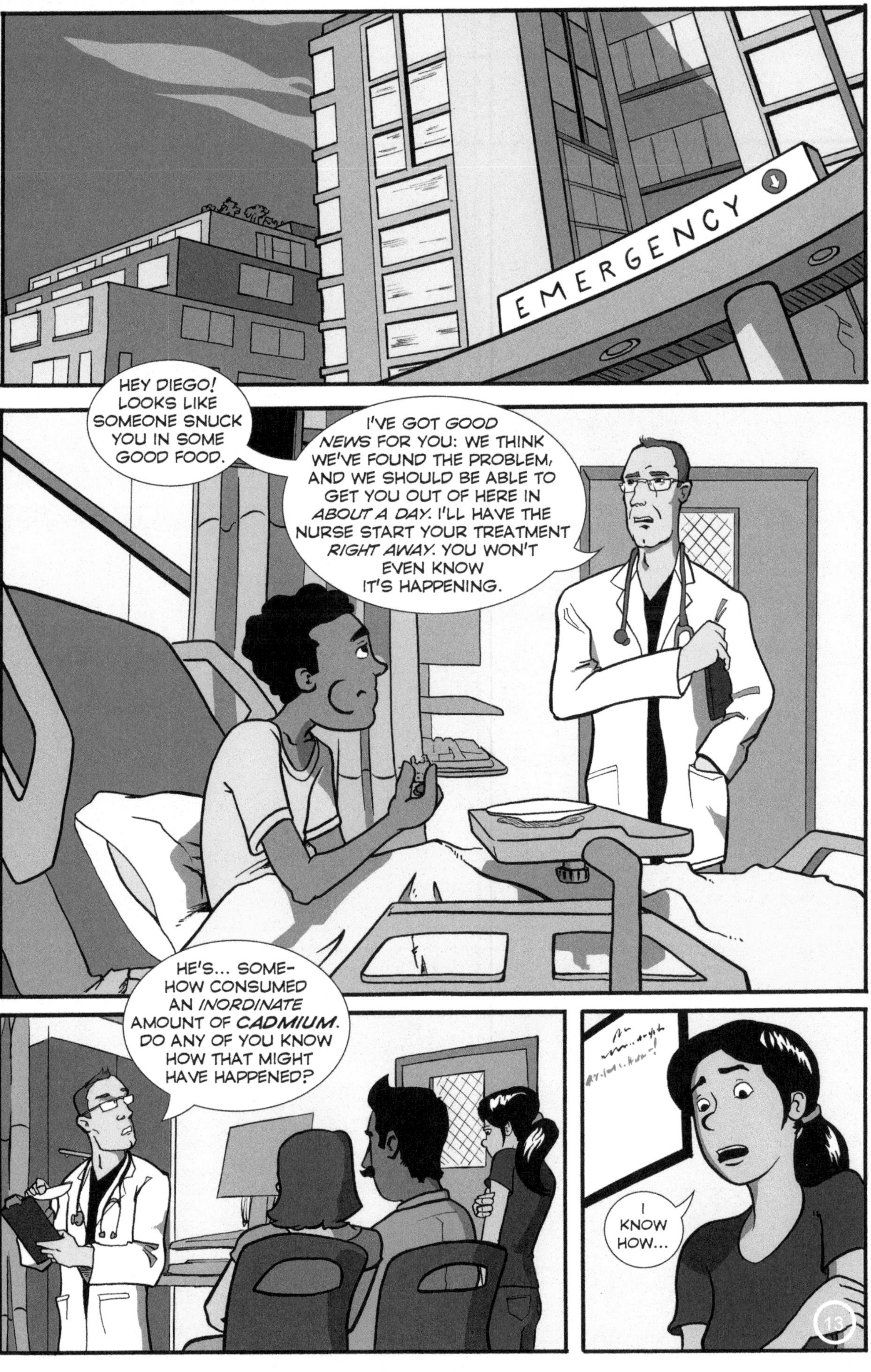
EMERGENCY
HEY DIEGO! LOOKS LIKE SOMEONE SNUCK YOU IN SOME GOOD FOOD.
I'VE GOT *GOOD NEWS* FOR YOU: WE THINK WE'VE FOUND THE PROBLEM, AND WE SHOULD BE ABLE TO GET YOU OUT OF HERE IN *ABOUT A DAY*. I'LL HAVE THE NURSE START YOUR TREATMENT *RIGHT AWAY*. YOU WON'T EVEN KNOW IT'S HAPPENING.
HE'S... SOMEHOW CONSUMED AN *INORDINATE* AMOUNT OF ***CADMIUM***. DO ANY OF YOU KNOW HOW THAT MIGHT HAVE HAPPENED?
I KNOW HOW...
13

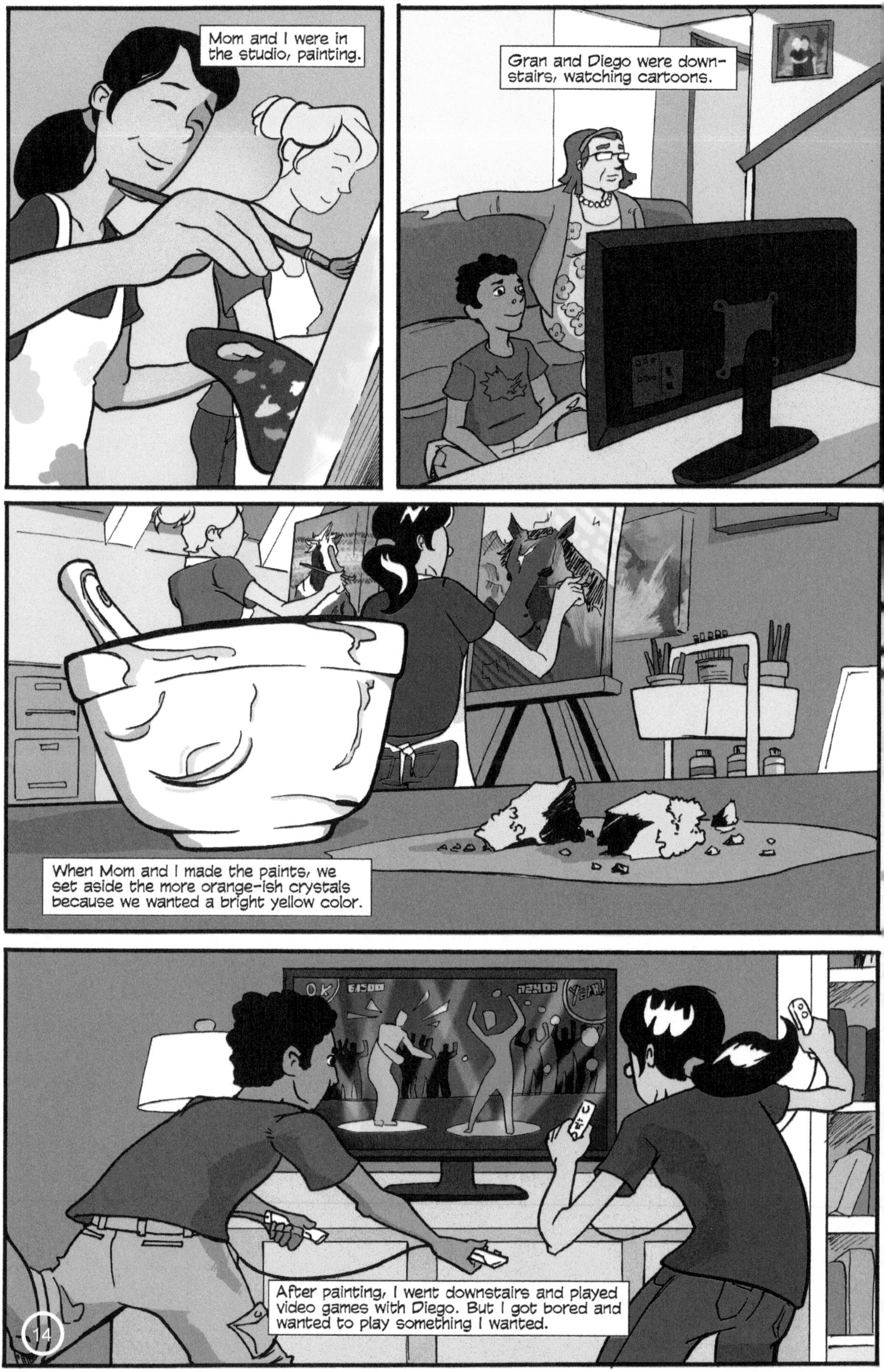
Mom and I were in the studio, painting.
Gran and Diego were downstairs, watching cartoons.
When Mom and I made the paints, we set aside the more orange-ish crystals because we wanted a bright yellow color.
After painting, I went downstairs and played video games with Diego. But I got bored and wanted to play something I wanted.

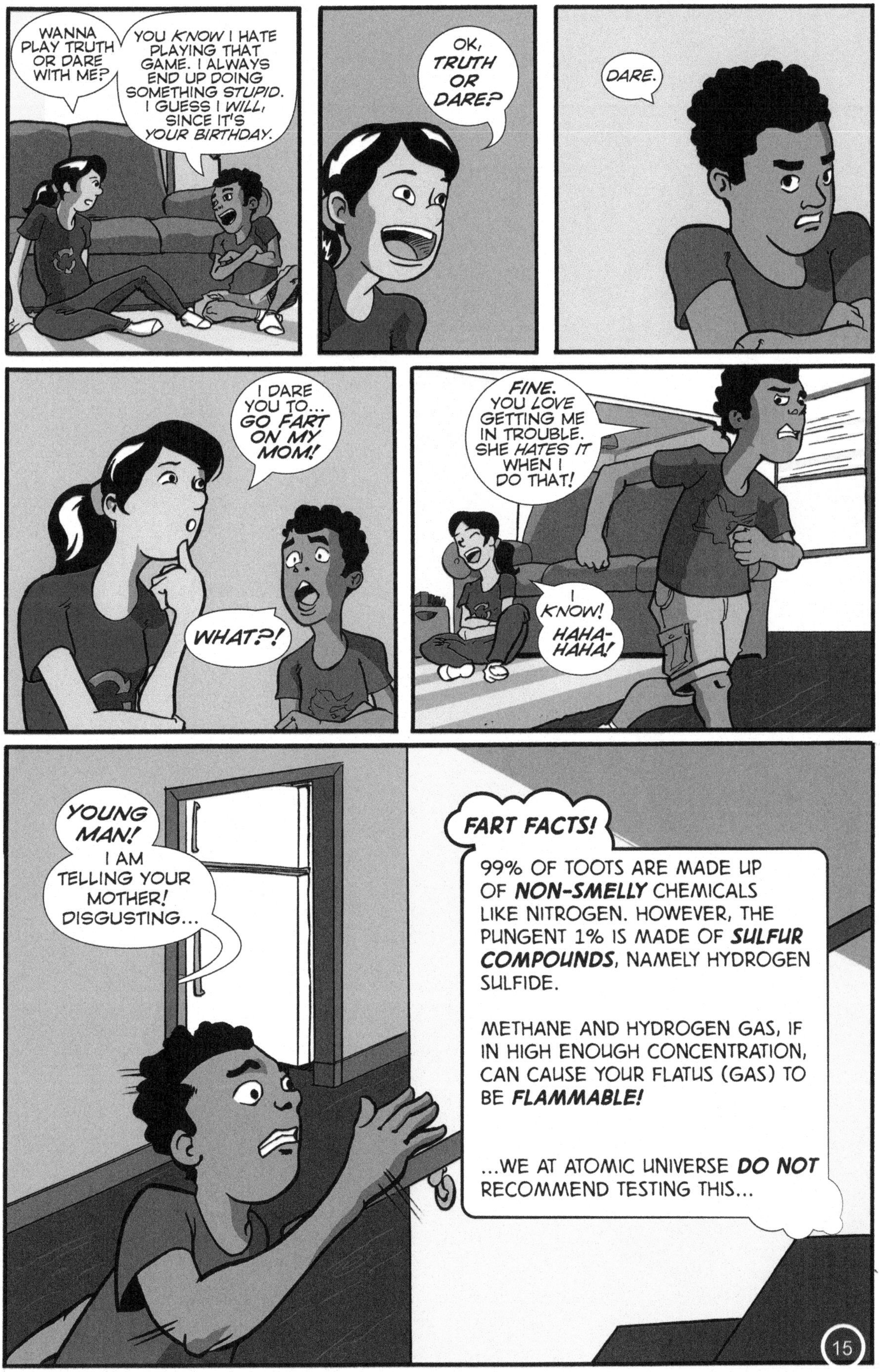
WANNA PLAY TRUTH OR DARE WITH ME?
YOU KNOW I HATE PLAYING THAT GAME. I ALWAYS END UP DOING SOMETHING STUPID. I GUESS I WILL, SINCE IT'S YOUR BIRTHDAY.
OK, TRUTH OR DARE?
DARE.
I DARE YOU TO... GO FART ON MY MOM!
WHAT?!
FINE. YOU LOVE GETTING ME IN TROUBLE. SHE HATES IT WHEN I DO THAT!
I KNOW! HAHA-HAHA!
YOUNG MAN! I AM TELLING YOUR MOTHER! DISGUSTING...
FART FACTS!
99% OF TOOTS ARE MADE UP OF NON-SMELLY CHEMICALS LIKE NITROGEN. HOWEVER, THE PUNGENT 1% IS MADE OF SULFUR COMPOUNDS, NAMELY HYDROGEN SULFIDE.
METHANE AND HYDROGEN GAS, IF IN HIGH ENOUGH CONCENTRATION, CAN CAUSE YOUR FLATUS (GAS) TO BE FLAMMABLE!
...WE AT ATOMIC UNIVERSE DO NOT RECOMMEND TESTING THIS...

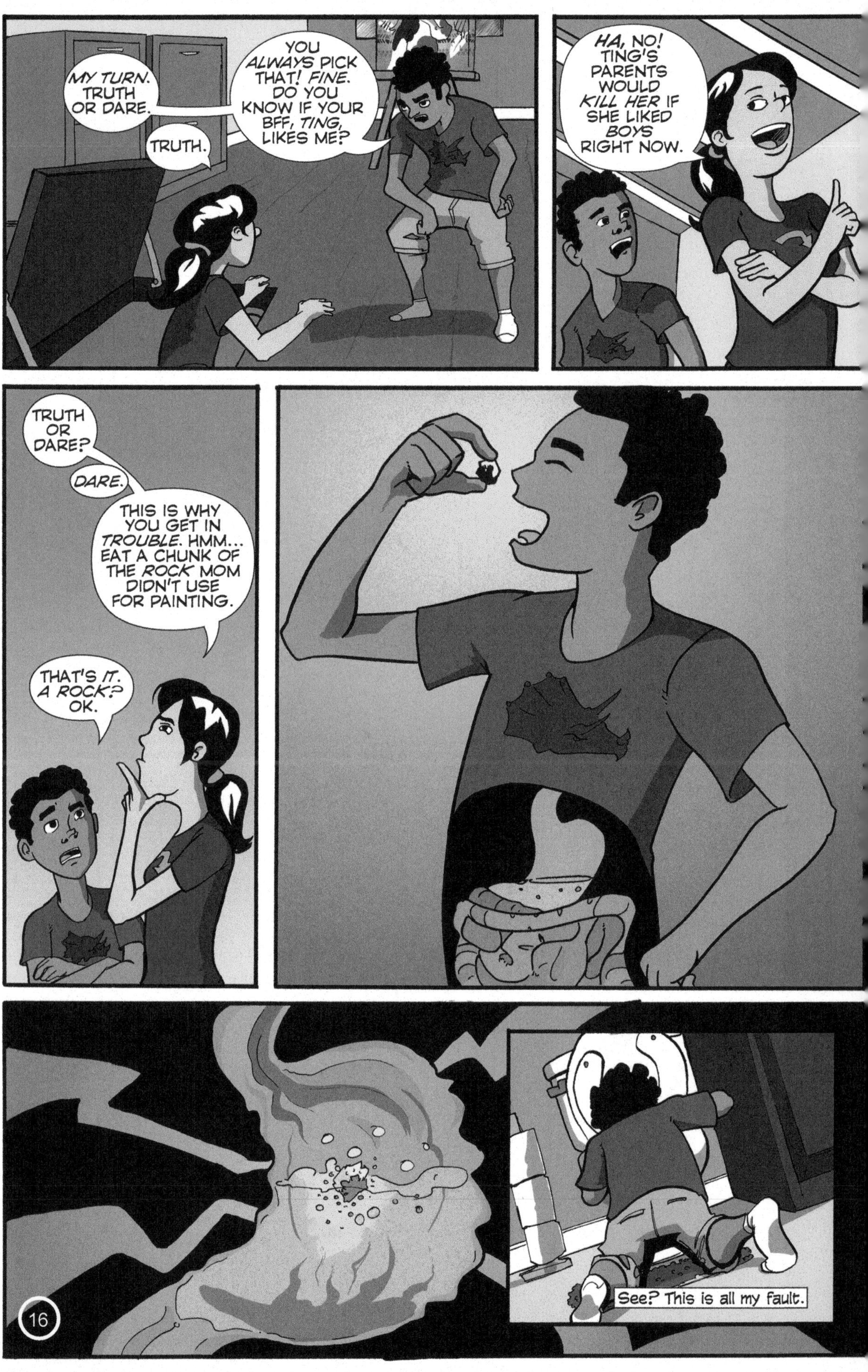
MY TURN. TRUTH OR DARE.
TRUTH.
YOU ALWAYS PICK THAT! FINE. DO YOU KNOW IF YOUR BFF, TING, LIKES ME?
HA, NO! TING'S PARENTS WOULD KILL HER IF SHE LIKED BOYS RIGHT NOW.
TRUTH OR DARE?
DARE.
THIS IS WHY YOU GET IN TROUBLE. HMM... EAT A CHUNK OF THE ROCK MOM DIDN'T USE FOR PAINTING.
THAT'S IT. A ROCK? OK.
See? This is all my fault.

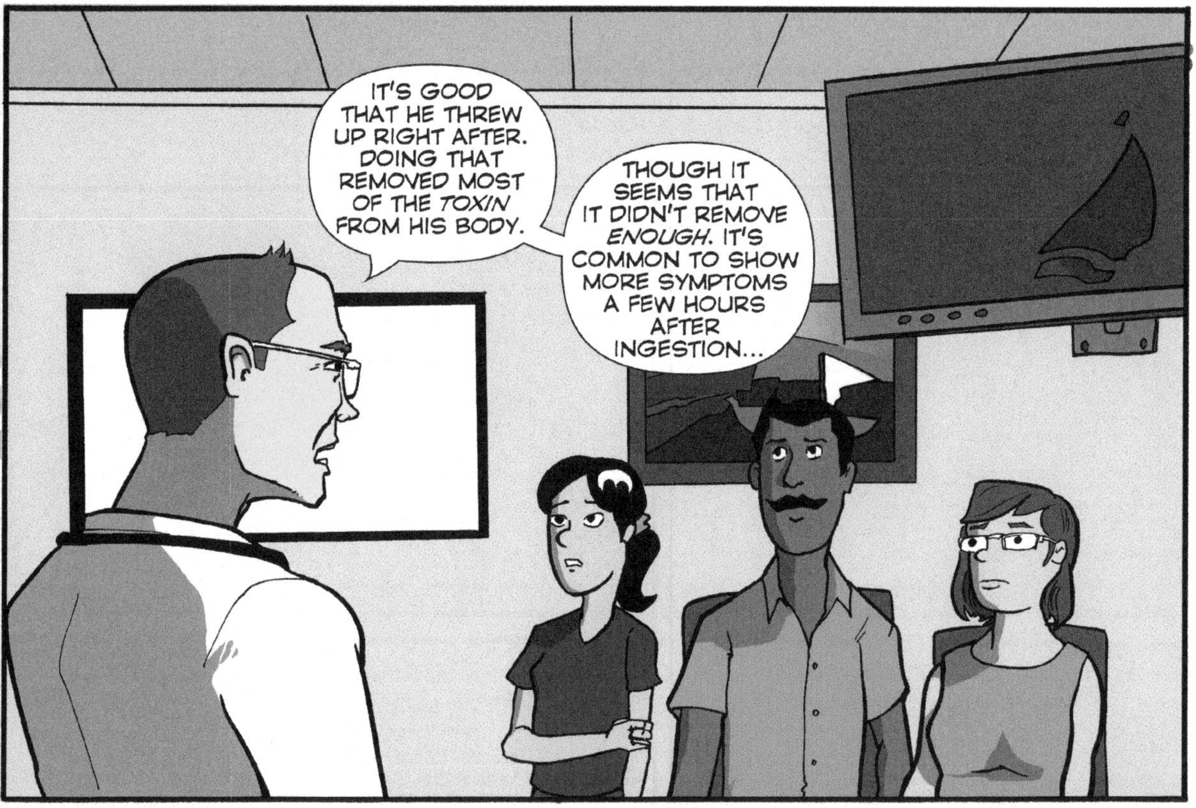
IT'S GOOD THAT HE THREW UP RIGHT AFTER. DOING THAT REMOVED MOST OF THE *TOXIN* FROM HIS BODY.
THOUGH IT SEEMS THAT IT DIDN'T REMOVE *ENOUGH*. IT'S COMMON TO SHOW MORE SYMPTOMS A FEW HOURS AFTER INGESTION...

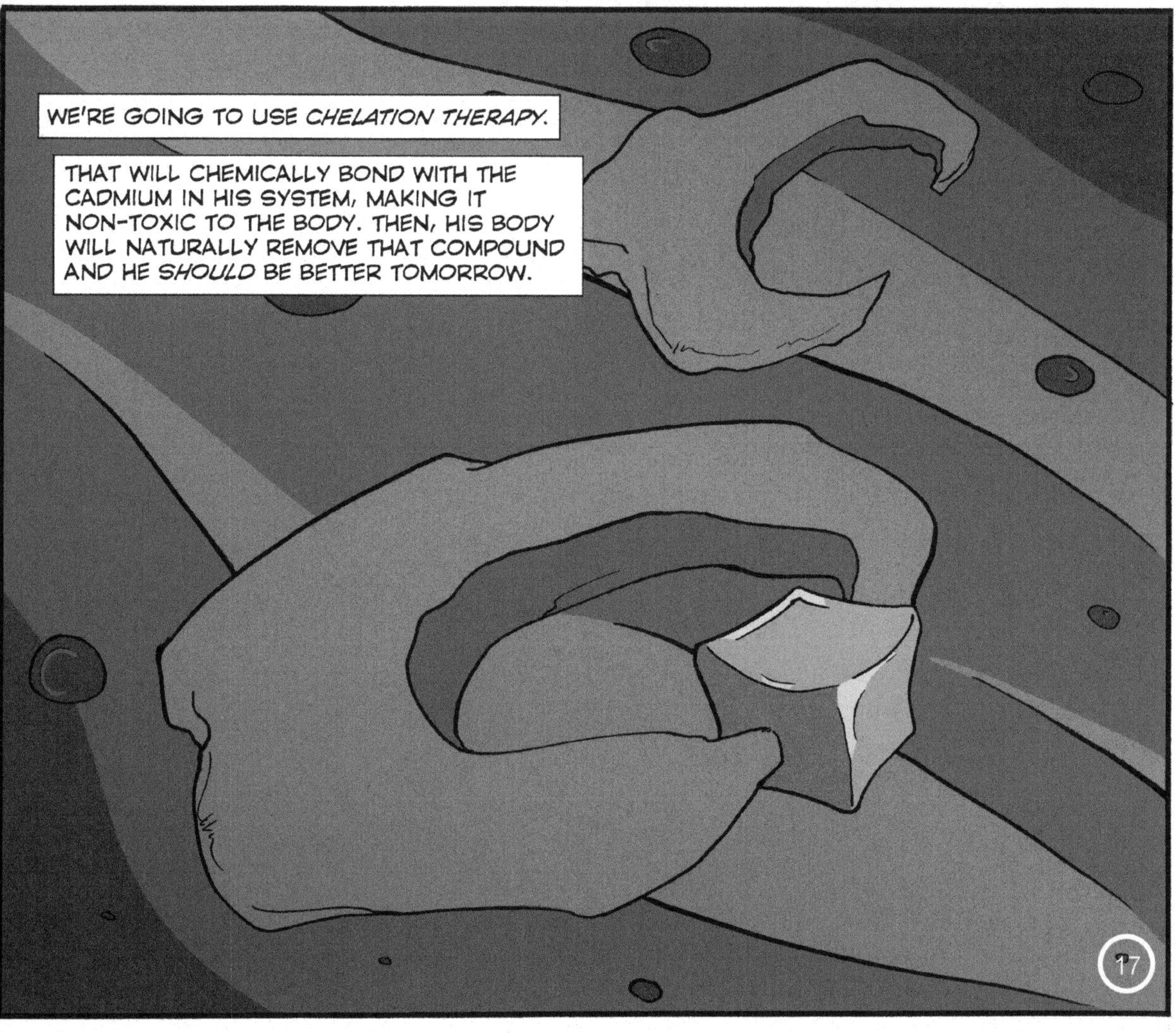
WE'RE GOING TO USE *CHELATION THERAPY*.
THAT WILL CHEMICALLY BOND WITH THE CADMIUM IN HIS SYSTEM, MAKING IT NON-TOXIC TO THE BODY. THEN, HIS BODY WILL NATURALLY REMOVE THAT COMPOUND AND HE *SHOULD* BE BETTER TOMORROW.

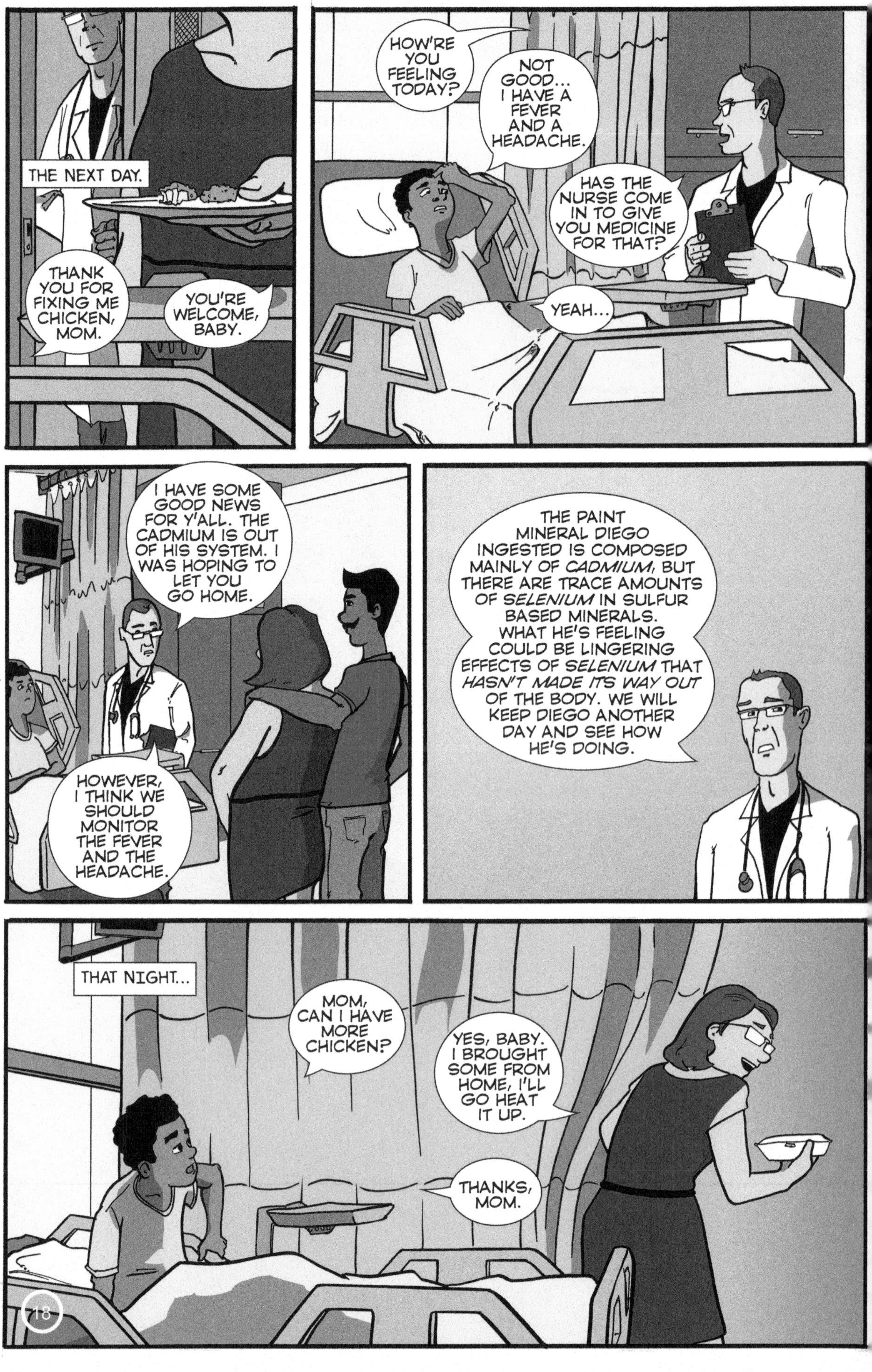
THE NEXT DAY.
THANK YOU FOR FIXING ME CHICKEN, MOM.
YOU'RE WELCOME, BABY.
HOW'RE YOU FEELING TODAY?
NOT GOOD... I HAVE A FEVER AND A HEADACHE.
HAS THE NURSE COME IN TO GIVE YOU MEDICINE FOR THAT?
YEAH...
I HAVE SOME GOOD NEWS FOR Y'ALL. THE CADMIUM IS OUT OF HIS SYSTEM. I WAS HOPING TO LET YOU GO HOME.
HOWEVER, I THINK WE SHOULD MONITOR THE FEVER AND THE HEADACHE.
THE PAINT MINERAL DIEGO INGESTED IS COMPOSED MAINLY OF *CADMIUM*, BUT THERE ARE TRACE AMOUNTS OF *SELENIUM* IN SULFUR BASED MINERALS. WHAT HE'S FEELING COULD BE LINGERING EFFECTS OF *SELENIUM* THAT *HASN'T MADE ITS WAY OUT* OF THE BODY. WE WILL KEEP DIEGO ANOTHER DAY AND SEE HOW HE'S DOING.
THAT NIGHT...
MOM, CAN I HAVE MORE CHICKEN?
YES, BABY. I BROUGHT SOME FROM HOME, I'LL GO HEAT IT UP.
THANKS, MOM.

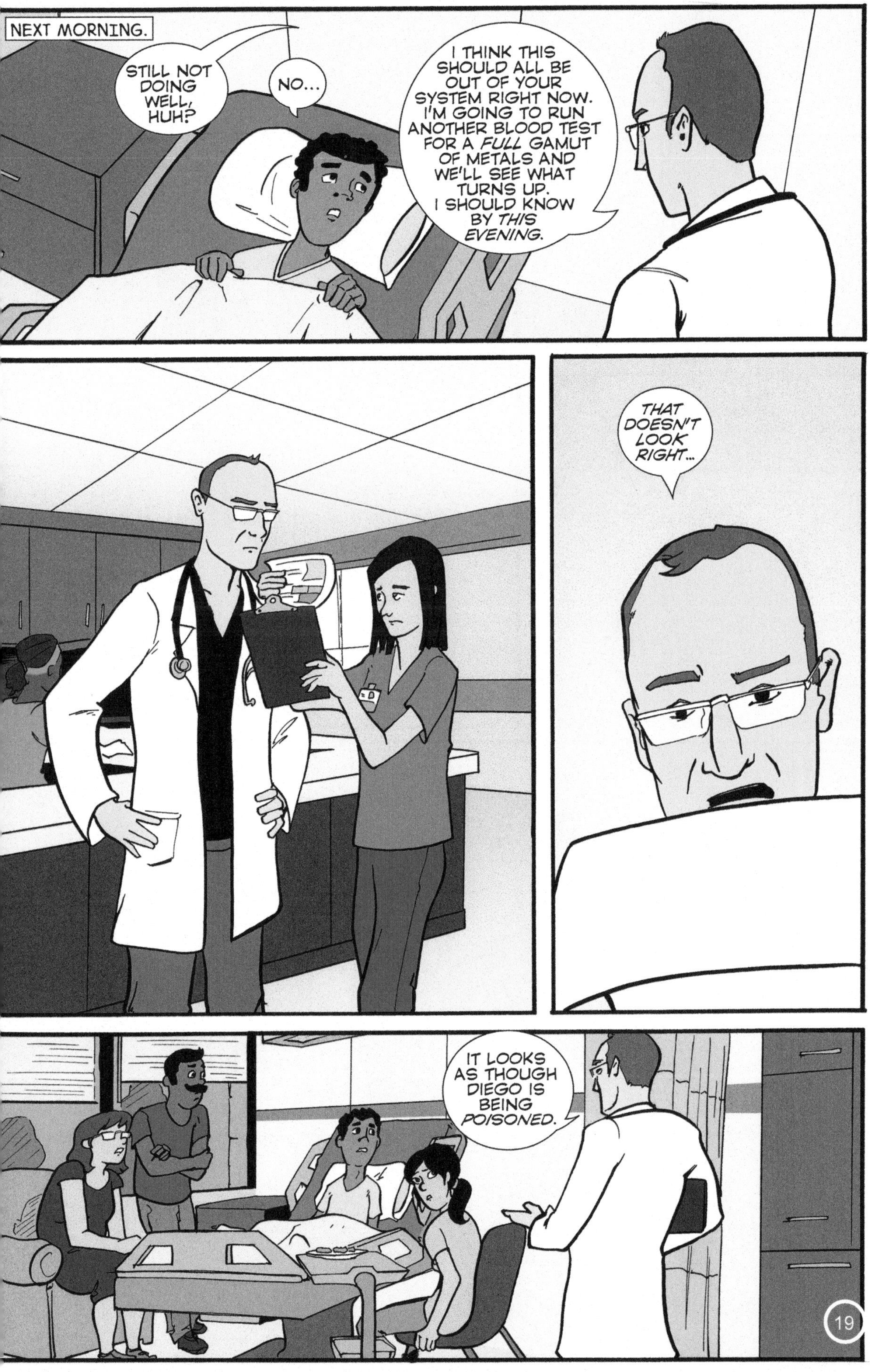
NEXT MORNING.
STILL NOT DOING WELL, HUH?
NO...
I THINK THIS SHOULD ALL BE OUT OF YOUR SYSTEM RIGHT NOW. I'M GOING TO RUN ANOTHER BLOOD TEST FOR A *FULL* GAMUT OF METALS AND WE'LL SEE WHAT TURNS UP. I SHOULD KNOW BY *THIS EVENING*.
THAT DOESN'T LOOK RIGHT...
IT LOOKS AS THOUGH DIEGO IS BEING *POISONED*.

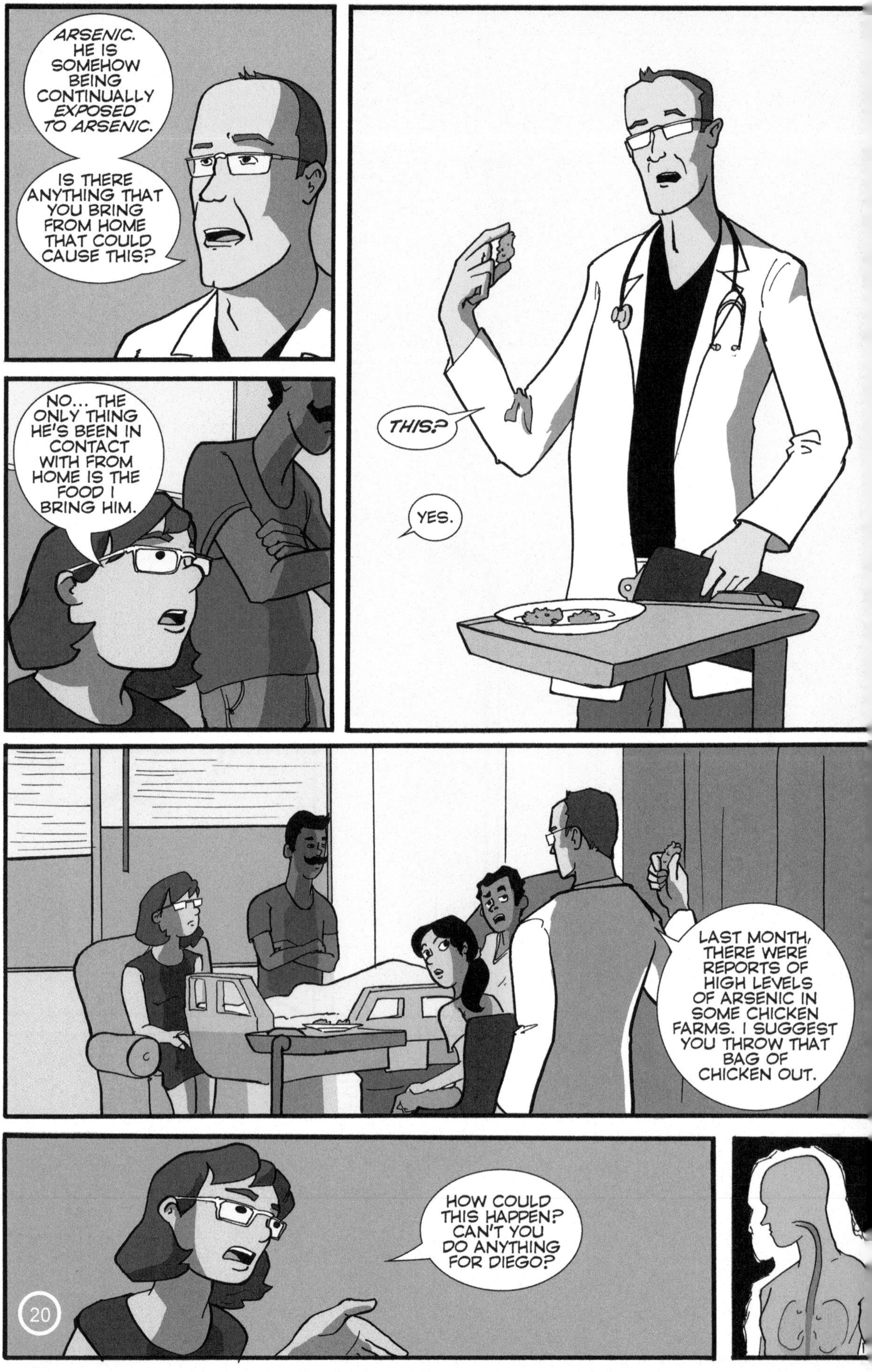
ARSENIC. HE IS SOMEHOW BEING CONTINUALLY EXPOSED TO ARSENIC.
IS THERE ANYTHING THAT YOU BRING FROM HOME THAT COULD CAUSE THIS?
THIS?
NO... THE ONLY THING HE'S BEEN IN CONTACT WITH FROM HOME IS THE FOOD I BRING HIM.
YES.
LAST MONTH, THERE WERE REPORTS OF HIGH LEVELS OF ARSENIC IN SOME CHICKEN FARMS. I SUGGEST YOU THROW THAT BAG OF CHICKEN OUT.
HOW COULD THIS HAPPEN? CAN'T YOU DO ANYTHING FOR DIEGO?

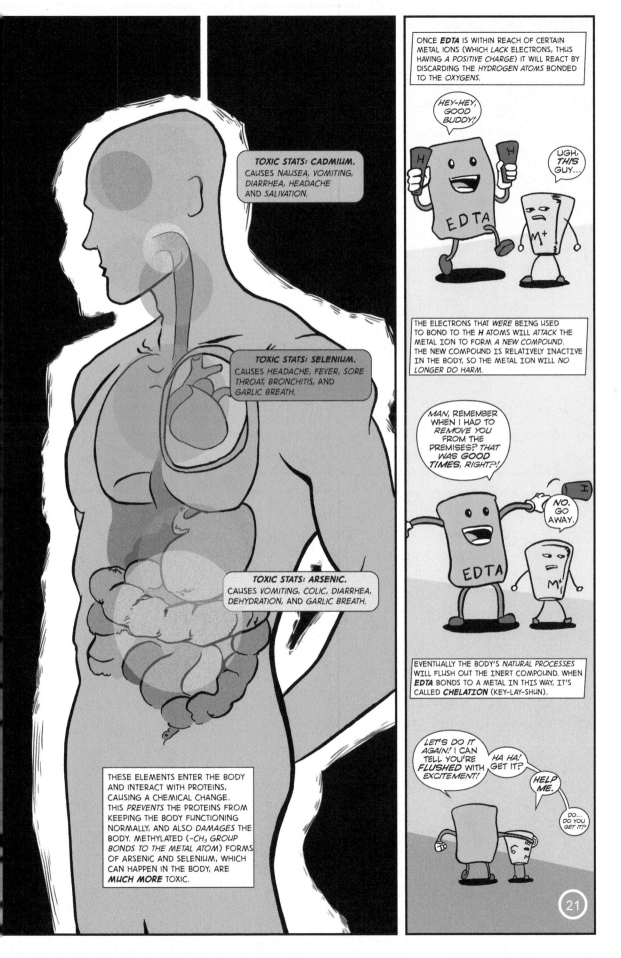

TOXIC STATS: CADMIUM. CAUSES NAUSEA, VOMITING, DIARRHEA, HEADACHE AND SALIVATION.

TOXIC STATS: SELENIUM. CAUSES HEADACHE, FEVER, SORE THROAT, BRONCHITIS, AND GARLIC BREATH.

TOXIC STATS: ARSENIC. CAUSES VOMITING, COLIC, DIARRHEA, DEHYDRATION, AND GARLIC BREATH.

THESE ELEMENTS ENTER THE BODY AND INTERACT WITH PROTEINS, CAUSING A CHEMICAL CHANGE. THIS PREVENTS THE PROTEINS FROM KEEPING THE BODY FUNCTIONING NORMALLY, AND ALSO DAMAGES THE BODY. METHYLATED ($-CH_3$ GROUP BONDS TO THE METAL ATOM) FORMS OF ARSENIC AND SELENIUM, WHICH CAN HAPPEN IN THE BODY, ARE MUCH MORE TOXIC.

ONCE EDTA IS WITHIN REACH OF CERTAIN METAL IONS (WHICH LACK ELECTRONS, THUS HAVING A POSITIVE CHARGE) IT WILL REACT BY DISCARDING THE HYDROGEN ATOMS BONDED TO THE OXYGENS.

HEY-HEY, GOOD BUDDY!

UGH, THIS GUY...

THE ELECTRONS THAT WERE BEING USED TO BOND TO THE H ATOMS WILL ATTACK THE METAL ION TO FORM A NEW COMPOUND. THE NEW COMPOUND IS RELATIVELY INACTIVE IN THE BODY, SO THE METAL ION WILL NO LONGER DO HARM.

MAN, REMEMBER WHEN I HAD TO REMOVE YOU FROM THE PREMISES? THAT WAS GOOD TIMES, RIGHT?!

NO. GO AWAY.

EVENTUALLY THE BODY'S NATURAL PROCESSES WILL FLUSH OUT THE INERT COMPOUND. WHEN EDTA BONDS TO A METAL IN THIS WAY, IT'S CALLED CHELATION (KEY-LAY-SHUN).

LET'S DO IT AGAIN! I CAN TELL YOU'RE FLUSHED WITH EXCITEMENT!

HA HA! GET IT?

HELP ME.

DO... DO YOU GET IT?

21

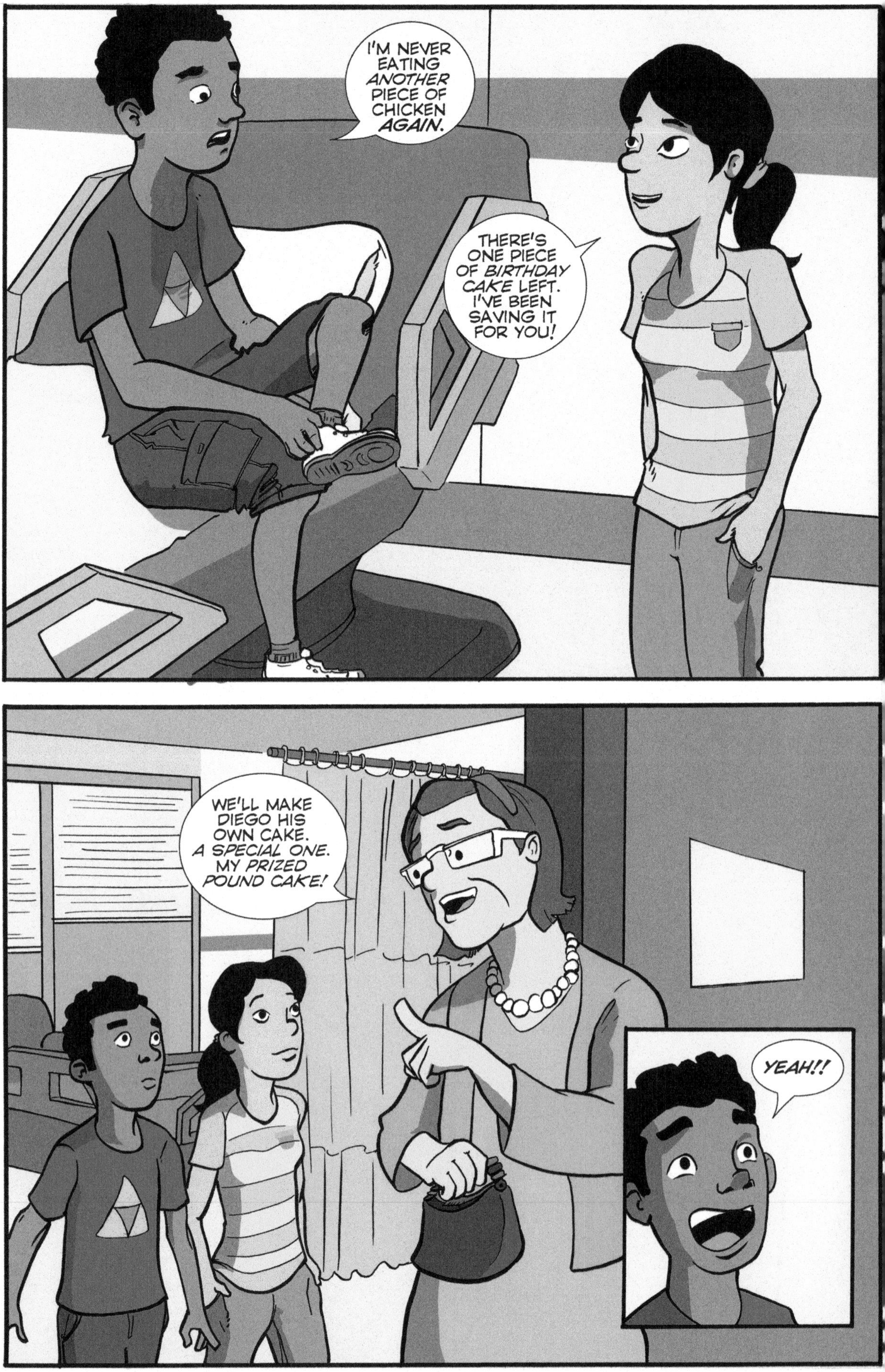
I'M NEVER EATING *ANOTHER* PIECE OF CHICKEN *AGAIN*.
THERE'S ONE PIECE OF *BIRTHDAY CAKE* LEFT. I'VE BEEN SAVING IT FOR YOU!
WE'LL MAKE DIEGO HIS OWN CAKE. *A SPECIAL ONE.* MY *PRIZED POUND CAKE!*
YEAH!!

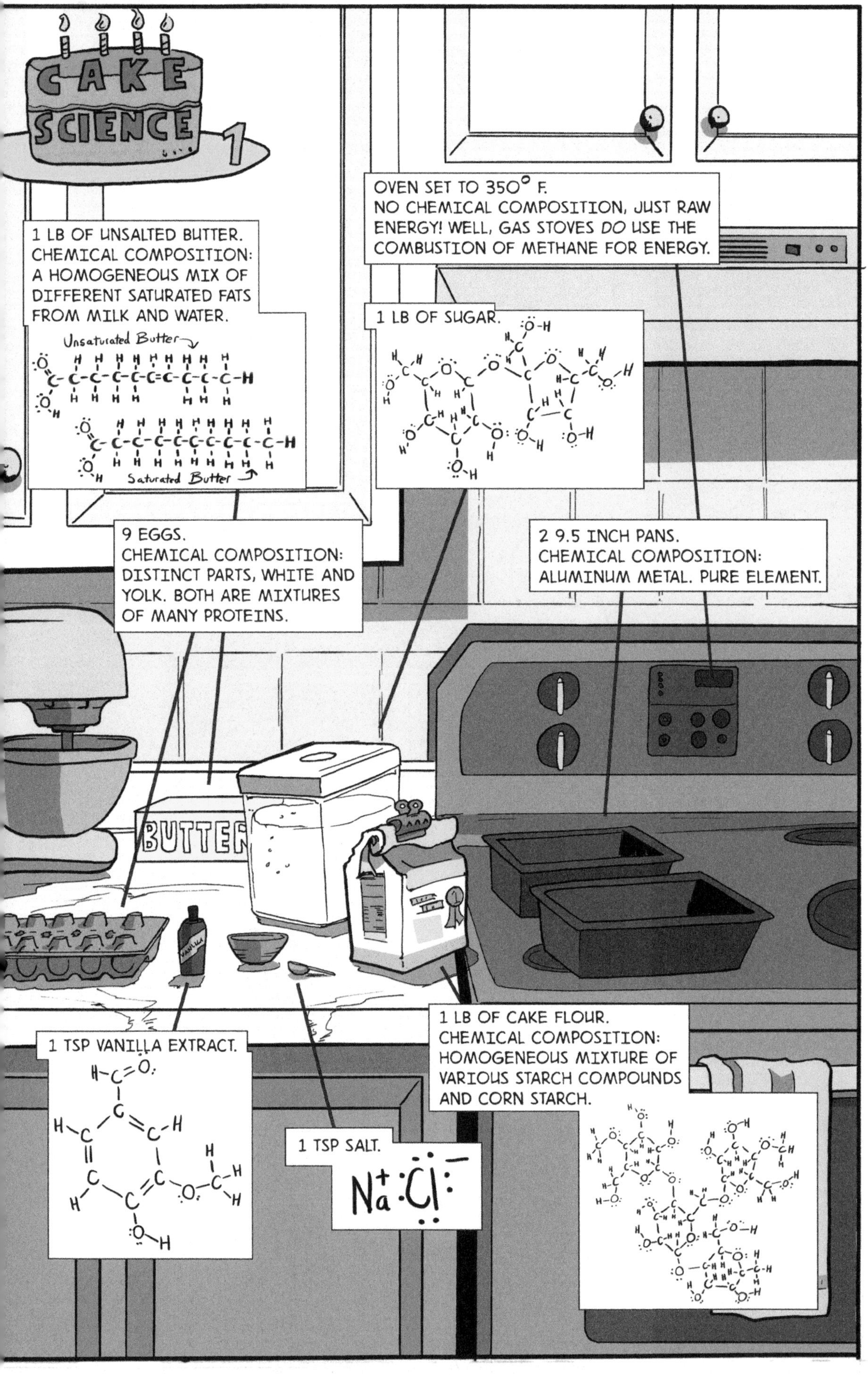
CAKE SCIENCE 1
1 LB OF UNSALTED BUTTER. CHEMICAL COMPOSITION: A HOMOGENEOUS MIX OF DIFFERENT SATURATED FATS FROM MILK AND WATER.
Unsaturated Butter
Saturated Butter
OVEN SET TO 350° F. NO CHEMICAL COMPOSITION, JUST RAW ENERGY! WELL, GAS STOVES *DO* USE THE COMBUSTION OF METHANE FOR ENERGY.
1 LB OF SUGAR.
9 EGGS. CHEMICAL COMPOSITION: DISTINCT PARTS, WHITE AND YOLK. BOTH ARE MIXTURES OF MANY PROTEINS.
2 9.5 INCH PANS. CHEMICAL COMPOSITION: ALUMINUM METAL. PURE ELEMENT.
BUTTER
VANILLA
1 TSP VANILLA EXTRACT.
1 TSP SALT.
1 LB OF CAKE FLOUR. CHEMICAL COMPOSITION: HOMOGENEOUS MIXTURE OF VARIOUS STARCH COMPOUNDS AND CORN STARCH.

BUTTER AND FLOUR THE PANS.

SUGAR AND ROOM TEMPERATURE BUTTER GO IN THE MIXER ON MEDIUM FOR 5 MIN. *(IMPORTANT FOR FORMING LOTS OF BUBBLES)* A PHYSICAL CHANGE IS OCCURRING, AS THE BUTTER CHANGES FROM A SOLID TO A SOFTER SOLID, OR LIQUID, IF IT GETS TOO HOT.

ADD EGGS TO THE MIXTURE ONE AT A TIME WHILE MIXING SLOWLY IN THE MIXER. (MAKING AN EMULSION.) THROUGH THE FIRST FEW STIRS, A HETEROGENEOUS MIXTURE IS MADE UNTIL THE EGG UNDERGOES A PHYSICAL CHANGE IN BEING SEPARATED INTO SMALLER PIECES AND DISPERSED THROUGHOUT THE MIXTURE, TO MAKE IT LOOK HOMOGENEOUS.

ADD THE VANILLA AND SALT.

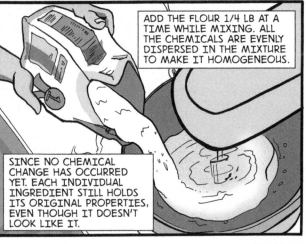

ADD THE FLOUR 1/4 LB AT A TIME WHILE MIXING. ALL THE CHEMICALS ARE EVENLY DISPERSED IN THE MIXTURE TO MAKE IT HOMOGENEOUS.

SINCE NO CHEMICAL CHANGE HAS OCCURRED YET. EACH INDIVIDUAL INGREDIENT STILL HOLDS ITS ORIGINAL PROPERTIES, EVEN THOUGH IT DOESN'T LOOK LIKE IT.

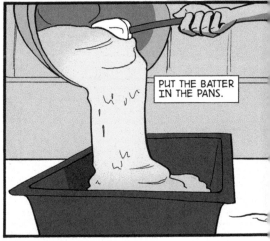

PUT THE BATTER IN THE PANS.

AND PUT THE PANS IN THE OVEN. TIME FOR A REACTION!

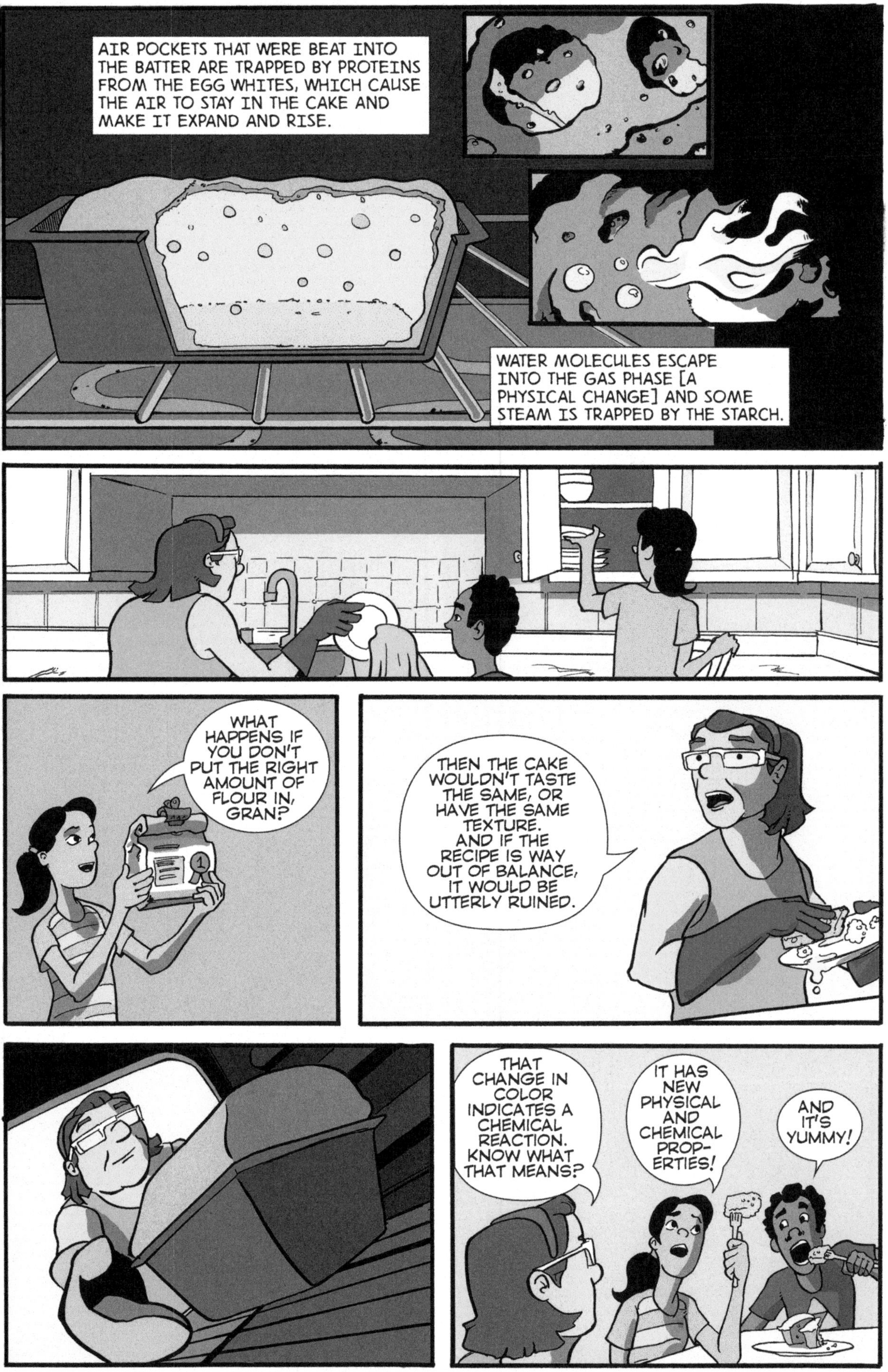
AIR POCKETS THAT WERE BEAT INTO THE BATTER ARE TRAPPED BY PROTEINS FROM THE EGG WHITES, WHICH CAUSE THE AIR TO STAY IN THE CAKE AND MAKE IT EXPAND AND RISE.
WATER MOLECULES ESCAPE INTO THE GAS PHASE [A PHYSICAL CHANGE] AND SOME STEAM IS TRAPPED BY THE STARCH.
WHAT HAPPENS IF YOU DON'T PUT THE RIGHT AMOUNT OF FLOUR IN, GRAN?
THEN THE CAKE WOULDN'T TASTE THE SAME, OR HAVE THE SAME TEXTURE. AND IF THE RECIPE IS WAY OUT OF BALANCE, IT WOULD BE UTTERLY RUINED.
THAT CHANGE IN COLOR INDICATES A CHEMICAL REACTION. KNOW WHAT THAT MEANS?
IT HAS NEW PHYSICAL AND CHEMICAL PROPERTIES!
AND IT'S YUMMY!

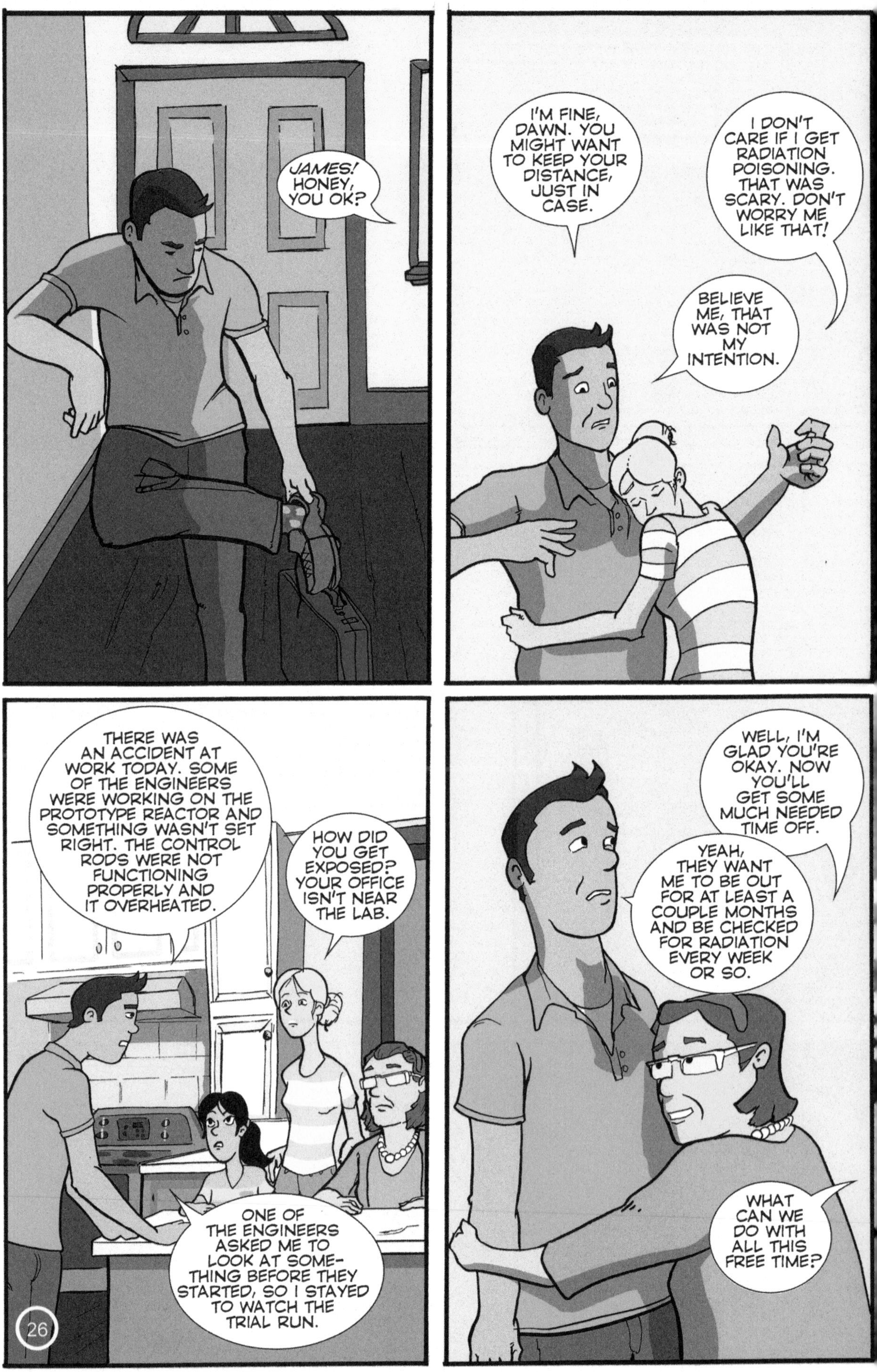
JAMES! HONEY, YOU OK?
I'M FINE, DAWN. YOU MIGHT WANT TO KEEP YOUR DISTANCE, JUST IN CASE.
I DON'T CARE IF I GET RADIATION POISONING. THAT WAS SCARY. DON'T WORRY ME LIKE THAT!
BELIEVE ME, THAT WAS NOT MY INTENTION.
THERE WAS AN ACCIDENT AT WORK TODAY. SOME OF THE ENGINEERS WERE WORKING ON THE PROTOTYPE REACTOR AND SOMETHING WASN'T SET RIGHT. THE CONTROL RODS WERE NOT FUNCTIONING PROPERLY AND IT OVERHEATED.
HOW DID YOU GET EXPOSED? YOUR OFFICE ISN'T NEAR THE LAB.
ONE OF THE ENGINEERS ASKED ME TO LOOK AT SOME-THING BEFORE THEY STARTED, SO I STAYED TO WATCH THE TRIAL RUN.
WELL, I'M GLAD YOU'RE OKAY. NOW YOU'LL GET SOME MUCH NEEDED TIME OFF.
YEAH, THEY WANT ME TO BE OUT FOR AT LEAST A COUPLE MONTHS AND BE CHECKED FOR RADIATION EVERY WEEK OR SO.
WHAT CAN WE DO WITH ALL THIS FREE TIME?

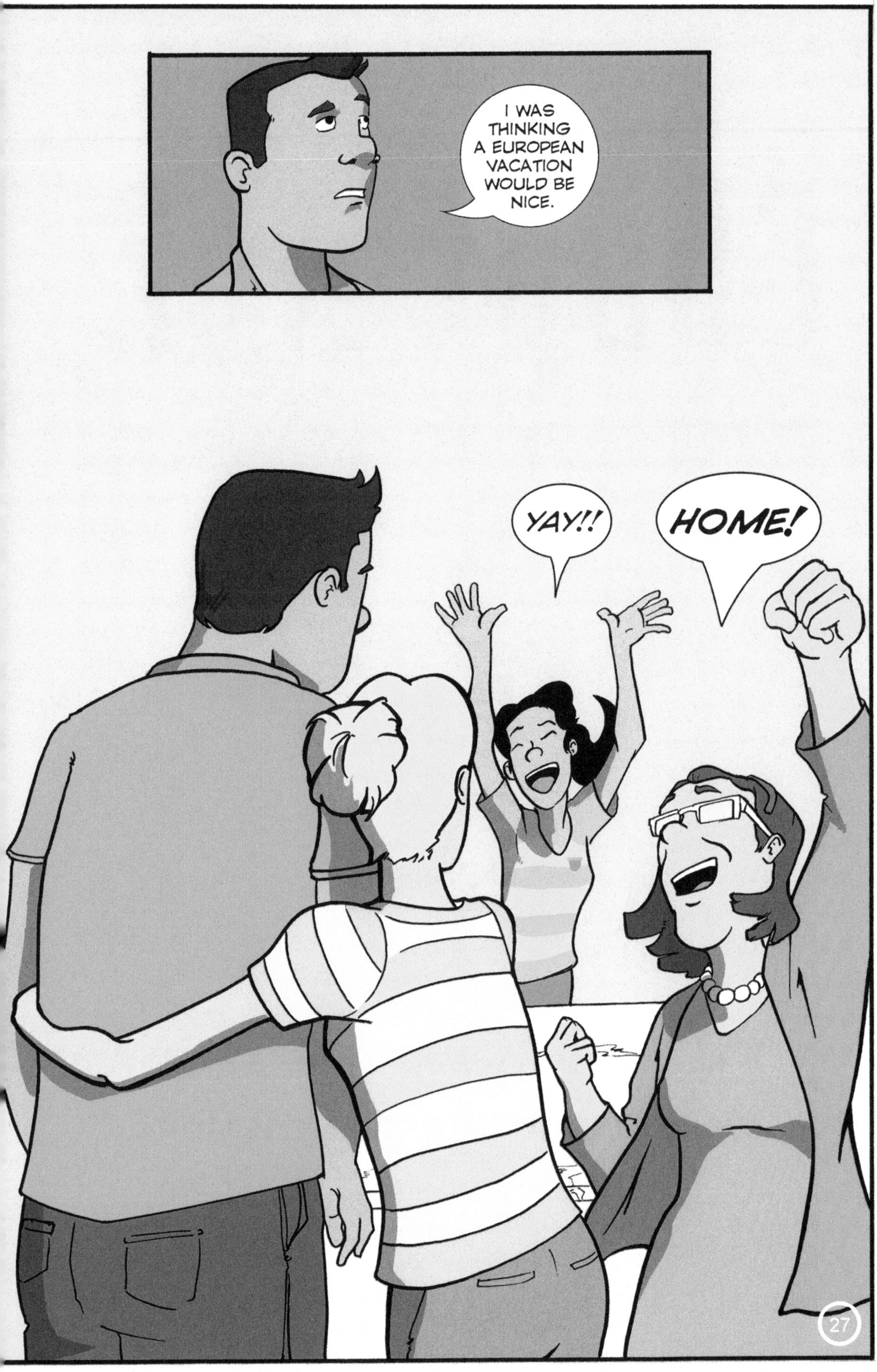
I WAS THINKING A EUROPEAN VACATION WOULD BE NICE.
YAY!!
HOME!

Chapter 2

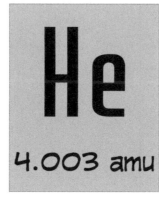

Neutrons have no charge and
weigh 1 amu (Atomic Mass Unit).

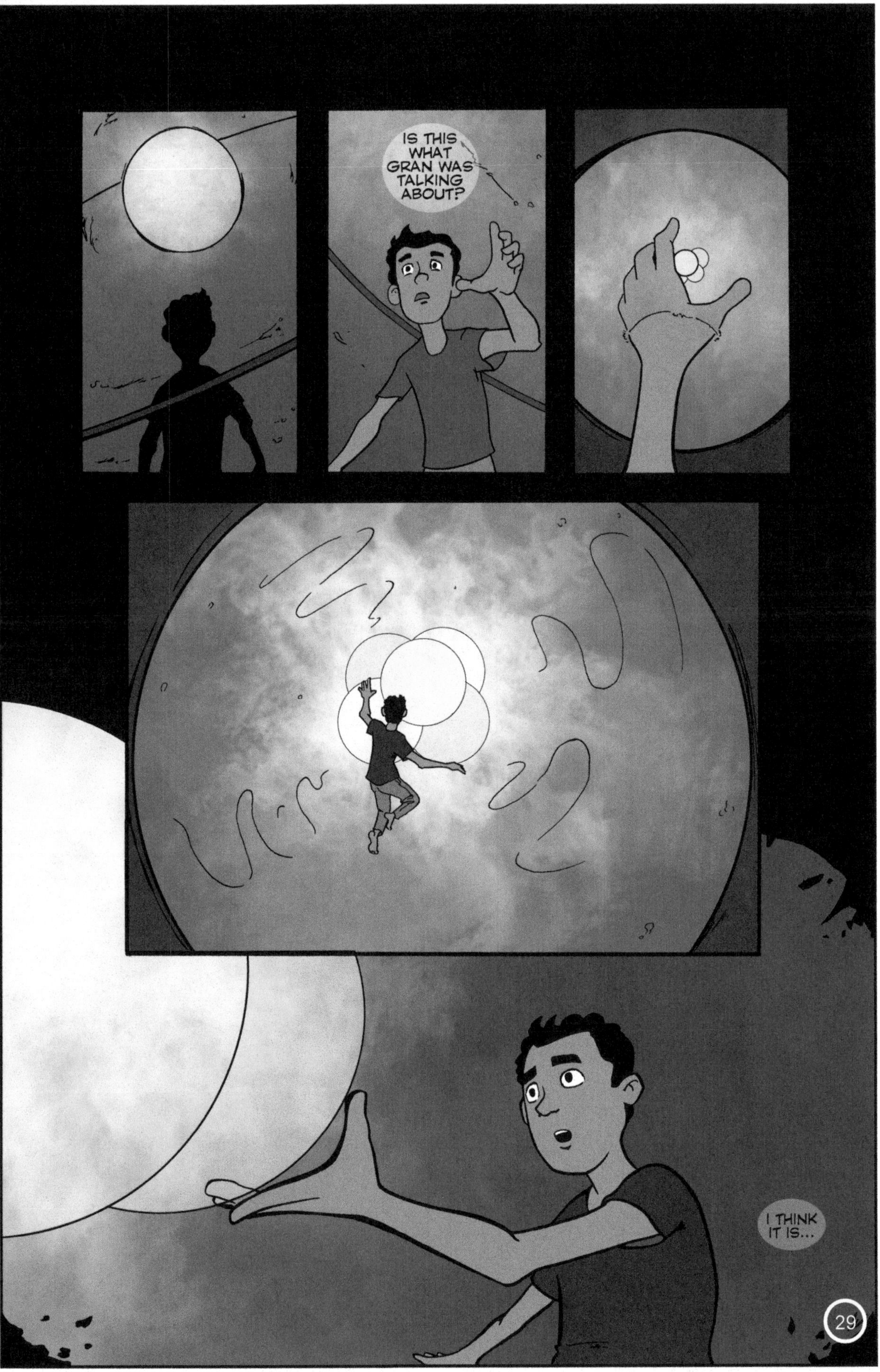
IS THIS WHAT GRAN WAS TALKING ABOUT?
I THINK IT IS...

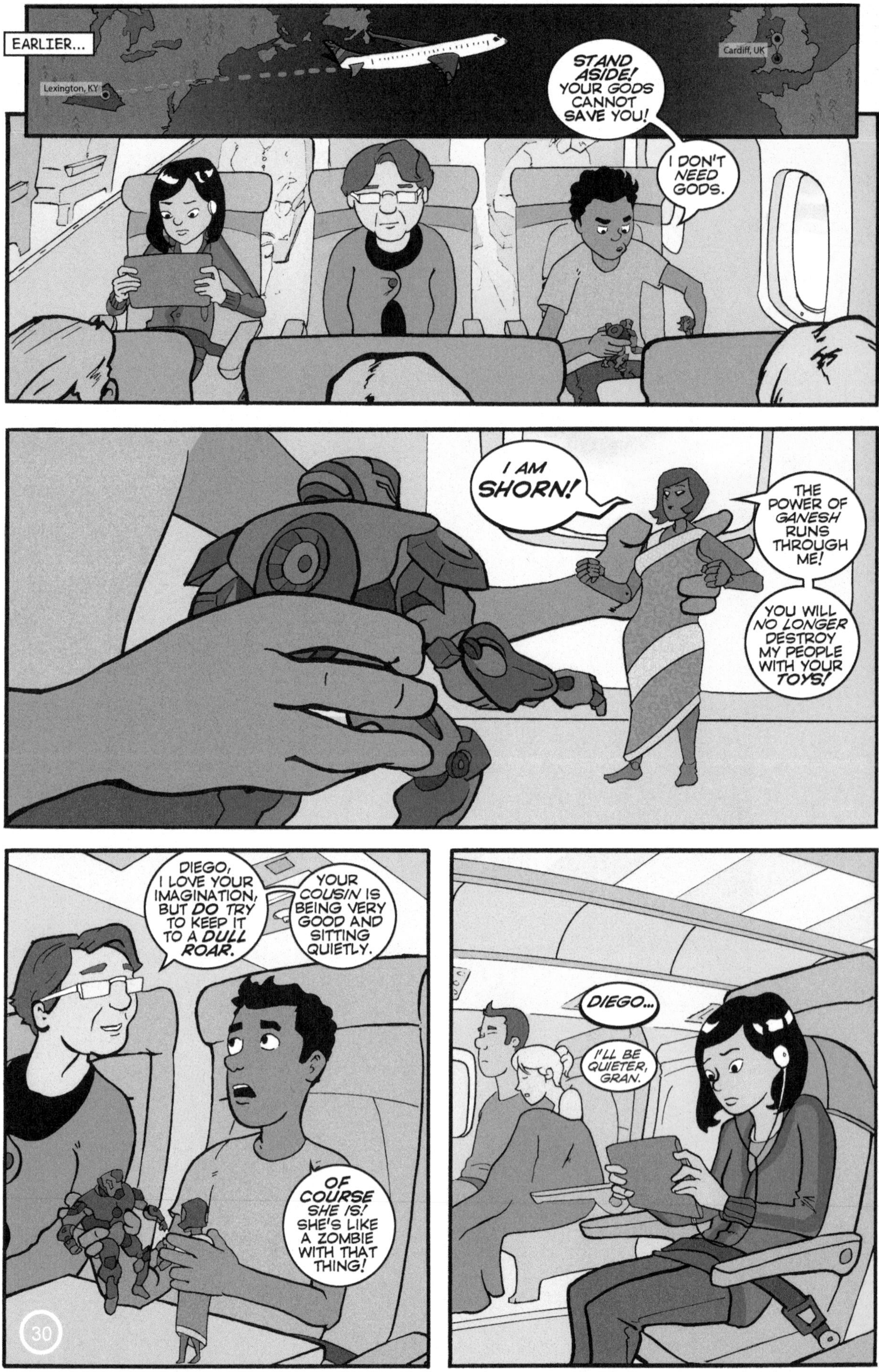

EARLIER...
Lexington, KY
Cardiff, UK
STAND ASIDE! YOUR GODS CANNOT SAVE YOU!
I DON'T NEED GODS.
I AM SHORN!
THE POWER OF GANESH RUNS THROUGH ME!
YOU WILL NO LONGER DESTROY MY PEOPLE WITH YOUR TOYS!
DIEGO, I LOVE YOUR IMAGINATION, BUT DO TRY TO KEEP IT TO A DULL ROAR.
YOUR COUSIN IS BEING VERY GOOD AND SITTING QUIETLY.
OF COURSE SHE IS! SHE'S LIKE A ZOMBIE WITH THAT THING!
DIEGO...
I'LL BE QUIETER, GRAN.

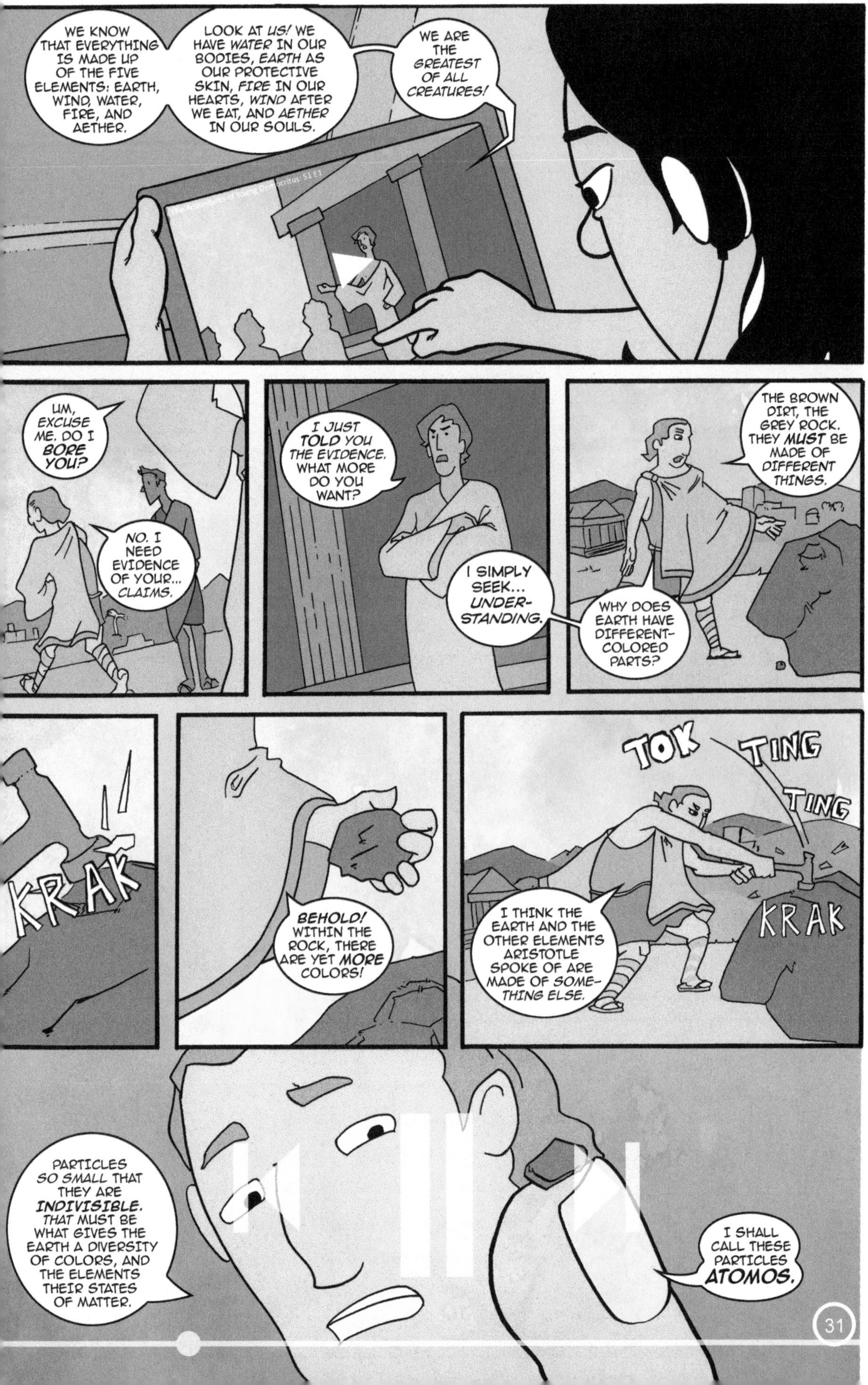
WE KNOW THAT EVERYTHING IS MADE UP OF THE FIVE ELEMENTS: EARTH, WIND, WATER, FIRE, AND AETHER.
LOOK AT *US!* WE HAVE *WATER* IN OUR BODIES, *EARTH* AS OUR PROTECTIVE SKIN, *FIRE* IN OUR HEARTS, *WIND* AFTER WE EAT, AND *AETHER* IN OUR SOULS.
WE ARE THE *GREATEST OF ALL CREATURES!*
The Adventures of Young Democritus: S1 E1
UM, *EXCUSE ME. DO I* ***BORE YOU?***
NO. I NEED EVIDENCE OF YOUR... *CLAIMS.*
I JUST ***TOLD*** *YOU THE EVIDENCE.* WHAT MORE DO YOU WANT?
I SIMPLY SEEK... *UNDER-STANDING.*
WHY DOES EARTH HAVE DIFFERENT-COLORED PARTS?
THE BROWN DIRT, THE GREY ROCK. THEY ***MUST*** BE MADE OF DIFFERENT THINGS.
KRAK
BEHOLD! WITHIN THE ROCK, THERE ARE YET ***MORE*** COLORS!
TOK
TING
TING
KRAK
I THINK THE EARTH AND THE OTHER ELEMENTS ARISTOTLE SPOKE OF ARE MADE OF *SOME-THING ELSE.*
PARTICLES *SO SMALL* THAT THEY ARE ***INDIVISIBLE.*** *THAT* MUST BE WHAT GIVES THE EARTH A DIVERSITY OF COLORS, AND THE ELEMENTS THEIR STATES OF MATTER.
I SHALL CALL THESE PARTICLES ***ATOMOS.***

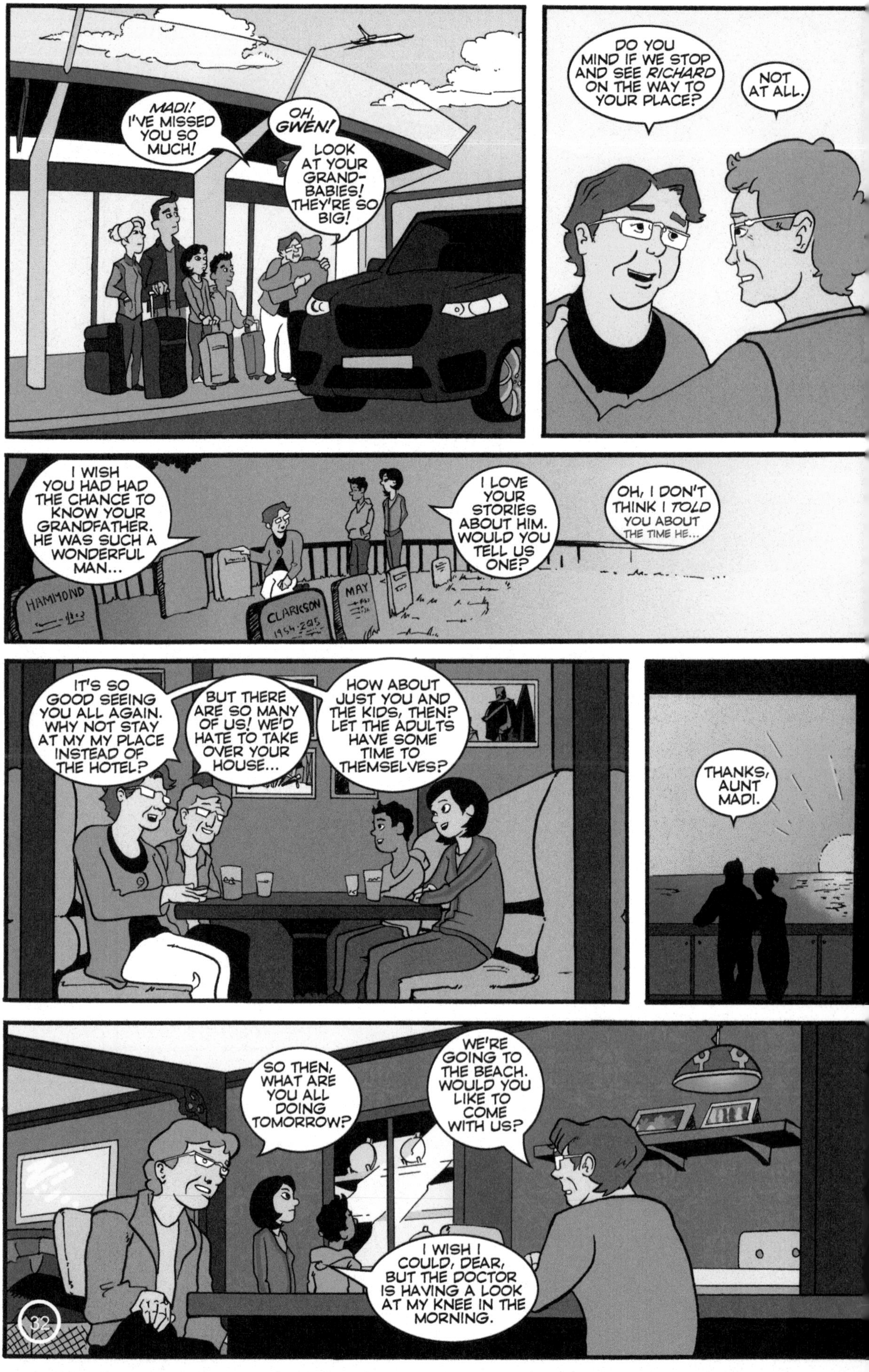
MADI! I'VE MISSED YOU SO MUCH!
OH, GWEN!
LOOK AT YOUR GRAND-BABIES! THEY'RE SO BIG!
DO YOU MIND IF WE STOP AND SEE RICHARD ON THE WAY TO YOUR PLACE?
NOT AT ALL.
I WISH YOU HAD HAD THE CHANCE TO KNOW YOUR GRANDFATHER. HE WAS SUCH A WONDERFUL MAN...
I LOVE YOUR STORIES ABOUT HIM. WOULD YOU TELL US ONE?
OH, I DON'T THINK I TOLD YOU ABOUT THE TIME HE...
HAMMOND
MAY
CLARKSON 1954-2015
IT'S SO GOOD SEEING YOU ALL AGAIN. WHY NOT STAY AT MY MY PLACE INSTEAD OF THE HOTEL?
BUT THERE ARE SO MANY OF US! WE'D HATE TO TAKE OVER YOUR HOUSE...
HOW ABOUT JUST YOU AND THE KIDS, THEN? LET THE ADULTS HAVE SOME TIME TO THEMSELVES?
THANKS, AUNT MADI.
SO THEN, WHAT ARE YOU ALL DOING TOMORROW?
WE'RE GOING TO THE BEACH. WOULD YOU LIKE TO COME WITH US?
I WISH I COULD, DEAR, BUT THE DOCTOR IS HAVING A LOOK AT MY KNEE IN THE MORNING.

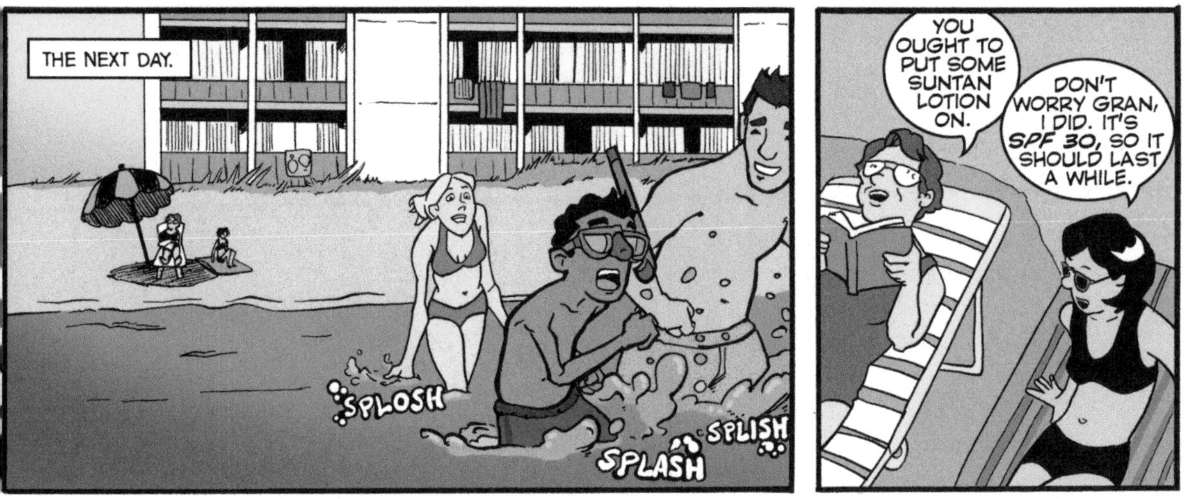
THE NEXT DAY.
SPLOSH
SPLASH
SPLISH
YOU OUGHT TO PUT SOME SUNTAN LOTION ON.
DON'T WORRY GRAN, I DID. IT'S SPF 30, SO IT SHOULD LAST A WHILE.

SCIENCE TIME! WHAT IS SPF, ANYWAY?

The Sunburn Protection Factor is a calculation of how well the chemicals in the lotion will be able to block ultra violet (UV) radiation from the sun. SPF 20 equates to only allowing 5 of every 100 photons to reach the skin. The primary active ingredients are zinc oxide, titanium oxide, and avobenzone.

$Zn^{2+}O^{2-}$ (Zinc Oxide)

$O^{2-}Ti^{4+}O^{2-}$ (Titanium Oxide)

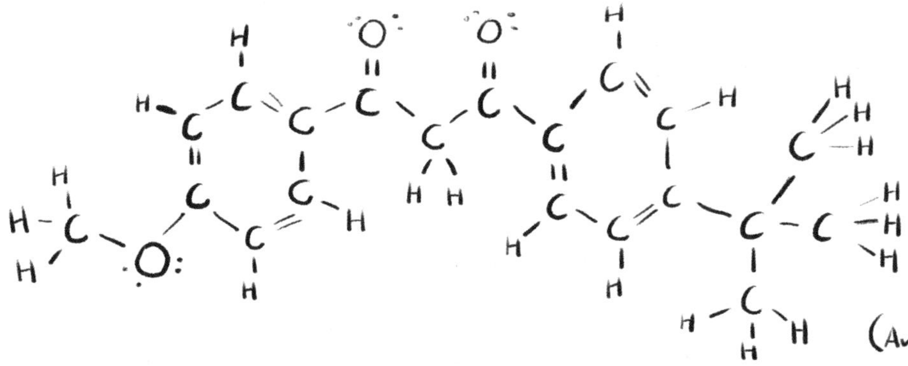

(Avobenzone)

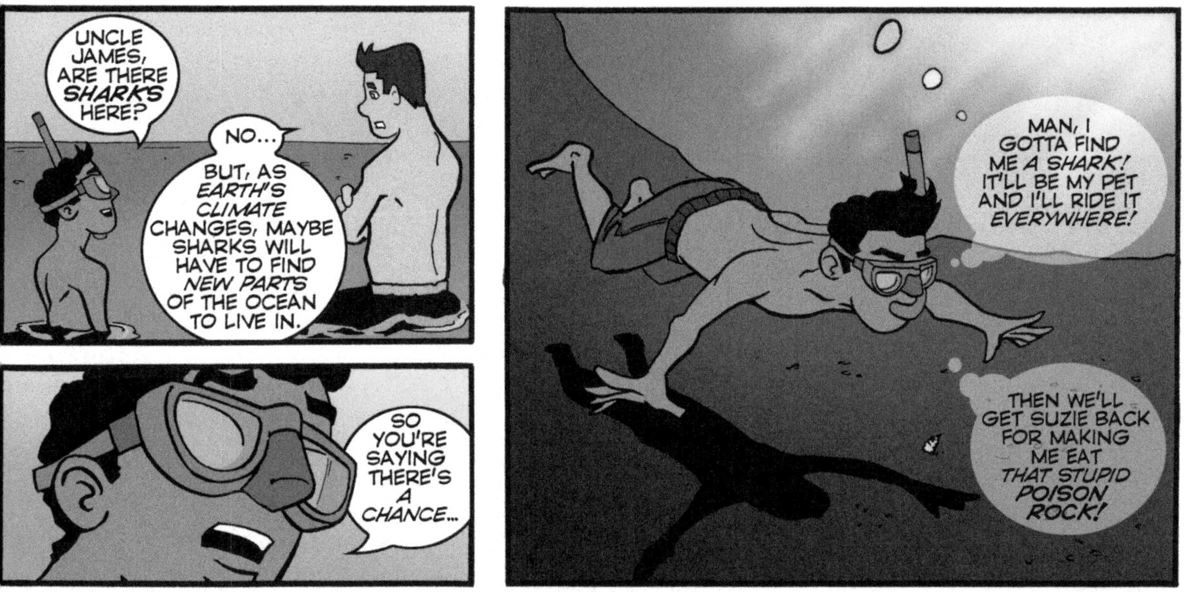
UNCLE JAMES, ARE THERE SHARKS HERE?
NO...
BUT, AS EARTH'S CLIMATE CHANGES, MAYBE SHARKS WILL HAVE TO FIND NEW PARTS OF THE OCEAN TO LIVE IN.
SO YOU'RE SAYING THERE'S A CHANCE...
MAN, I GOTTA FIND ME A SHARK! IT'LL BE MY PET AND I'LL RIDE IT EVERYWHERE!
THEN WE'LL GET SUZIE BACK FOR MAKING ME EAT THAT STUPID POISON ROCK!

GRAN! I'M SUNBURNT!

THE HOTEL SHOULD HAVE SOME ALOE. THAT WILL HELP WITH THE PAIN AND KEEP IT FROM PEELING.

I GUESS I SHOULD HAVE REAPPLIED... GRAN, HOW DOES THE SUN *BURN* US?

OUR *SKIN* CAN ONLY PROTECT US FROM SO MUCH. PIGMENT IN OUR SKIN SOAKS UP AS MUCH SUN AS IT CAN, BUT AFTER THAT, *UV RAYS* FROM *THE SUN* START TO DAMAGE CELLS, WHICH CAN CAUSE CANCER LATER IN LIFE.

EARTH'S ATMOSPHERE, AND OUR SKIN, DO A GOOD JOB OF PROTECTING US FROM A LOT, BUT THEY *CAN'T DO IT ALL...*

LOOK OUT BELOW, GRAN'S DROPPING SOME SCIENCE!

Our skin produces melanin to block harmful sunlight. Most of the UV rays are absorbed by the melanin and turned into heat. However, melanin on its own cannot stop all of the UV rays, which leads to skin burns that damage skin cells.

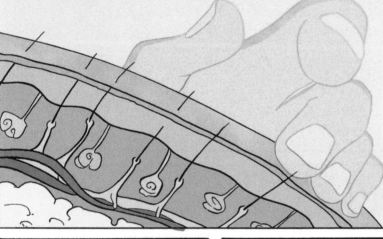

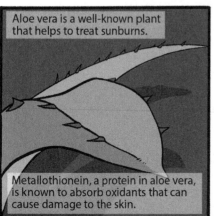

Aloe vera is a well-known plant that helps to treat sunburns.

Metallothionein, a protein in aloe vera, is known to absorb oxidants that can cause damage to the skin.

COME ALONG, DEARIES. WE NEED TO GET YOU OUT OF THE SUN. HOW ABOUT I SHOW YOU WHERE YOUR GRANDPA WORKED?

YES. PLEASE. I WANT OUT OF THIS DEATH-TRAP.

ARE YOU SURE YOU DON'T WANT TO STAY OUT A LITTLE LONGER? BE *EXTRA CRISPY?*

DID YOU KNOW THAT YOUR GRANDFATHER HELPED SOME OF THE WORLD'S MOST *RENOWNED* SCIENTISTS ON ATOMIC THEORY, BACK BEFORE WE EVEN KNEW THAT NEUTRONS EXISTED?

HE WAS ALWAYS TALKING TO THE STUDENTS AND PROFESSORS ABOUT THEIR EXPERIMENTS. HE FOUND THEIR WORK FASCINATING.

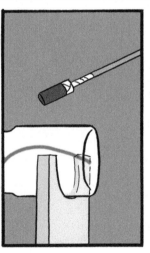

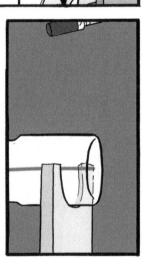

HE WOULD ALWAYS COME HOME AND TELL ME ABOUT THEIR WORK. HE HOPED TO BECOME AN ASSISTANT, BUT HE FELT HE *WASN'T SMART ENOUGH*.

BUT YOUR GRANDPA HELPED *WITHOUT EVEN KNOWING IT*. HIS STROKE OF GOOD LUCK GAVE HIM THE CONFIDENCE TO ASK TO BE A LAB ASSISTANT, AND *THEY AGREED!*

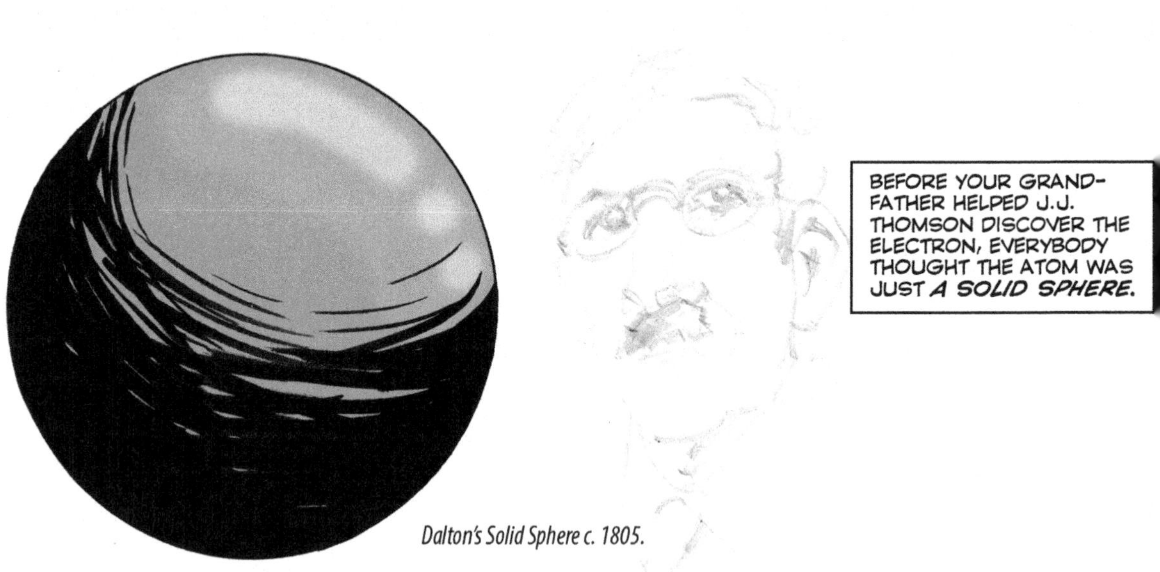
BEFORE YOUR GRANDFATHER HELPED J.J. THOMSON DISCOVER THE ELECTRON, EVERYBODY THOUGHT THE ATOM WAS JUST ***A SOLID SPHERE.***

Dalton's Solid Sphere c. 1805.

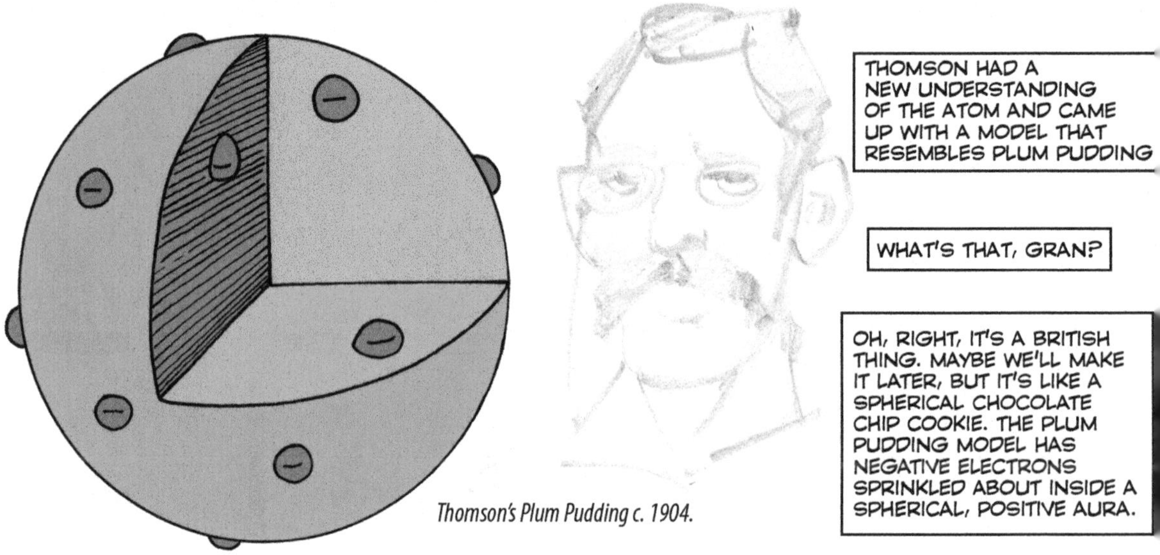
THOMSON HAD A NEW UNDERSTANDING OF THE ATOM AND CAME UP WITH A MODEL THAT RESEMBLES PLUM PUDDING
WHAT'S THAT, GRAN?
OH, RIGHT, IT'S A BRITISH THING. MAYBE WE'LL MAKE IT LATER, BUT IT'S LIKE A SPHERICAL CHOCOLATE CHIP COOKIE. THE PLUM PUDDING MODEL HAS NEGATIVE ELECTRONS SPRINKLED ABOUT INSIDE A SPHERICAL, POSITIVE AURA.

Thomson's Plum Pudding c. 1904.

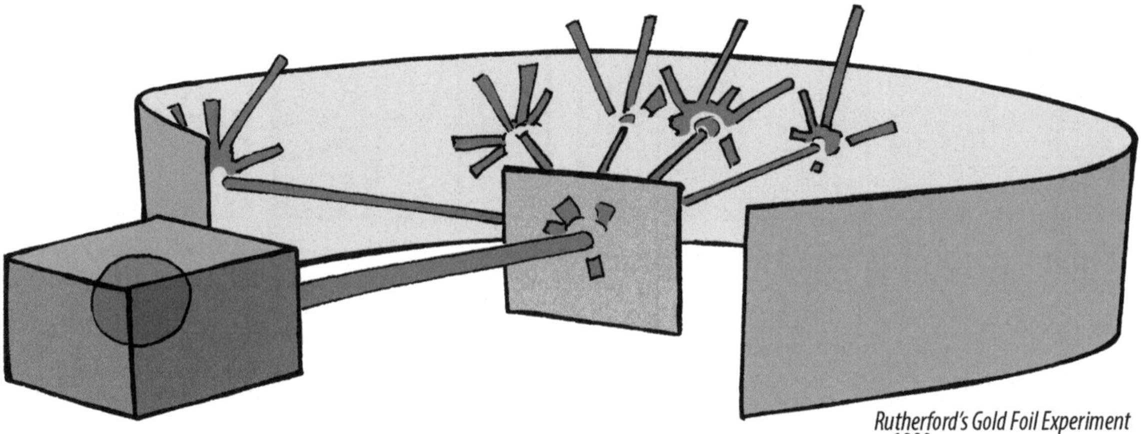

Rutherford's Gold Foil Experiment c. 1909.

ERNEST RUTHERFORD, ONE OF THOMSON'S STUDENTS, WENT ON TO DO AN EXPERIMENT WITH GOLD FOIL. IT SHOWED THAT THE POSITIVE PART OF AN ATOM ISN'T LIKE AN AURA, BUT A VERY SMALL DENSE SPHERE IN THE CENTER OF AN ATOM THAT WE CALL THE NUCLEUS, AND THAT THE ELECTRONS FLOAT AROUND IT.

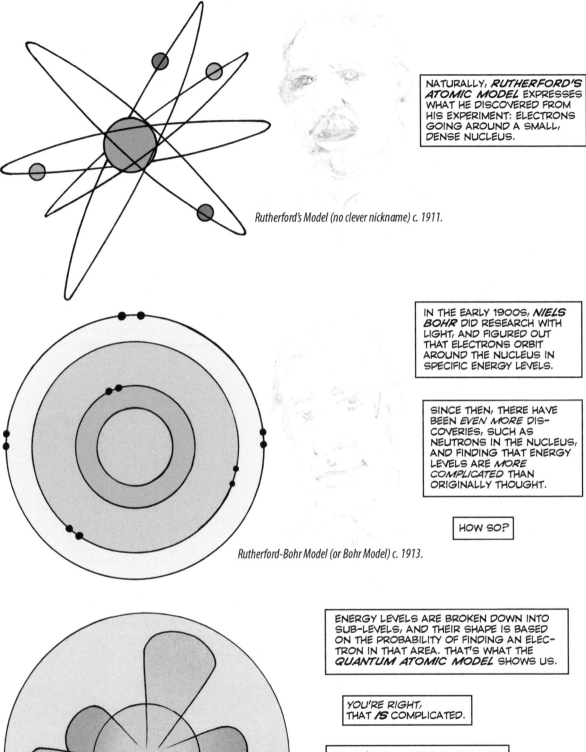

NATURALLY, **RUTHERFORD'S ATOMIC MODEL** EXPRESSES WHAT HE DISCOVERED FROM HIS EXPERIMENT: ELECTRONS GOING AROUND A SMALL, DENSE NUCLEUS.

Rutherford's Model (no clever nickname) c. 1911.

IN THE EARLY 1900s, **NIELS BOHR** DID RESEARCH WITH LIGHT, AND FIGURED OUT THAT ELECTRONS ORBIT AROUND THE NUCLEUS IN SPECIFIC ENERGY LEVELS.

SINCE THEN, THERE HAVE BEEN *EVEN MORE* DISCOVERIES, SUCH AS NEUTRONS IN THE NUCLEUS, AND FINDING THAT ENERGY LEVELS ARE *MORE COMPLICATED* THAN ORIGINALLY THOUGHT.

HOW SO?

Rutherford-Bohr Model (or Bohr Model) c. 1913.

ENERGY LEVELS ARE BROKEN DOWN INTO SUB-LEVELS, AND THEIR SHAPE IS BASED ON THE PROBABILITY OF FINDING AN ELECTRON IN THAT AREA. THAT'S WHAT THE **QUANTUM ATOMIC MODEL** SHOWS US.

YOU'RE RIGHT, THAT *IS* COMPLICATED.

HA HA! IT CAN BE, BUT YOU *ARE* MY SMARTEST GRANDDAUGHTER!

THE BOHR MODEL IS VISUALLY EASIER TO SHOW WHAT IS HAPPENING WITH AN ATOM, SO THAT MODEL WILL BE USED THROUGHOUT THE COMIC.

Quantum Mechanical model (Current model)

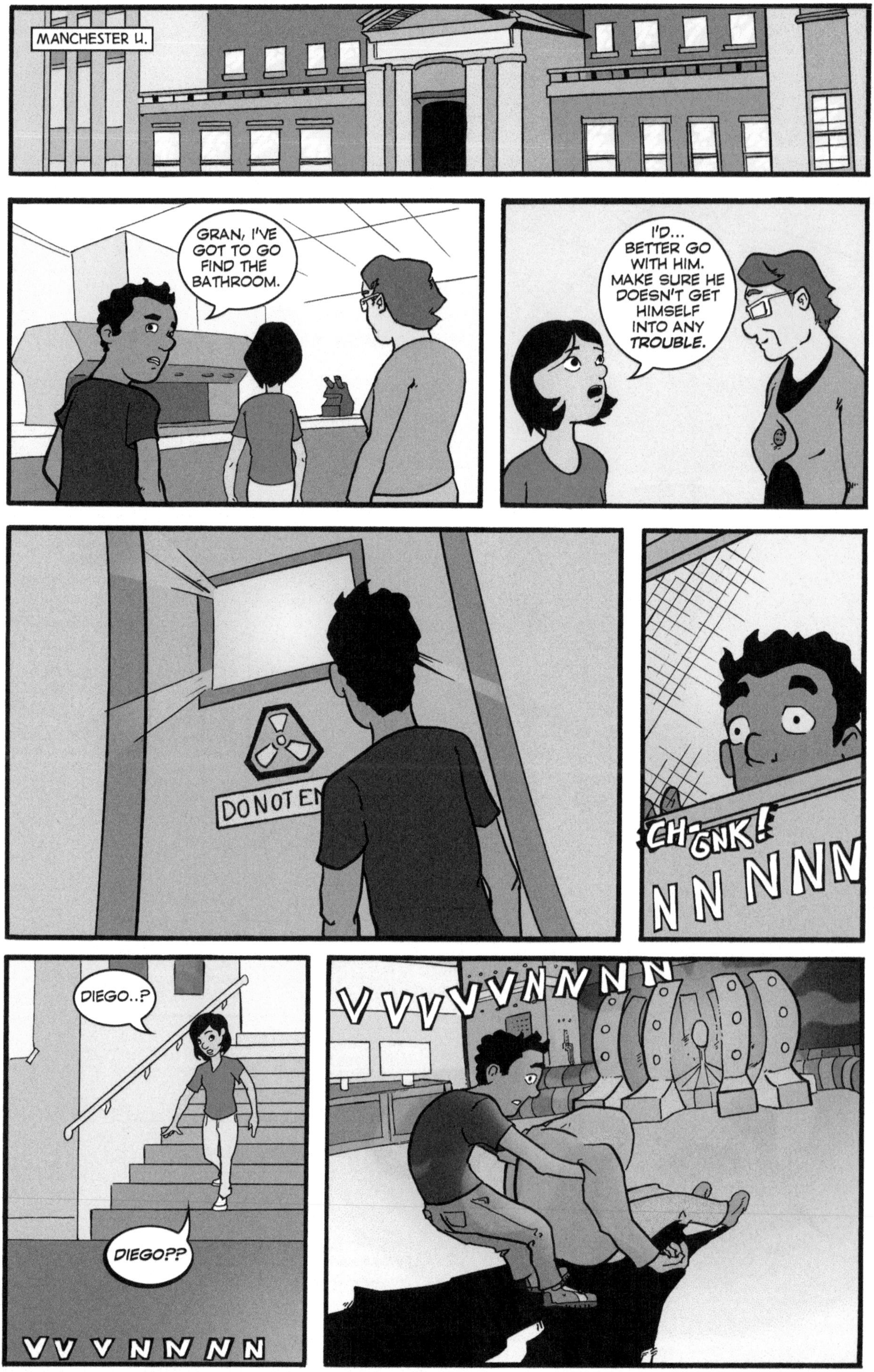
MANCHESTER U.
GRAN, I'VE GOT TO GO FIND THE BATHROOM.
I'D... BETTER GO WITH HIM. MAKE SURE HE DOESN'T GET HIMSELF INTO ANY TROUBLE.
DO NOT EN
CH-GNK!
N N NNN
DIEGO..?
DIEGO??
VV V NNNNN
V V V VVNNNNN

DIEGO!
NO!!!

BWAA

BWAA

BWA

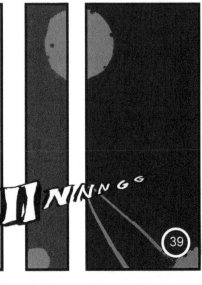

BRRIINNNGG

39

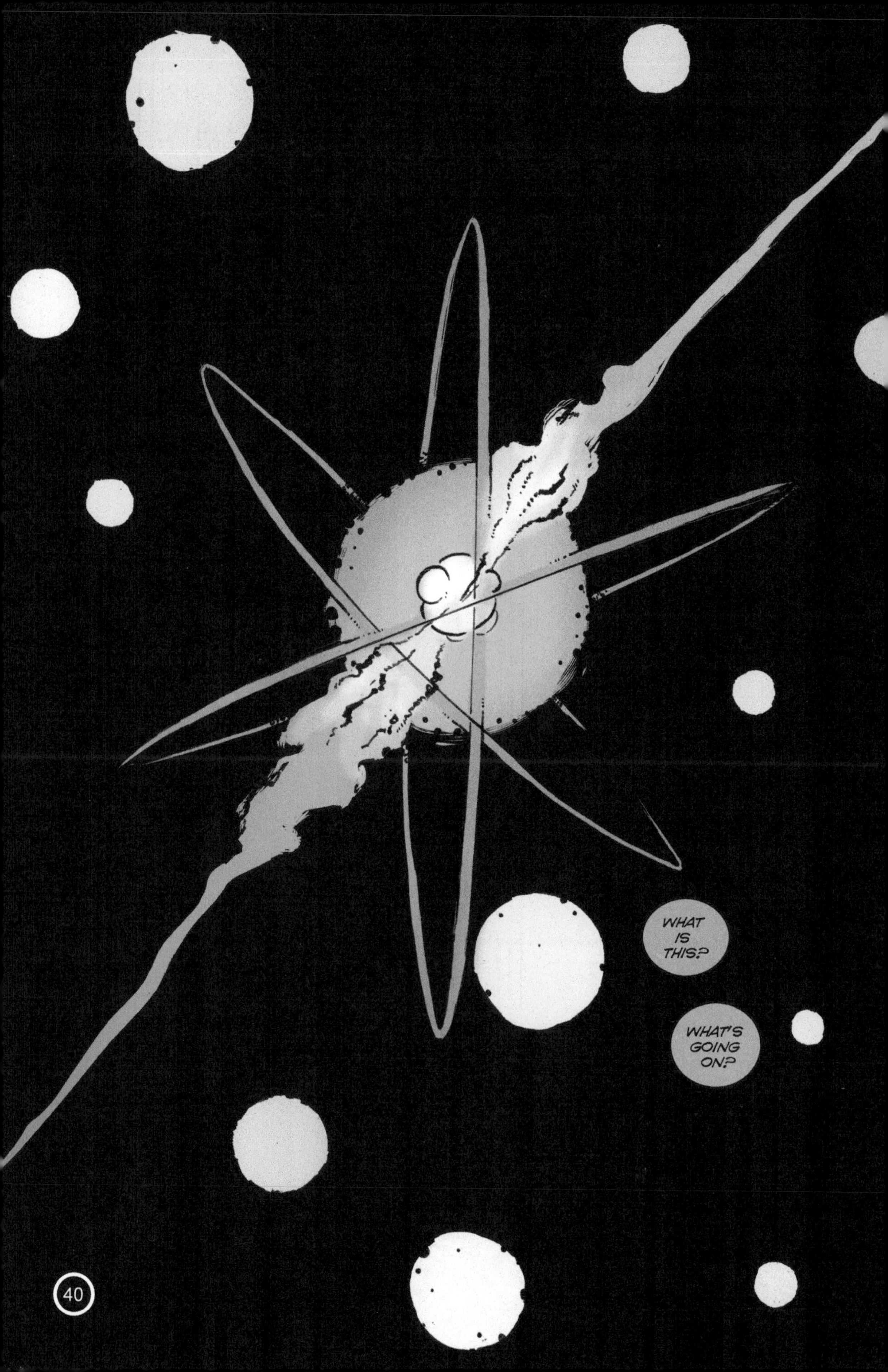
WHAT IS THIS?
WHAT'S GOING ON?

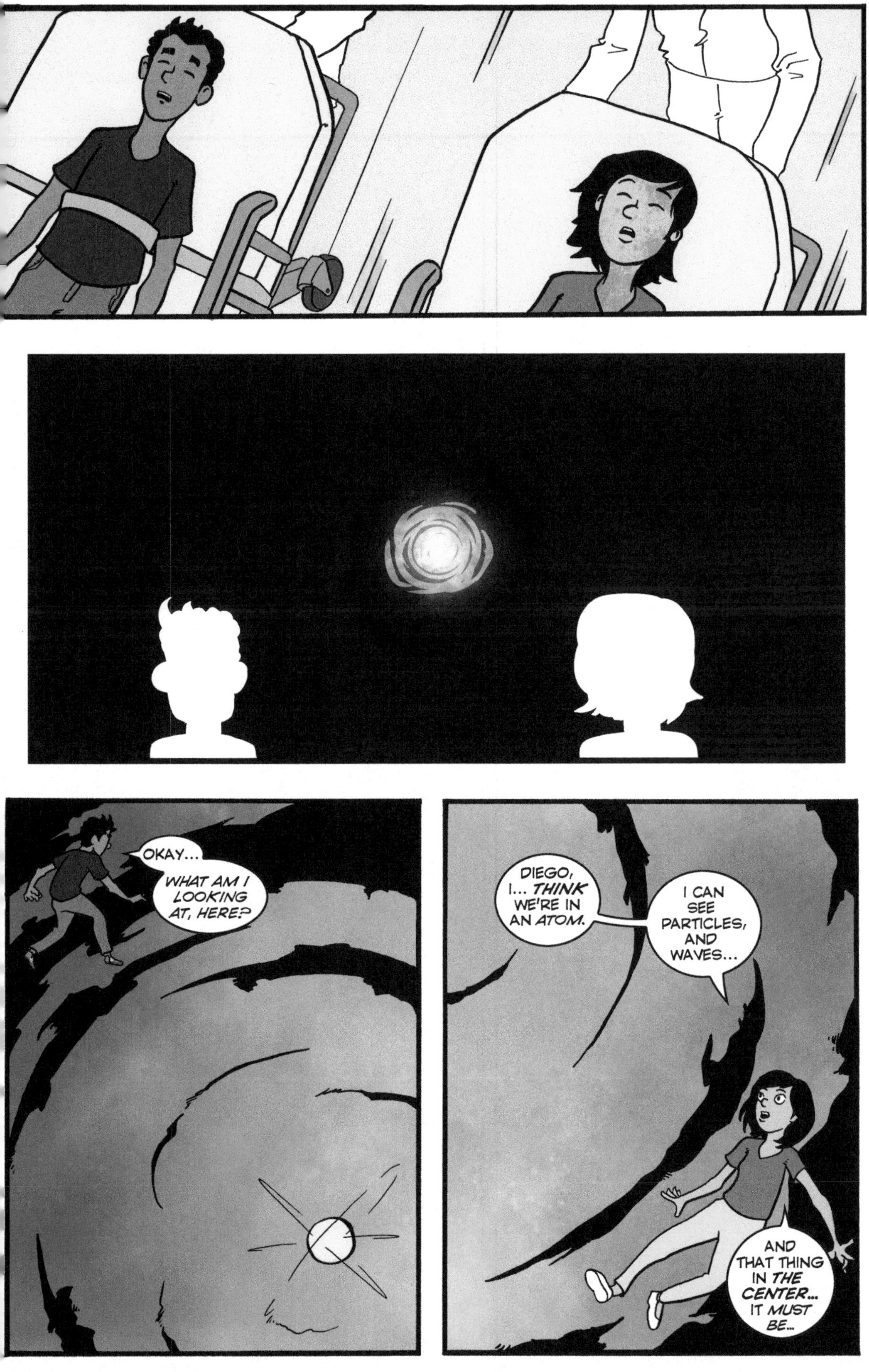
OKAY...
WHAT AM I LOOKING AT, HERE?
DIEGO, I... THINK WE'RE IN AN ATOM.
I CAN SEE PARTICLES, AND WAVES...
AND THAT THING IN THE CENTER... IT MUST BE...

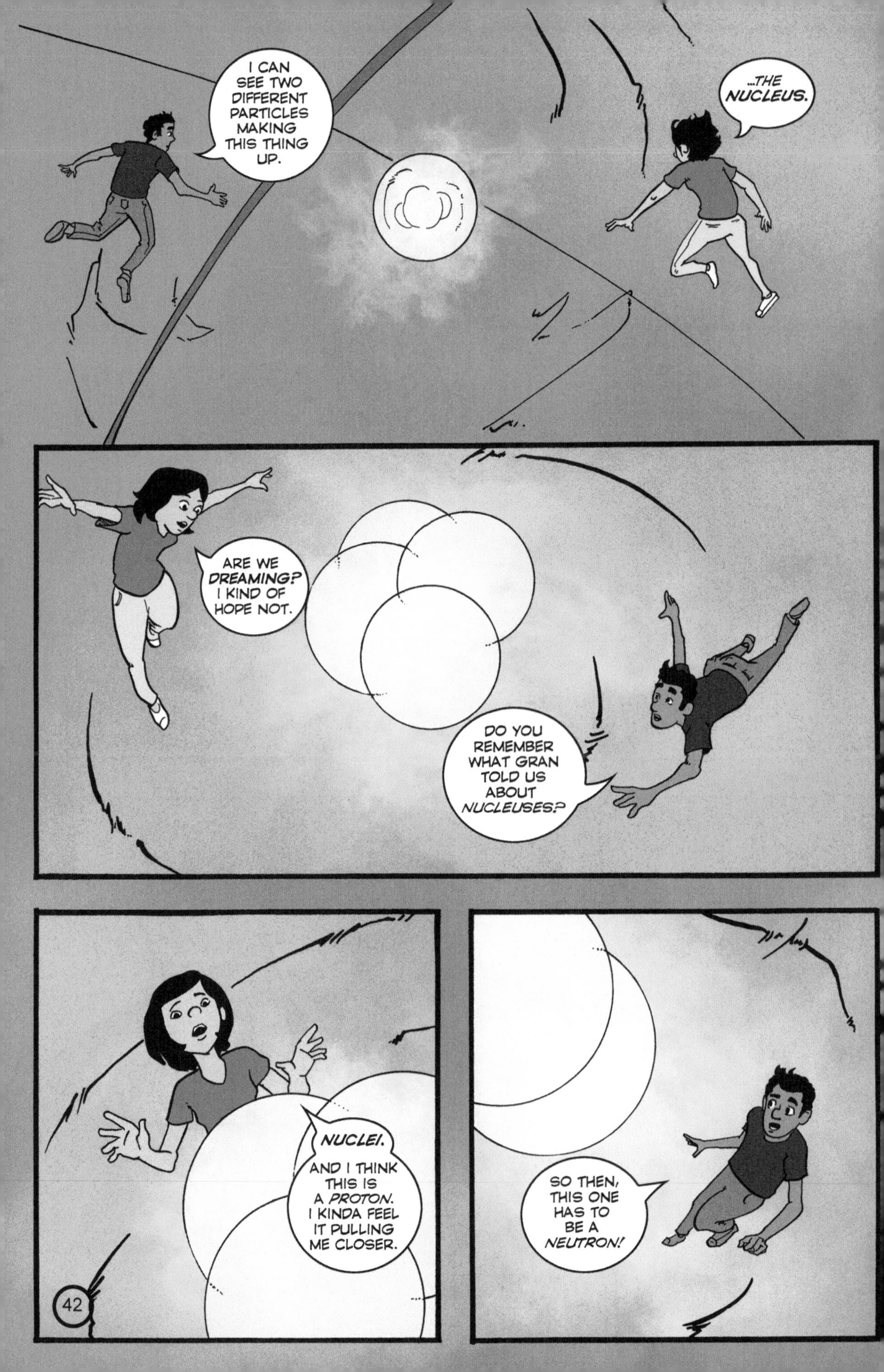
I CAN SEE TWO DIFFERENT PARTICLES MAKING THIS THING UP.
...THE NUCLEUS.
ARE WE DREAMING? I KIND OF HOPE NOT.
DO YOU REMEMBER WHAT GRAN TOLD US ABOUT NUCLEUSES?
NUCLEI.
AND I THINK THIS IS A PROTON. I KINDA FEEL IT PULLING ME CLOSER.
SO THEN, THIS ONE HAS TO BE A NEUTRON!

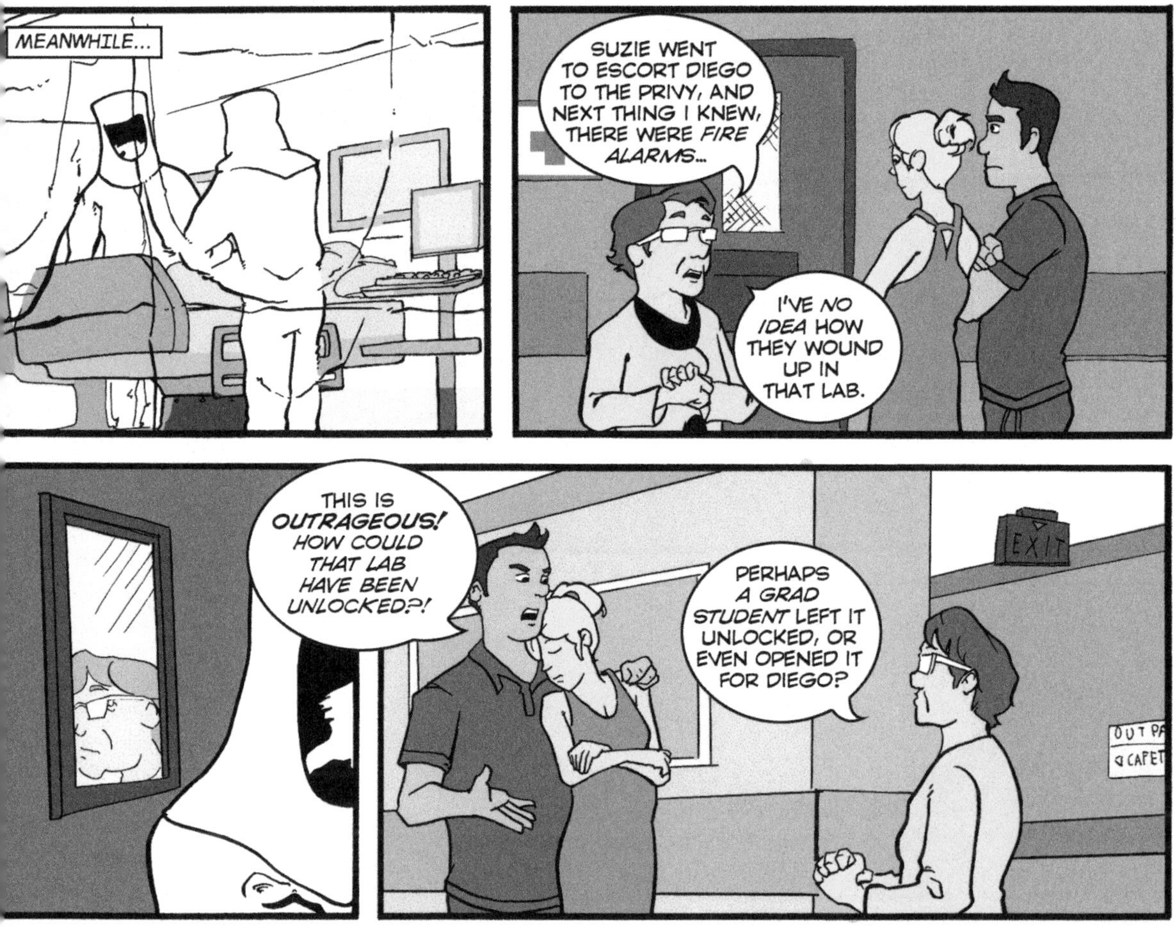
MEANWHILE...
SUZIE WENT TO ESCORT DIEGO TO THE PRIVY, AND NEXT THING I KNEW, THERE WERE *FIRE ALARMS*...
I'VE *NO IDEA* HOW THEY WOUND UP IN THAT LAB.
THIS IS ***OUTRAGEOUS!*** *HOW COULD THAT LAB HAVE BEEN UNLOCKED?!*
PERHAPS *A GRAD STUDENT* LEFT IT UNLOCKED, OR EVEN OPENED IT FOR DIEGO?
EXIT

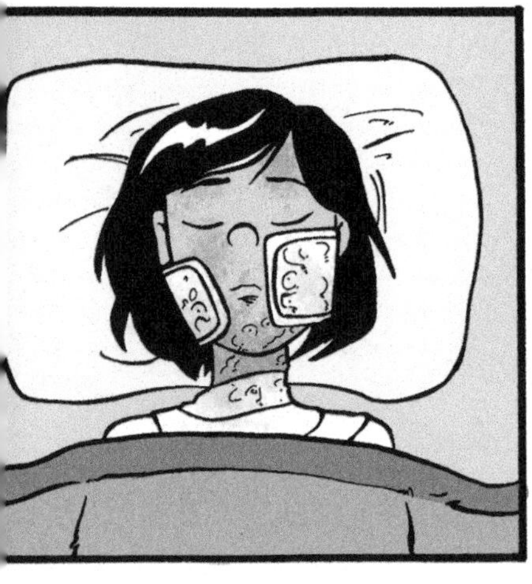

AT THE PLANTS, THERE ARE MAJOR RESTRICTIONS ON AREAS WITH A RISK OF RADIATION EXPOSURE. I KNOW THE UNIVERSITY MUST HAVE SIMILAR RESTRICTIONS, IF NOT *EVEN MORE* STRINGENT. ALL WE CAN DO IS HOPE AND PRAY THEY'RE GOING TO BE OKAY. WITH THAT HIGH LEVEL OF EXPOSURE, WE'RE LUCKY THEY'RE STILL ALIVE.

THIS LEVEL OF EXPOSURE HAD TO BE FROM EITHER A MECHANICAL MALFUNCTION, OR A GROSS MIS-CALCULATION.

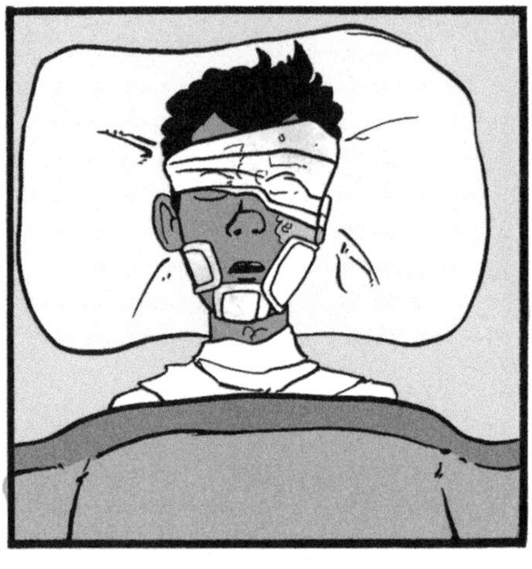

Depth of damaged skin, due to radiation burns:

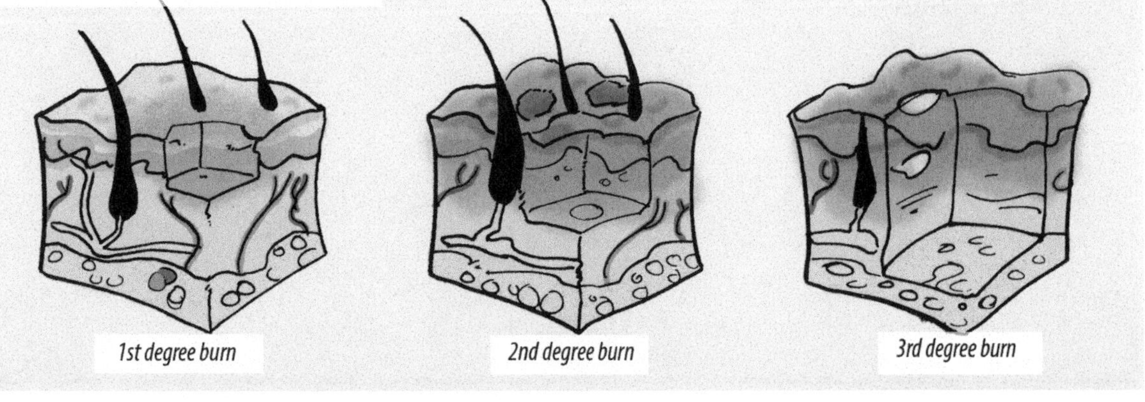
1st degree burn
2nd degree burn
3rd degree burn

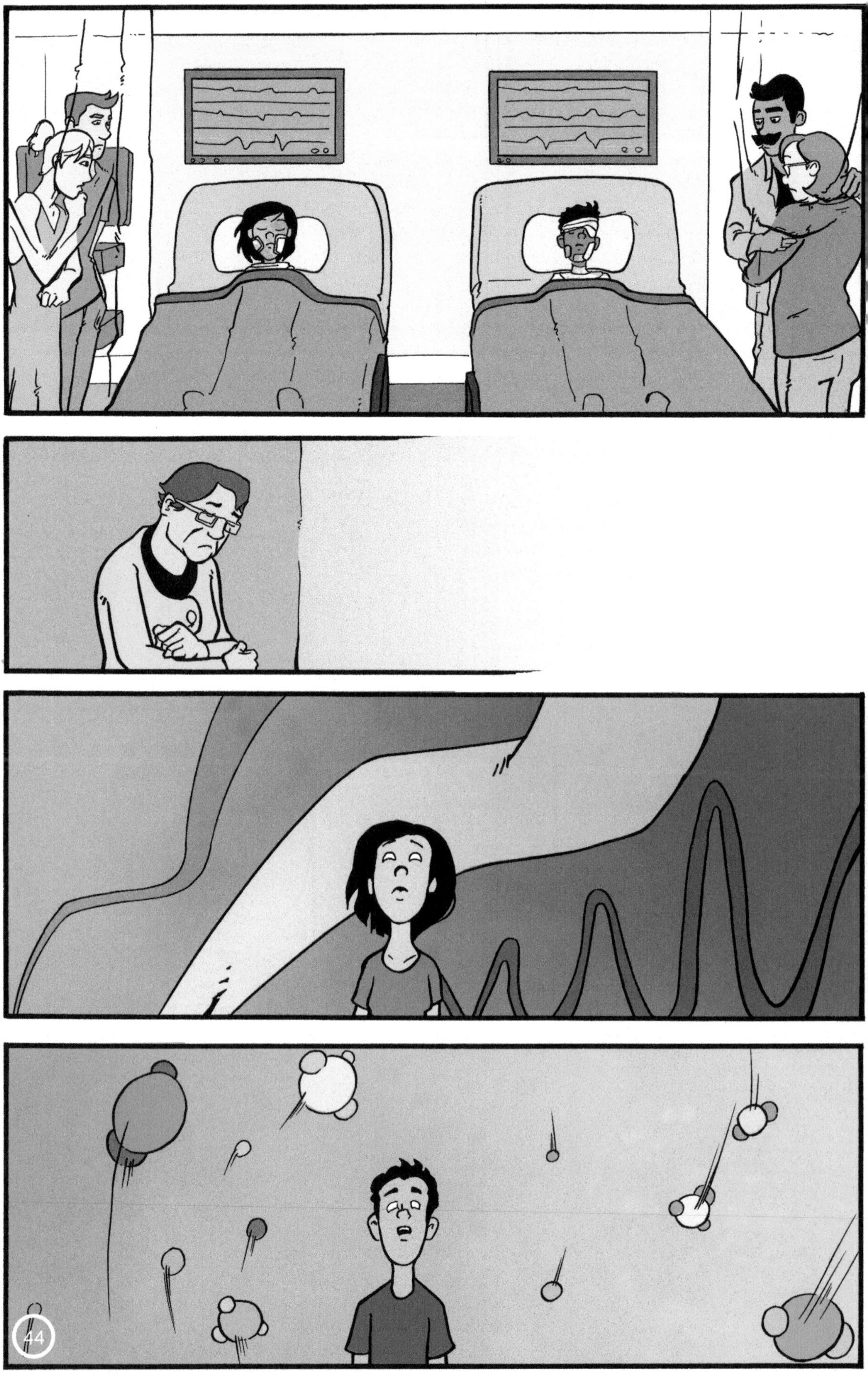

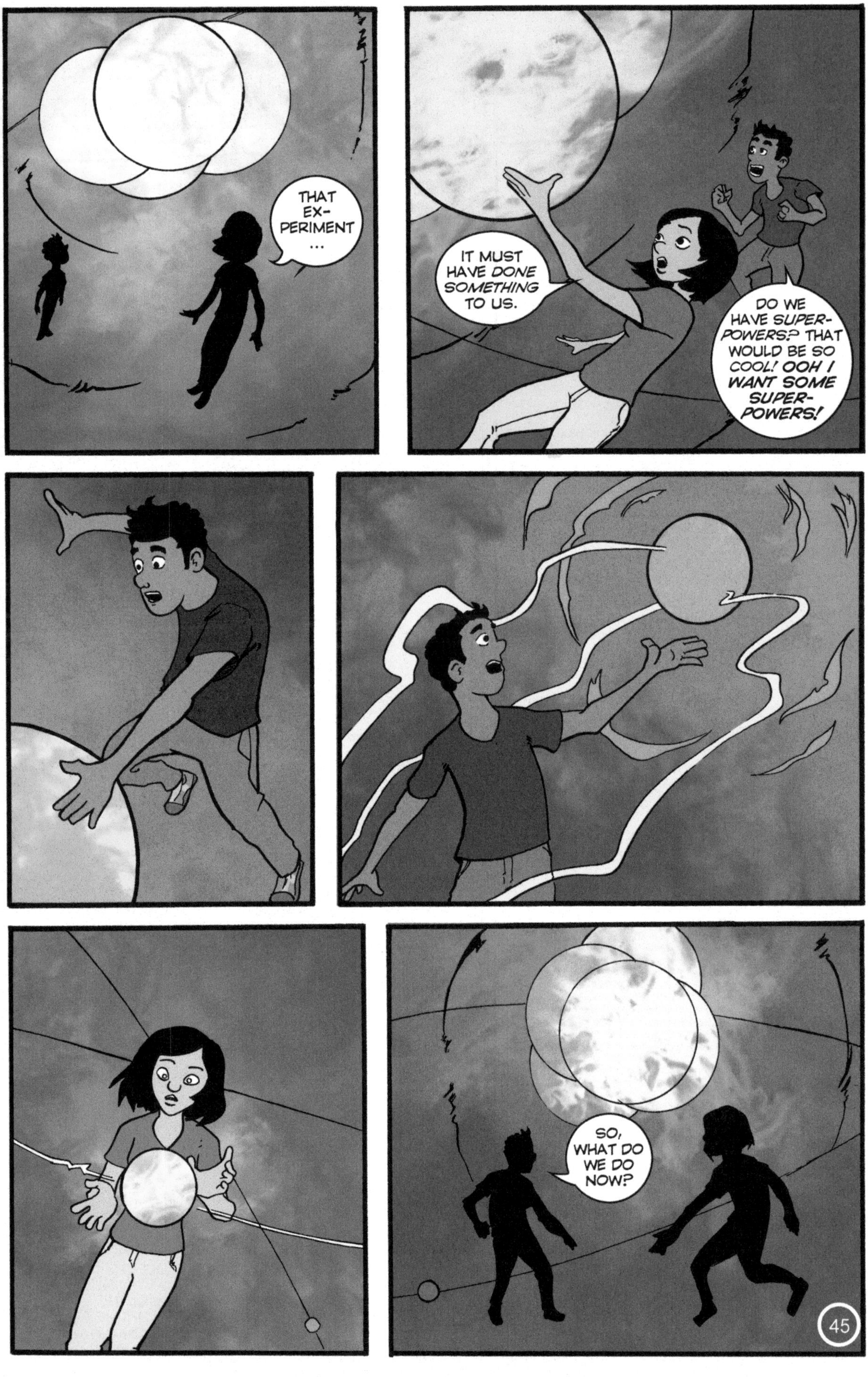
THAT EX-PERIMENT ...
IT MUST HAVE DONE SOMETHING TO US.
DO WE HAVE SUPER-POWERS? THAT WOULD BE SO COOL! OOH I WANT SOME SUPER-POWERS!
SO, WHAT DO WE DO NOW?

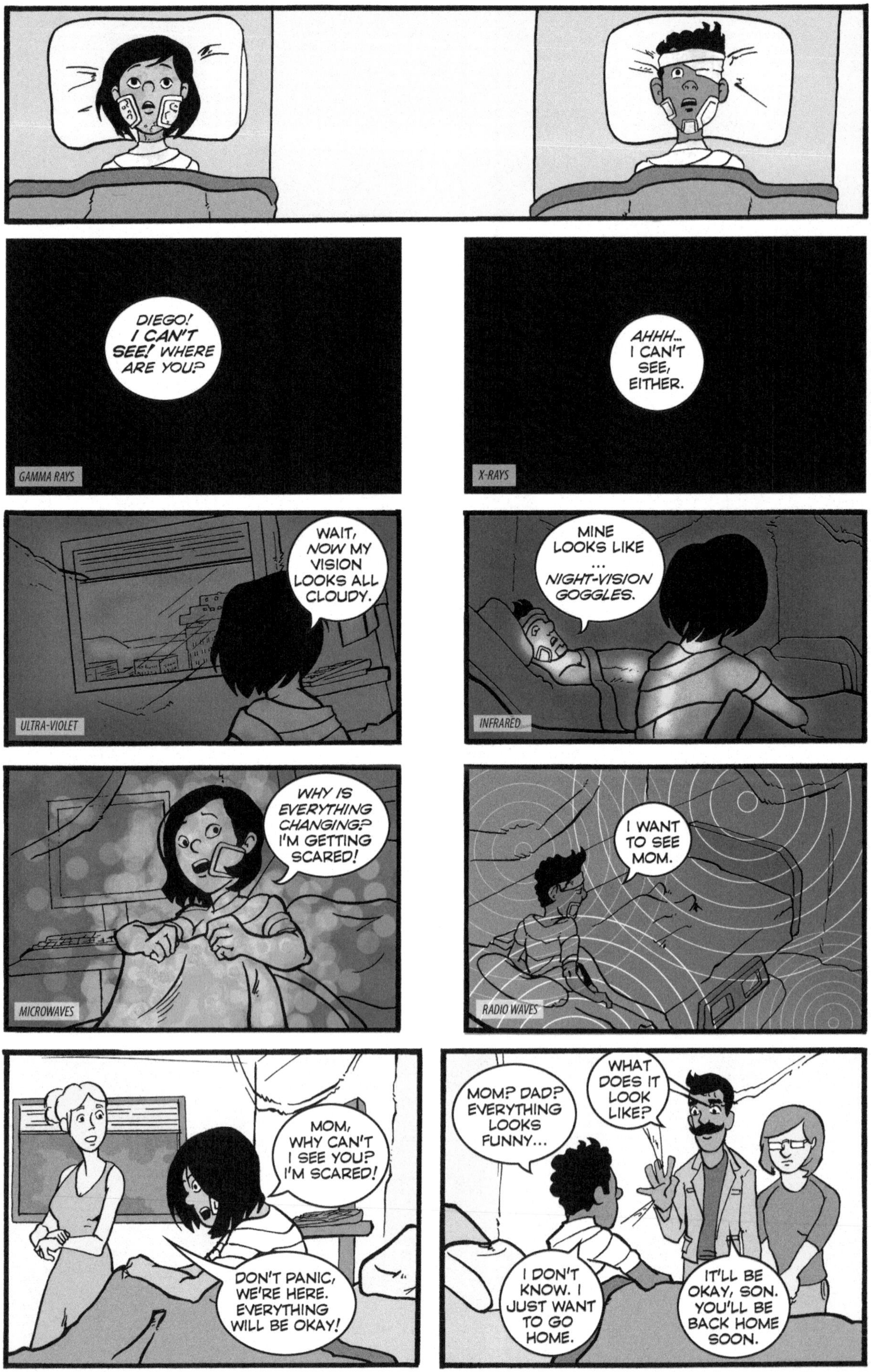

DIEGO! I CAN'T SEE! WHERE ARE YOU?
GAMMA RAYS
AHHH... I CAN'T SEE, EITHER.
X-RAYS
WAIT, NOW MY VISION LOOKS ALL CLOUDY.
ULTRA-VIOLET
MINE LOOKS LIKE ... NIGHT-VISION GOGGLES.
INFRARED
WHY IS EVERYTHING CHANGING? I'M GETTING SCARED!
MICROWAVES
I WANT TO SEE MOM.
RADIO WAVES
MOM, WHY CAN'T I SEE YOU? I'M SCARED!
DON'T PANIC, WE'RE HERE. EVERYTHING WILL BE OKAY!
MOM? DAD? EVERYTHING LOOKS FUNNY...
WHAT DOES IT LOOK LIKE?
I DON'T KNOW. I JUST WANT TO GO HOME.
IT'LL BE OKAY, SON. YOU'LL BE BACK HOME SOON.

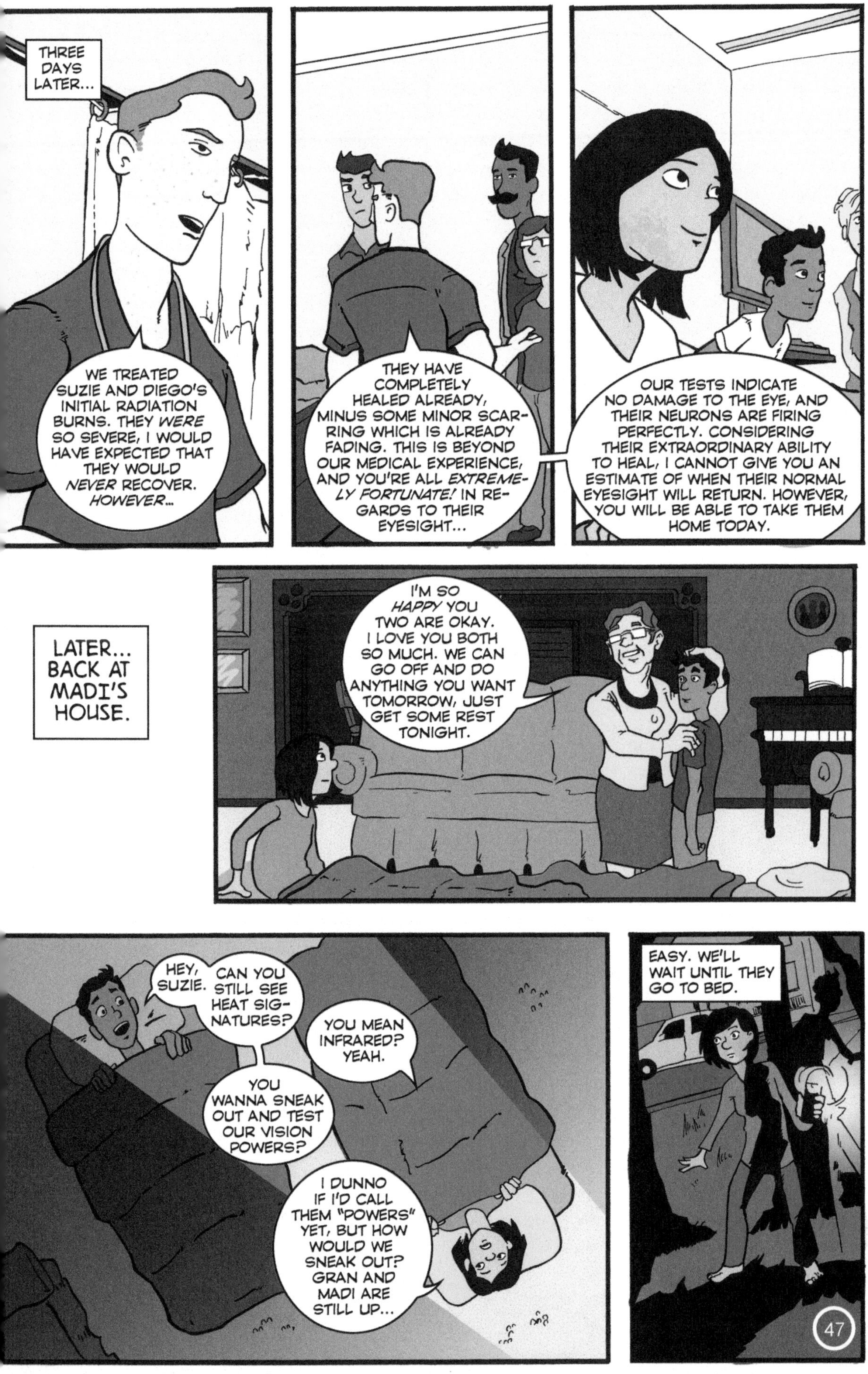
THREE DAYS LATER...
WE TREATED SUZIE AND DIEGO'S INITIAL RADIATION BURNS. THEY *WERE* SO SEVERE, I WOULD HAVE EXPECTED THAT THEY WOULD *NEVER* RECOVER. *HOWEVER*...
THEY HAVE COMPLETELY HEALED ALREADY, MINUS SOME MINOR SCARRING WHICH IS ALREADY FADING. THIS IS BEYOND OUR MEDICAL EXPERIENCE, AND YOU'RE ALL *EXTREMELY FORTUNATE!* IN REGARDS TO THEIR EYESIGHT...
OUR TESTS INDICATE NO DAMAGE TO THE EYE, AND THEIR NEURONS ARE FIRING PERFECTLY. CONSIDERING THEIR EXTRAORDINARY ABILITY TO HEAL, I CANNOT GIVE YOU AN ESTIMATE OF WHEN THEIR NORMAL EYESIGHT WILL RETURN. HOWEVER, YOU WILL BE ABLE TO TAKE THEM HOME TODAY.
LATER... BACK AT MADI'S HOUSE.
I'M SO *HAPPY* YOU TWO ARE OKAY. I LOVE YOU BOTH SO MUCH. WE CAN GO OFF AND DO ANYTHING YOU WANT TOMORROW, JUST GET SOME REST TONIGHT.
HEY, SUZIE.
CAN YOU STILL SEE HEAT SIGNATURES?
YOU MEAN INFRARED? YEAH.
YOU WANNA SNEAK OUT AND TEST OUR VISION POWERS?
I DUNNO IF I'D CALL THEM "POWERS" YET, BUT HOW WOULD WE SNEAK OUT? GRAN AND MADI ARE STILL UP...
EASY. WE'LL WAIT UNTIL THEY GO TO BED.

OXYGEN ATOMS?
I WISH GRAN COULD SEE THIS.
LOOK AT HOW THESE ELECTRON ORBITALS REARRANGE WHEN THE ATOMS LINK UP.
I THINK I JUST MADE OZONE!
AHH, *BEAUTIFUL!* AND TOASTY! IT'S AN *EXO-THERMIC REACTION!*

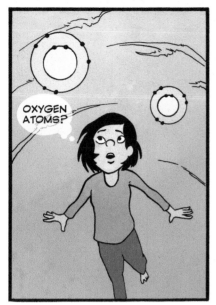

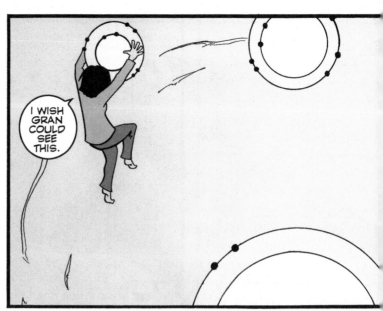

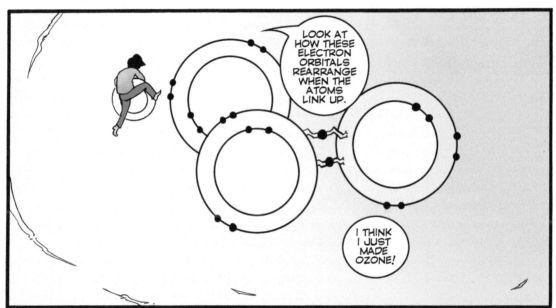

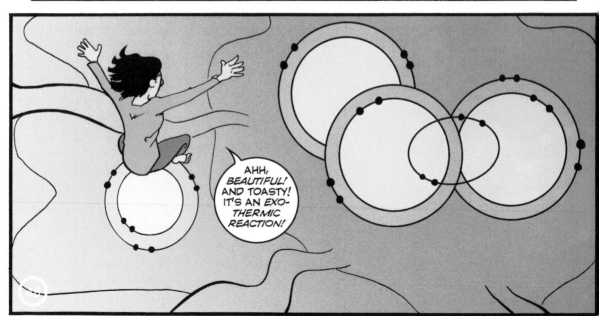

I CAN SEE...
EVERYTHING.
THE CELLS...
THEIR PROTEINS...
EVEN ATOMS!
WHAT IS THAT? WHY DOES THAT CARBON HAVE EIGHT NEUTRONS? IS IT A DIFFERENT TYPE OF ATOM?
IT'S AN ISOTOPE. AS LONG AS THERE ARE SIX PROTONS IT'S A CARBON ATOM, BUT THEY CAN VARY IN NEUTRONS, WHICH GIVES THEM A DIFFERENT MASS.
WE SHOULD GET BACK BEFORE GRAN AND MADI WAKE UP!

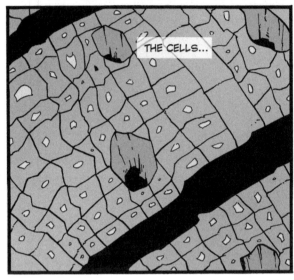

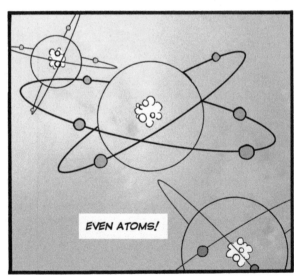

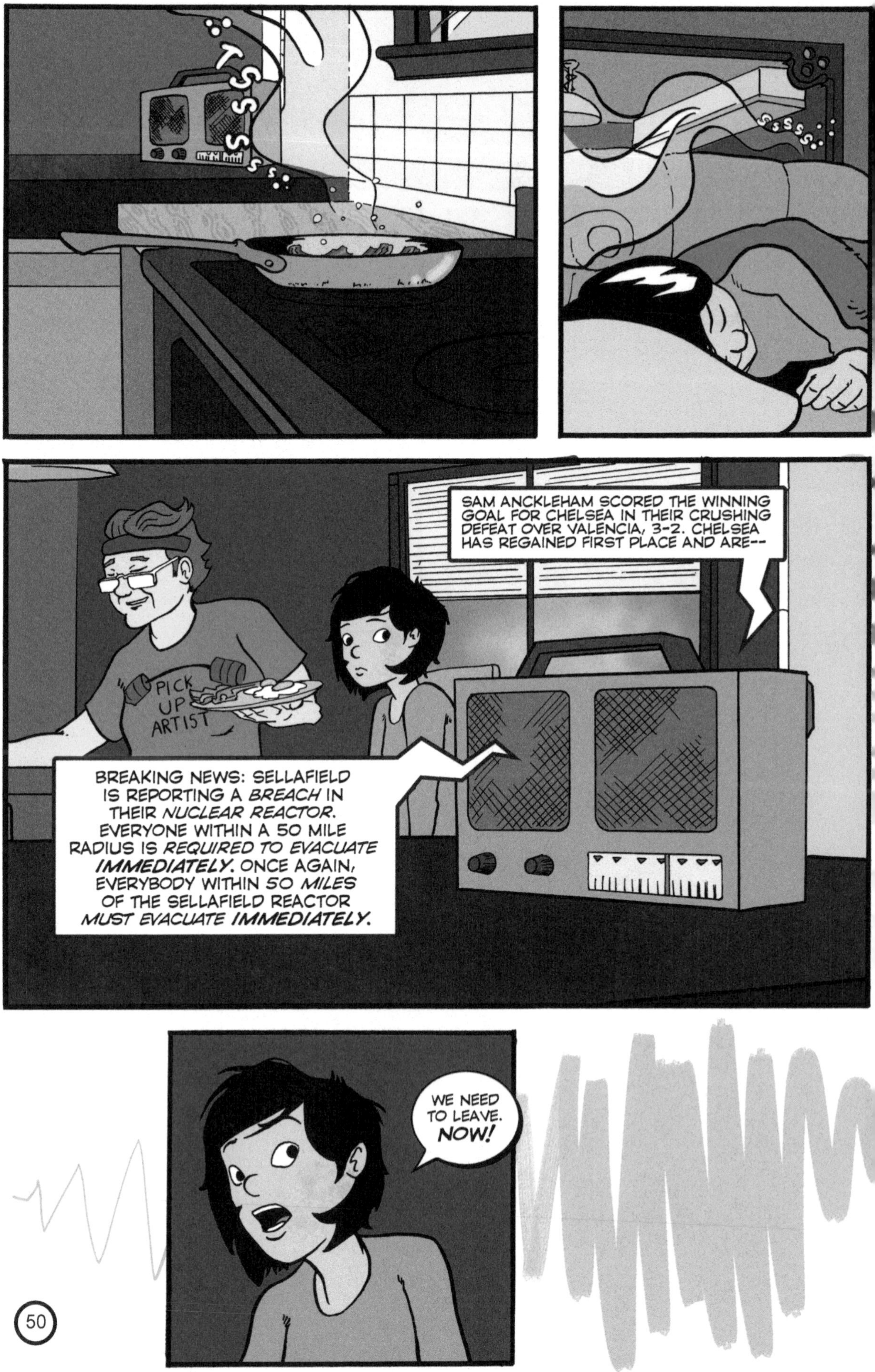
SAM ANCKLEHAM SCORED THE WINNING GOAL FOR CHELSEA IN THEIR CRUSHING DEFEAT OVER VALENCIA, 3-2. CHELSEA HAS REGAINED FIRST PLACE AND ARE--
PICK UP ARTIST
BREAKING NEWS: SELLAFIELD IS REPORTING A *BREACH* IN THEIR *NUCLEAR REACTOR*. EVERYONE WITHIN A 50 MILE RADIUS IS *REQUIRED TO EVACUATE* ***IMMEDIATELY***. ONCE AGAIN, EVERYBODY WITHIN 50 *MILES* OF THE SELLAFIELD REACTOR *MUST EVACUATE* ***IMMEDIATELY***.
WE NEED TO LEAVE. ***NOW!***

Chapter 3

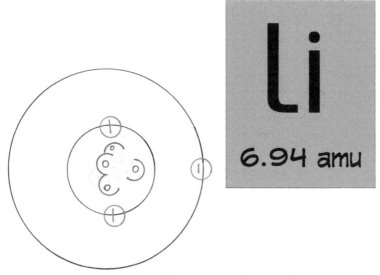

Li

6.94 amu

Lithium has been used as a coolant in experimental fusion reactors.

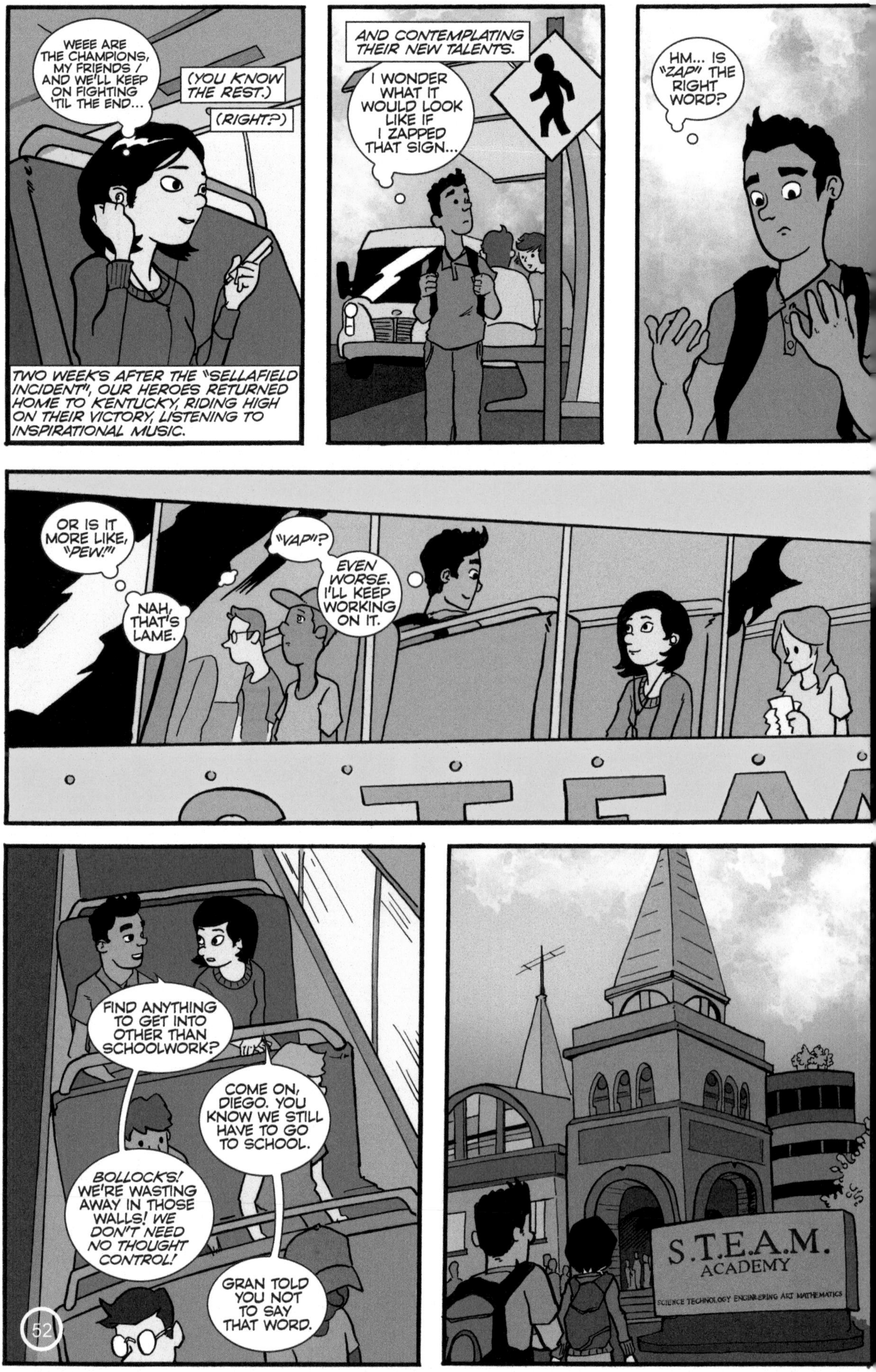
WEEE ARE THE CHAMPIONS, MY FRIENDS / AND WE'LL KEEP ON FIGHTING 'TIL THE END...
(YOU KNOW THE REST.)
(RIGHT?)
TWO WEEKS AFTER THE "SELLAFIELD INCIDENT", OUR HEROES RETURNED HOME TO KENTUCKY, RIDING HIGH ON THEIR VICTORY, LISTENING TO INSPIRATIONAL MUSIC.
AND CONTEMPLATING THEIR NEW TALENTS.
I WONDER WHAT IT WOULD LOOK LIKE IF I ZAPPED THAT SIGN...
HM... IS "ZAP" THE RIGHT WORD?
OR IS IT MORE LIKE, "PEW!"
NAH, THAT'S LAME.
"VAP"?
EVEN WORSE. I'LL KEEP WORKING ON IT.
FIND ANYTHING TO GET INTO OTHER THAN SCHOOLWORK?
COME ON, DIEGO. YOU KNOW WE STILL HAVE TO GO TO SCHOOL.
BOLLOCKS! WE'RE WASTING AWAY IN THOSE WALLS! WE DON'T NEED NO THOUGHT CONTROL!
GRAN TOLD YOU NOT TO SAY THAT WORD.
S.T.E.A.M.
ACADEMY
SCIENCE TECHNOLOGY ENGINEERING ART MATHEMATICS

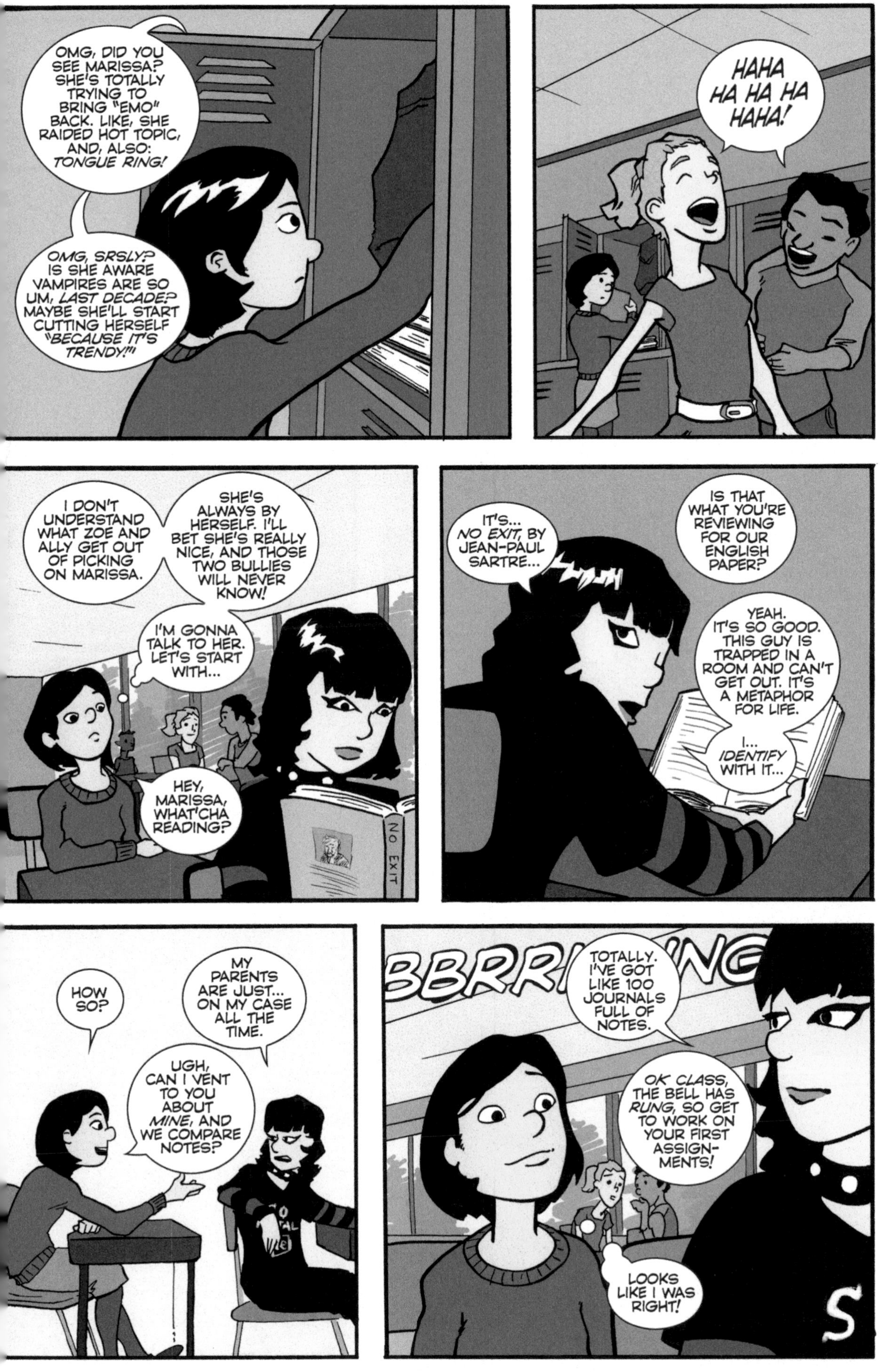
OMG, DID YOU SEE MARISSA? SHE'S TOTALLY TRYING TO BRING "EMO" BACK. LIKE, SHE RAIDED HOT TOPIC, AND, ALSO: *TONGUE RING!*
OMG, SRSLY? IS SHE AWARE VAMPIRES ARE SO UM, *LAST DECADE?* MAYBE SHE'LL START CUTTING HERSELF *"BECAUSE IT'S TRENDY!"*
HAHA HA HA HA HAHA!
I DON'T UNDERSTAND WHAT ZOE AND ALLY GET OUT OF PICKING ON MARISSA.
SHE'S ALWAYS BY HERSELF. I'LL BET SHE'S REALLY NICE, AND THOSE TWO BULLIES WILL NEVER KNOW!
I'M GONNA TALK TO HER. LET'S START WITH...
HEY, MARISSA, WHAT'CHA READING?
NO EXIT
IT'S... *NO EXIT,* BY JEAN-PAUL SARTRE...
IS THAT WHAT YOU'RE REVIEWING FOR OUR ENGLISH PAPER?
YEAH. IT'S SO GOOD. THIS GUY IS TRAPPED IN A ROOM AND CAN'T GET OUT. IT'S A METAPHOR FOR LIFE.
I... *IDENTIFY* WITH IT...
HOW SO?
MY PARENTS ARE JUST... ON MY CASE ALL THE TIME.
UGH, CAN I VENT TO YOU ABOUT *MINE,* AND WE COMPARE NOTES?
BBRRI
NG
TOTALLY. I'VE GOT LIKE 100 JOURNALS FULL OF NOTES.
OK CLASS, THE BELL HAS *RUNG,* SO GET TO WORK ON YOUR FIRST ASSIGN-MENTS!
LOOKS LIKE I WAS RIGHT!

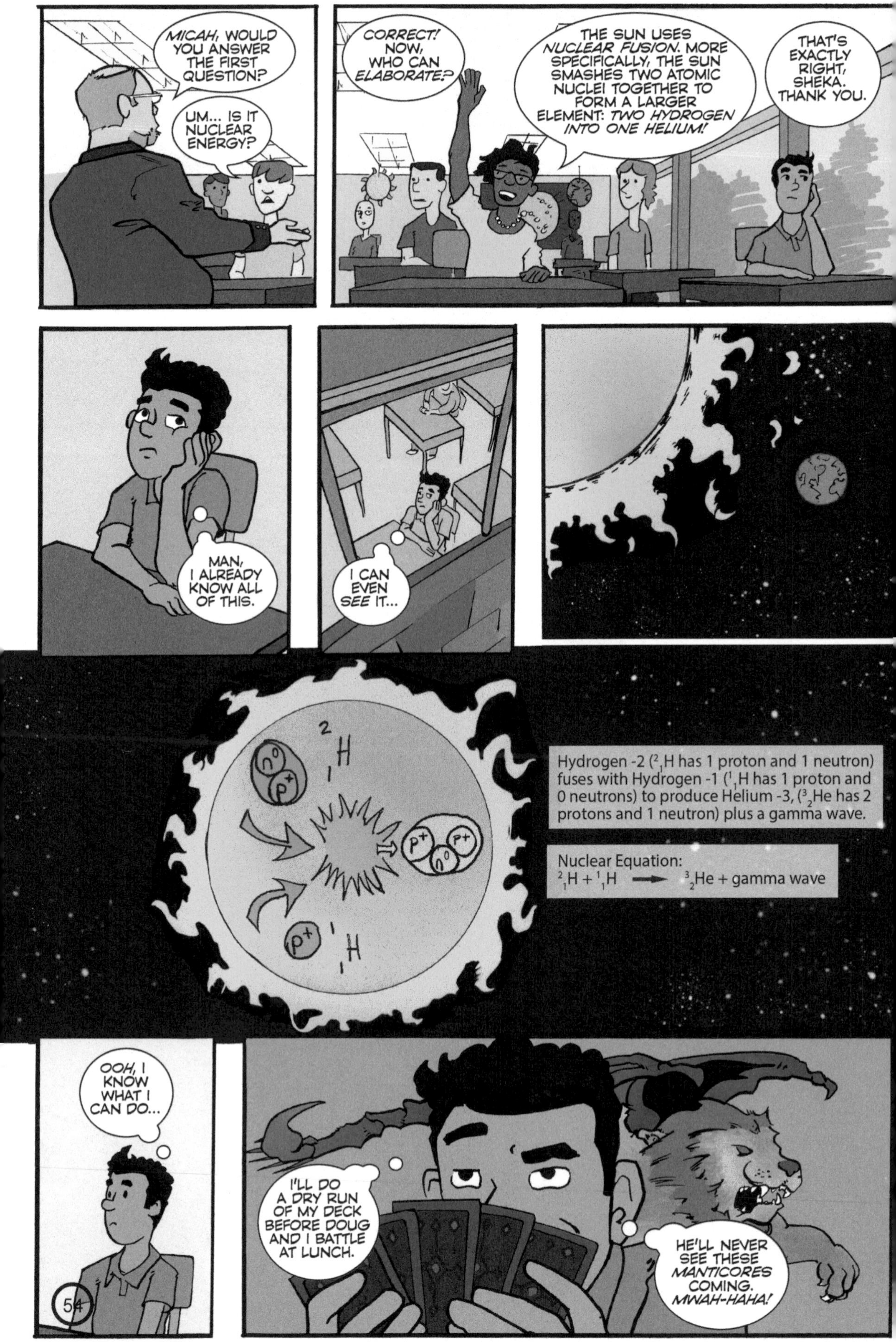
MICAH, WOULD YOU ANSWER THE FIRST QUESTION?
UM... IS IT NUCLEAR ENERGY?
CORRECT! NOW, WHO CAN ELABORATE?
THE SUN USES NUCLEAR FUSION. MORE SPECIFICALLY, THE SUN SMASHES TWO ATOMIC NUCLEI TOGETHER TO FORM A LARGER ELEMENT: TWO HYDROGEN INTO ONE HELIUM!
THAT'S EXACTLY RIGHT, SHEKA. THANK YOU.
MAN, I ALREADY KNOW ALL OF THIS.
I CAN EVEN SEE IT...
$^{2}_{1}H$
$^{1}_{1}H$
Hydrogen -2 ($^{2}_{1}H$ has 1 proton and 1 neutron) fuses with Hydrogen -1 ($^{1}_{1}H$ has 1 proton and 0 neutrons) to produce Helium -3, ($^{3}_{2}He$ has 2 protons and 1 neutron) plus a gamma wave.
Nuclear Equation:
$^{2}_{1}H + ^{1}_{1}H \longrightarrow ^{3}_{2}He$ + gamma wave
OOH, I KNOW WHAT I CAN DO...
I'LL DO A DRY RUN OF MY DECK BEFORE DOUG AND I BATTLE AT LUNCH.
HE'LL NEVER SEE THESE MANTICORES COMING. MWAH-HAHA!

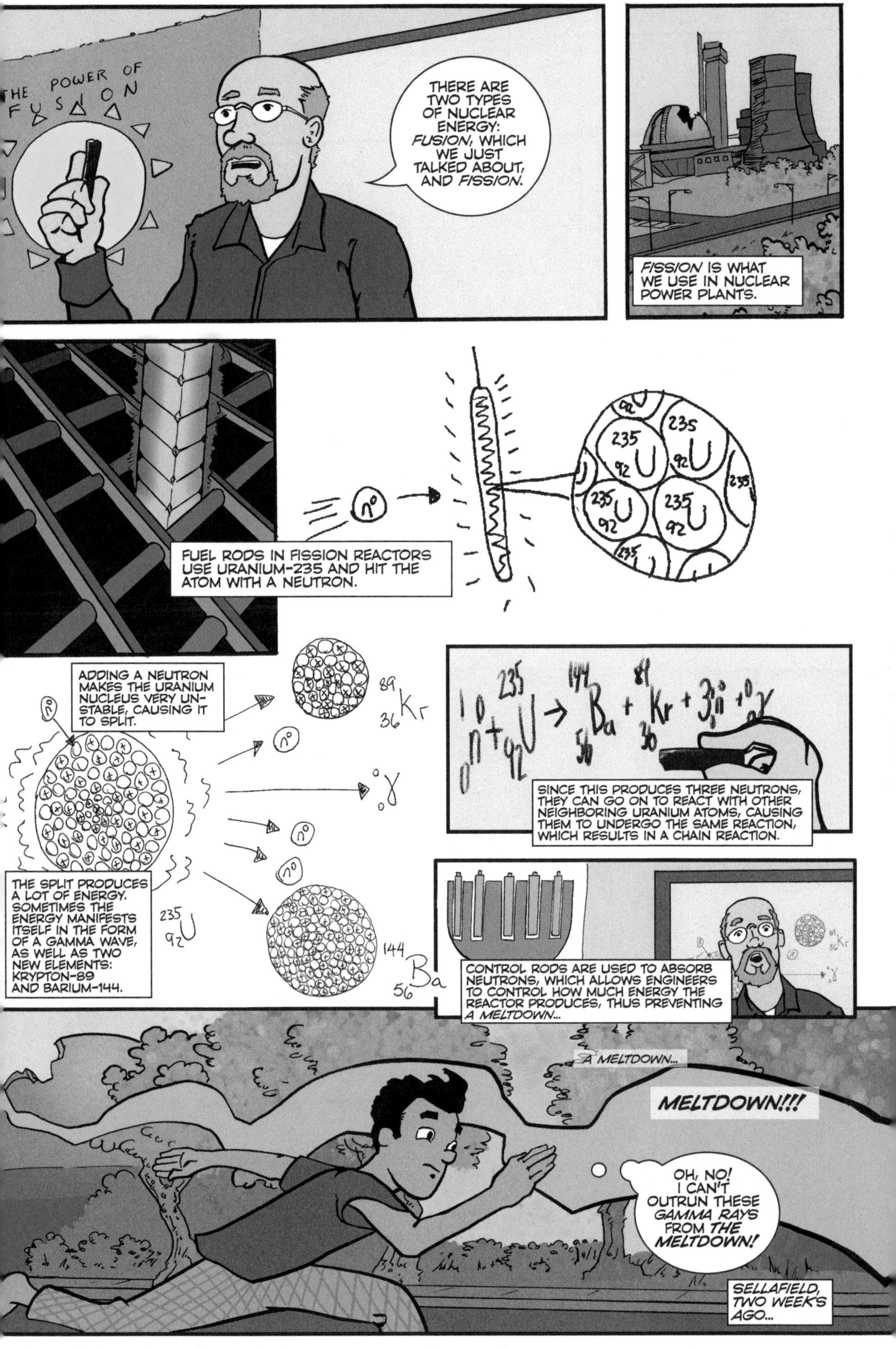
THE POWER OF FUSION
THERE ARE TWO TYPES OF NUCLEAR ENERGY: *FUSION*, WHICH WE JUST TALKED ABOUT, AND *FISSION*.
FISSION IS WHAT WE USE IN NUCLEAR POWER PLANTS.
FUEL RODS IN FISSION REACTORS USE URANIUM-235 AND HIT THE ATOM WITH A NEUTRON.
ADDING A NEUTRON MAKES THE URANIUM NUCLEUS VERY UNSTABLE, CAUSING IT TO SPLIT.
$^{89}_{36}Kr$
$^{235}_{92}U$
$^{144}_{56}Ba$
THE SPLIT PRODUCES A LOT OF ENERGY. SOMETIMES THE ENERGY MANIFESTS ITSELF IN THE FORM OF A GAMMA WAVE, AS WELL AS TWO NEW ELEMENTS: KRYPTON-89 AND BARIUM-144.
$^{1}_{0}n + ^{235}_{92}U \rightarrow ^{144}_{56}Ba + ^{89}_{36}Kr + 3^{1}_{0}n + ^{0}_{0}\gamma$
SINCE THIS PRODUCES THREE NEUTRONS, THEY CAN GO ON TO REACT WITH OTHER NEIGHBORING URANIUM ATOMS, CAUSING THEM TO UNDERGO THE SAME REACTION, WHICH RESULTS IN A CHAIN REACTION.
CONTROL RODS ARE USED TO ABSORB NEUTRONS, WHICH ALLOWS ENGINEERS TO CONTROL HOW MUCH ENERGY THE REACTOR PRODUCES, THUS PREVENTING *A MELTDOWN*...
A MELTDOWN...
MELTDOWN!!!
OH, NO! I CAN'T OUTRUN THESE *GAMMA RAYS* FROM ***THE MELTDOWN!***
SELLAFIELD, TWO WEEKS AGO...

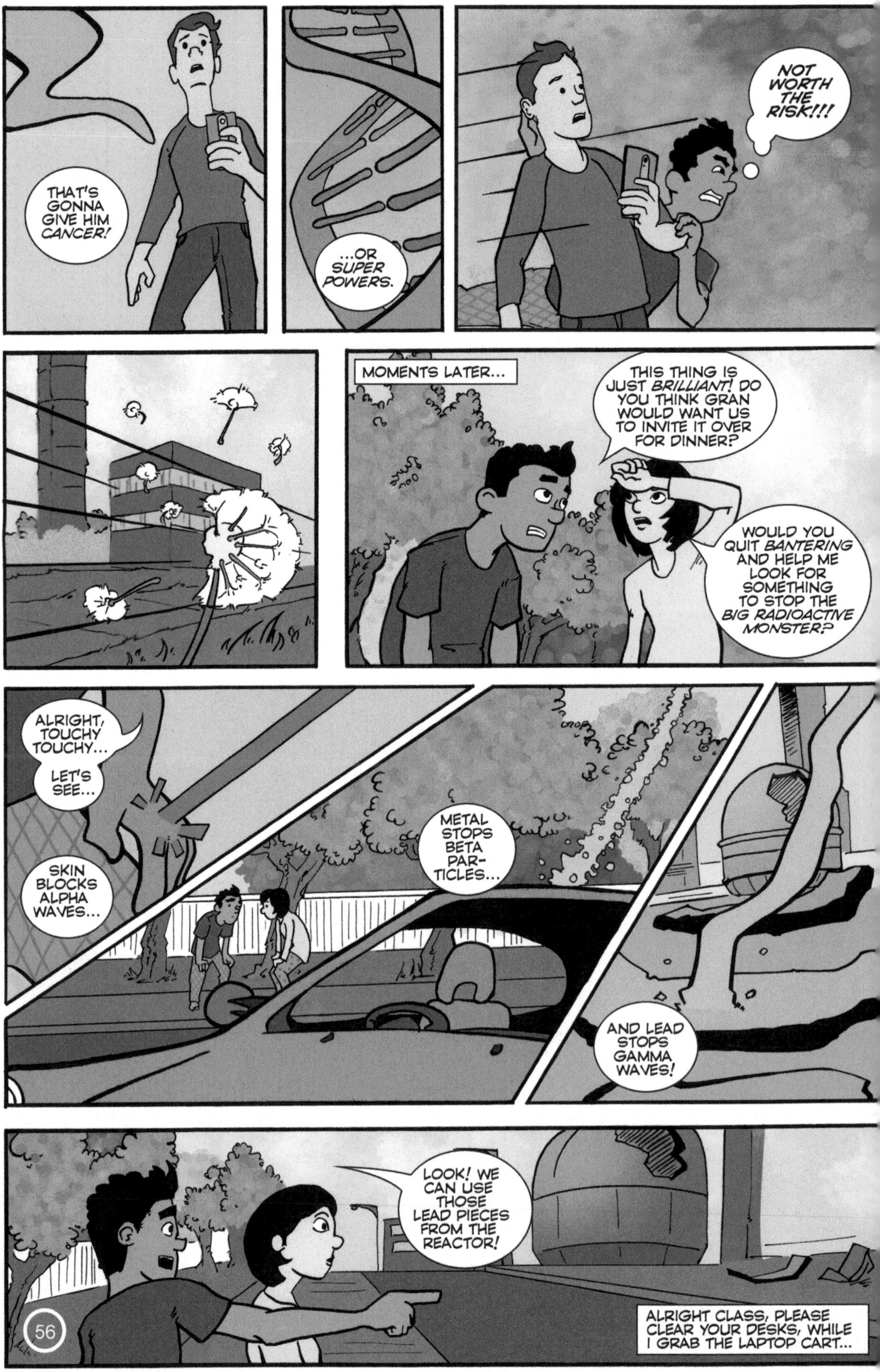

THAT'S GONNA GIVE HIM CANCER!
...OR SUPER POWERS.
NOT WORTH THE RISK!!!
MOMENTS LATER...
THIS THING IS JUST BRILLIANT! DO YOU THINK GRAN WOULD WANT US TO INVITE IT OVER FOR DINNER?
WOULD YOU QUIT BANTERING AND HELP ME LOOK FOR SOMETHING TO STOP THE BIG RADIOACTIVE MONSTER?
ALRIGHT, TOUCHY TOUCHY...
LET'S SEE...
SKIN BLOCKS ALPHA WAVES...
METAL STOPS BETA PAR-TICLES...
AND LEAD STOPS GAMMA WAVES!
LOOK! WE CAN USE THOSE LEAD PIECES FROM THE REACTOR!
ALRIGHT CLASS, PLEASE CLEAR YOUR DESKS, WHILE I GRAB THE LAPTOP CART...

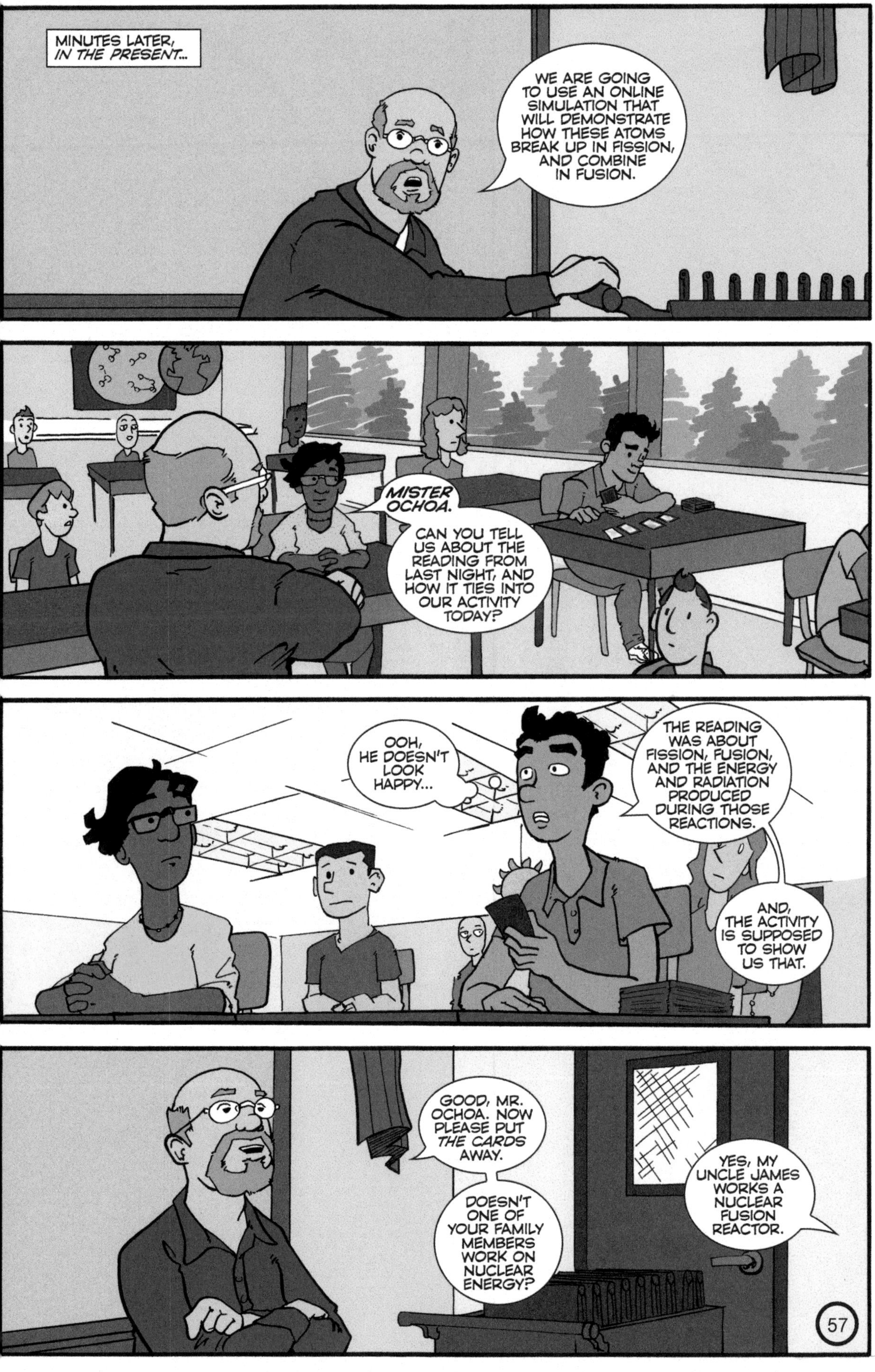
MINUTES LATER, IN THE PRESENT...
WE ARE GOING TO USE AN ONLINE SIMULATION THAT WILL DEMONSTRATE HOW THESE ATOMS BREAK UP IN FISSION, AND COMBINE IN FUSION.
MISTER OCHOA.
CAN YOU TELL US ABOUT THE READING FROM LAST NIGHT, AND HOW IT TIES INTO OUR ACTIVITY TODAY?
OOH, HE DOESN'T LOOK HAPPY...
THE READING WAS ABOUT FISSION, FUSION, AND THE ENERGY AND RADIATION PRODUCED DURING THOSE REACTIONS.
AND, THE ACTIVITY IS SUPPOSED TO SHOW US THAT.
GOOD, MR. OCHOA. NOW PLEASE PUT THE CARDS AWAY.
DOESN'T ONE OF YOUR FAMILY MEMBERS WORK ON NUCLEAR ENERGY?
YES, MY UNCLE JAMES WORKS A NUCLEAR FUSION REACTOR.

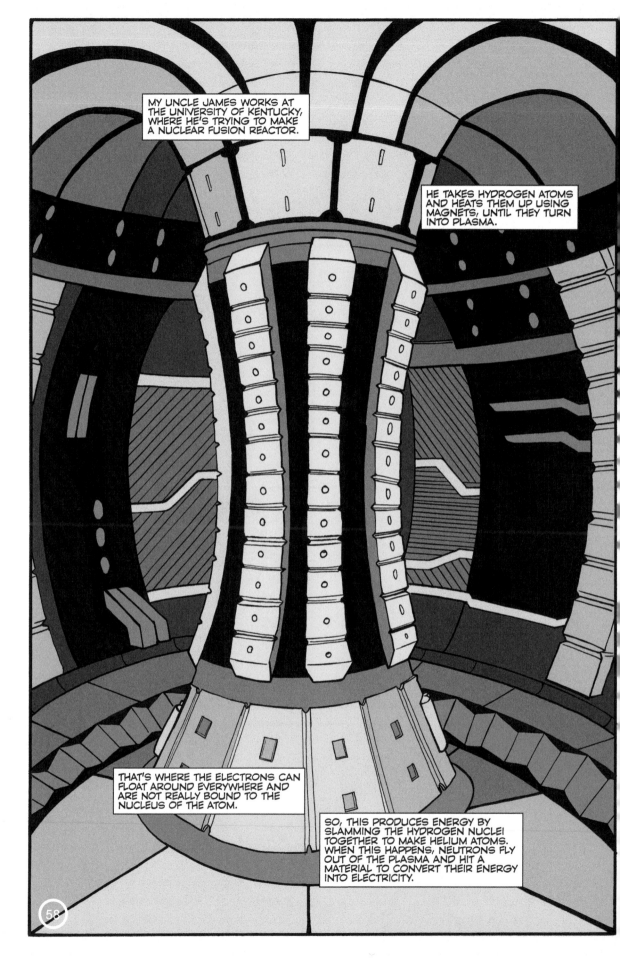

MY UNCLE JAMES WORKS AT THE UNIVERSITY OF KENTUCKY, WHERE HE'S TRYING TO MAKE A NUCLEAR FUSION REACTOR.

HE TAKES HYDROGEN ATOMS AND HEATS THEM UP USING MAGNETS, UNTIL THEY TURN INTO PLASMA.

THAT'S WHERE THE ELECTRONS CAN FLOAT AROUND EVERYWHERE AND ARE NOT REALLY BOUND TO THE NUCLEUS OF THE ATOM.

SO, THIS PRODUCES ENERGY BY SLAMMING THE HYDROGEN NUCLEI TOGETHER TO MAKE HELIUM ATOMS. WHEN THIS HAPPENS, NEUTRONS FLY OUT OF THE PLASMA AND HIT A MATERIAL TO CONVERT THEIR ENERGY INTO ELECTRICITY.

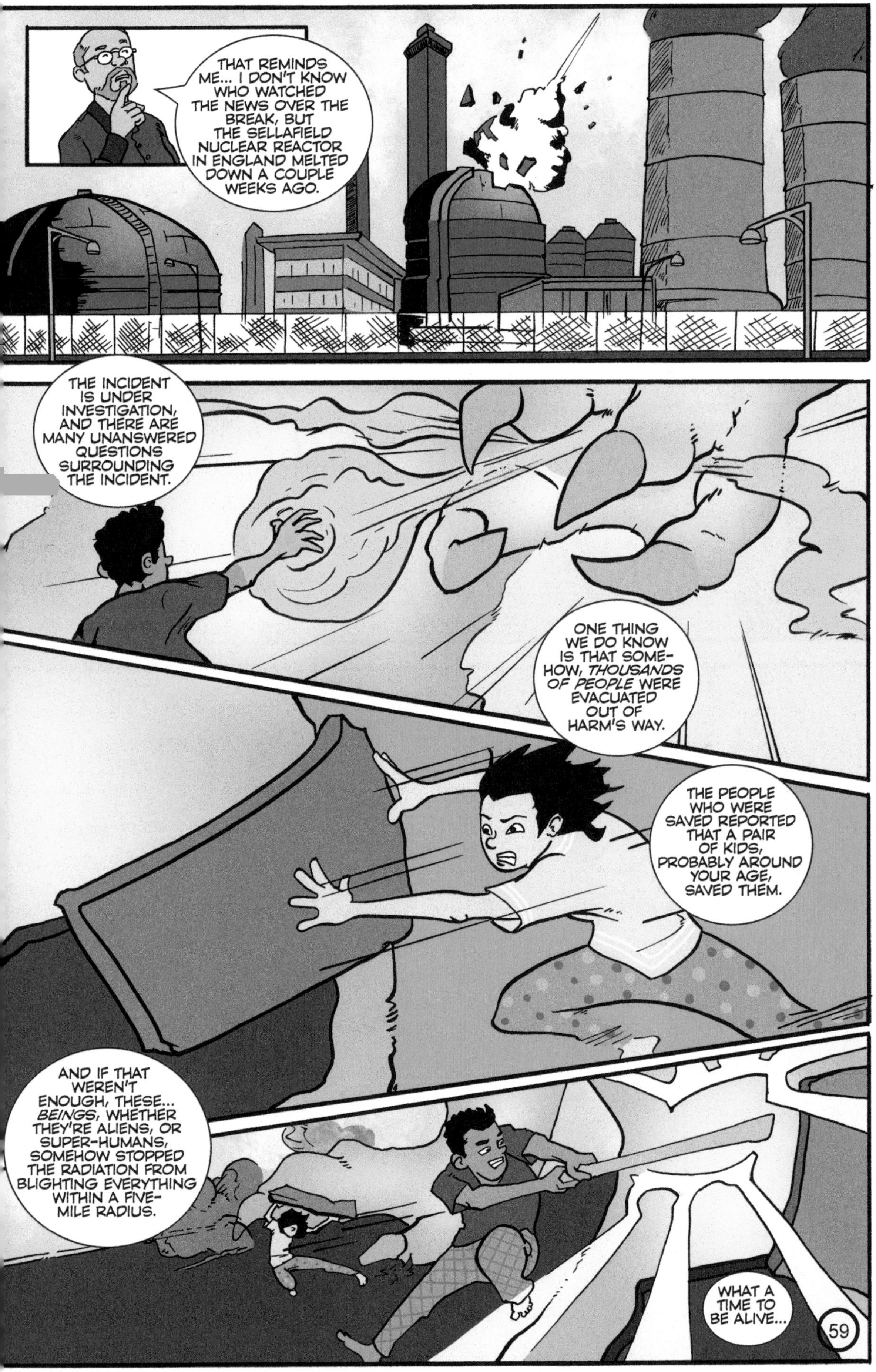
THAT REMINDS ME... I DON'T KNOW WHO WATCHED THE NEWS OVER THE BREAK, BUT THE SELLAFIELD NUCLEAR REACTOR IN ENGLAND MELTED DOWN A COUPLE WEEKS AGO.
THE INCIDENT IS UNDER INVESTIGATION, AND THERE ARE MANY UNANSWERED QUESTIONS SURROUNDING THE INCIDENT.
ONE THING WE DO KNOW IS THAT SOME-HOW, *THOUSANDS OF PEOPLE* WERE EVACUATED OUT OF HARM'S WAY.
THE PEOPLE WHO WERE SAVED REPORTED THAT A PAIR OF KIDS, PROBABLY AROUND YOUR AGE, SAVED THEM.
AND IF THAT WEREN'T ENOUGH, THESE... *BEINGS*, WHETHER THEY'RE ALIENS, OR SUPER-HUMANS, SOMEHOW STOPPED THE RADIATION FROM BLIGHTING EVERYTHING WITHIN A FIVE-MILE RADIUS.
WHAT A TIME TO BE ALIVE...

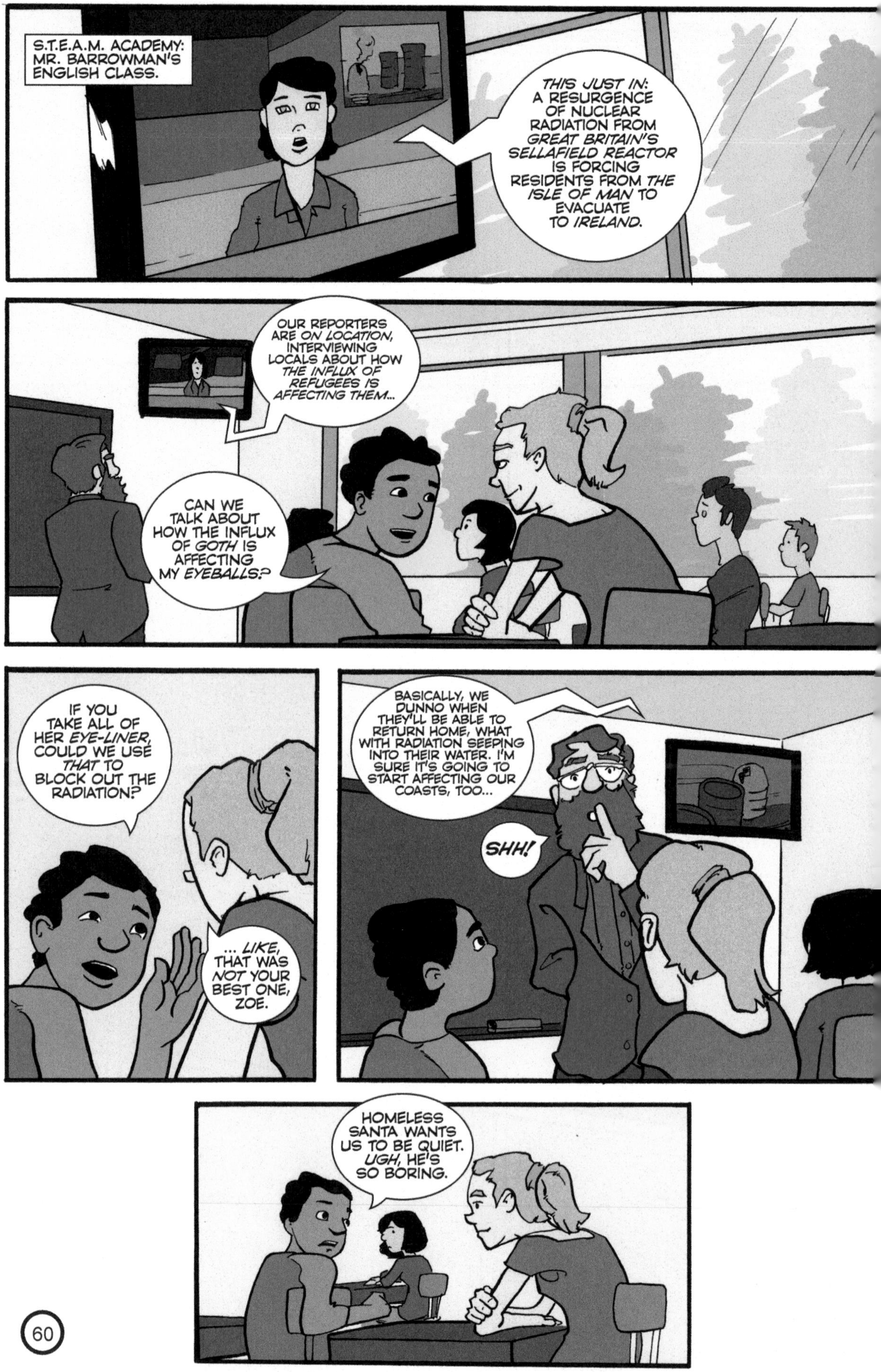
S.T.E.A.M. ACADEMY: MR. BARROWMAN'S ENGLISH CLASS.
THIS JUST IN: A RESURGENCE OF NUCLEAR RADIATION FROM GREAT BRITAIN'S SELLAFIELD REACTOR IS FORCING RESIDENTS FROM THE ISLE OF MAN TO EVACUATE TO IRELAND.
OUR REPORTERS ARE ON LOCATION, INTERVIEWING LOCALS ABOUT HOW THE INFLUX OF REFUGEES IS AFFECTING THEM...
CAN WE TALK ABOUT HOW THE INFLUX OF GOTH IS AFFECTING MY EYEBALLS?
IF YOU TAKE ALL OF HER EYE-LINER, COULD WE USE THAT TO BLOCK OUT THE RADIATION?
... LIKE, THAT WAS NOT YOUR BEST ONE, ZOE.
BASICALLY, WE DUNNO WHEN THEY'LL BE ABLE TO RETURN HOME, WHAT WITH RADIATION SEEPING INTO THEIR WATER. I'M SURE IT'S GOING TO START AFFECTING OUR COASTS, TOO...
SHH!
HOMELESS SANTA WANTS US TO BE QUIET. UGH, HE'S SO BORING.

SIGH... ALLY AND ZOE... I SHOULD STAND UP TO THEM.

IT'S WHAT *ANY HERO* WOULD DO.

HEROES HAVE THE GUTS TO HELP THE INNOCENT.

THEY DON'T JUST SIT BACK AND WATCH.

AND THEY NEVER, EVER EVER...

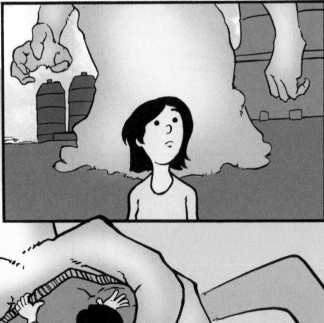

...EVER GIVE UP!

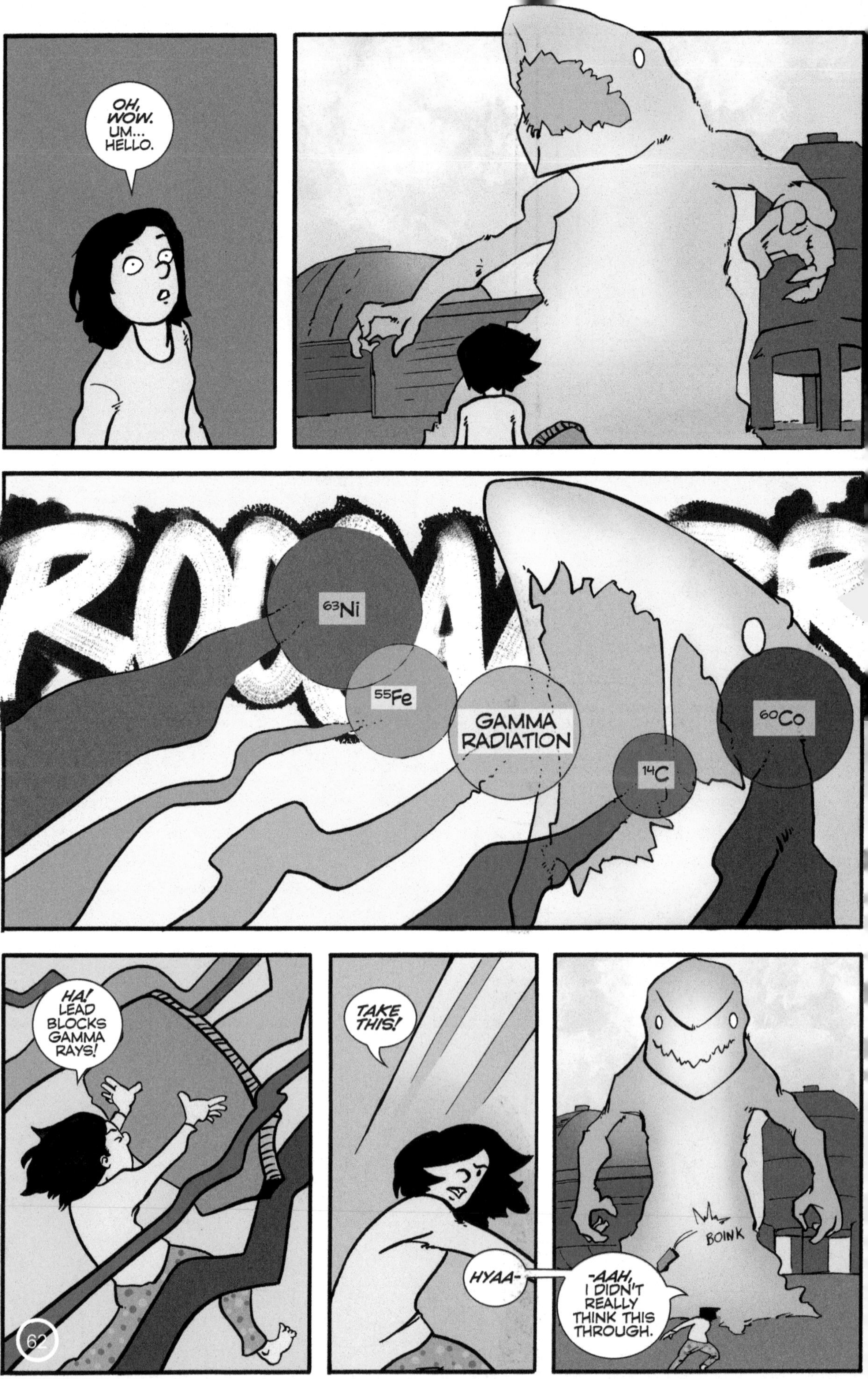
OH, WOW. UM... HELLO.
63Ni
55Fe
GAMMA RADIATION
14C
60Co
HA! LEAD BLOCKS GAMMA RAYS!
TAKE THIS!
BOINK
HYAA-
-AAH, I DIDN'T REALLY THINK THIS THROUGH.

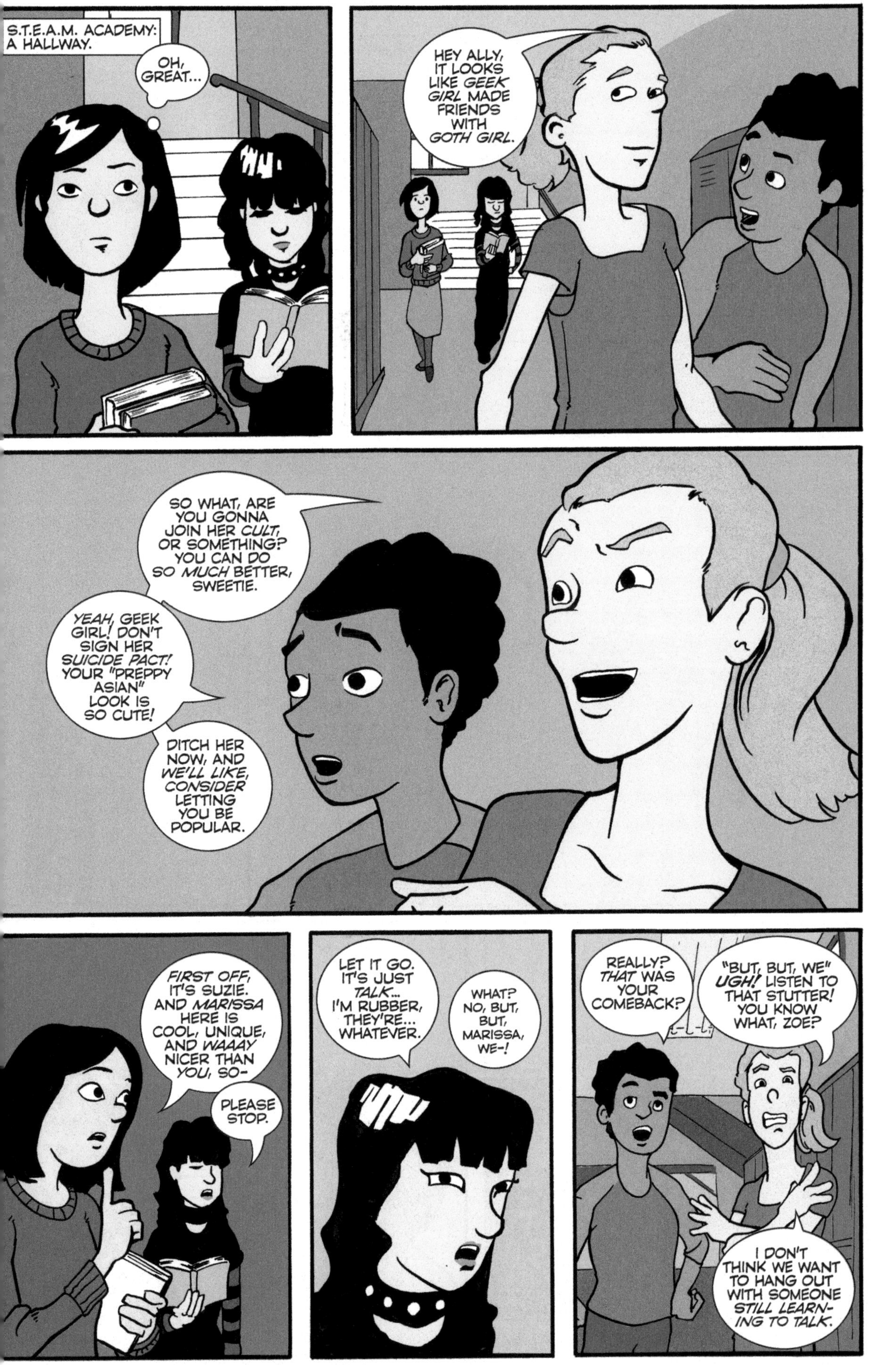
S.T.E.A.M. ACADEMY: A HALLWAY.
OH, GREAT...
HEY ALLY, IT LOOKS LIKE GEEK GIRL MADE FRIENDS WITH GOTH GIRL.
SO WHAT, ARE YOU GONNA JOIN HER CULT, OR SOMETHING? YOU CAN DO SO MUCH BETTER, SWEETIE.
YEAH, GEEK GIRL! DON'T SIGN HER SUICIDE PACT! YOUR "PREPPY ASIAN" LOOK IS SO CUTE!
DITCH HER NOW, AND WE'LL LIKE, CONSIDER LETTING YOU BE POPULAR.
FIRST OFF, IT'S SUZIE. AND MARISSA HERE IS COOL, UNIQUE, AND WAAAY NICER THAN YOU, SO-
PLEASE STOP.
LET IT GO. IT'S JUST TALK... I'M RUBBER, THEY'RE... WHATEVER.
WHAT? NO, BUT, BUT, MARISSA, WE-!
REALLY? THAT WAS YOUR COMEBACK?
"BUT, BUT, WE" UGH! LISTEN TO THAT STUTTER! YOU KNOW WHAT, ZOE?
I DON'T THINK WE WANT TO HANG OUT WITH SOMEONE STILL LEARNING TO TALK.

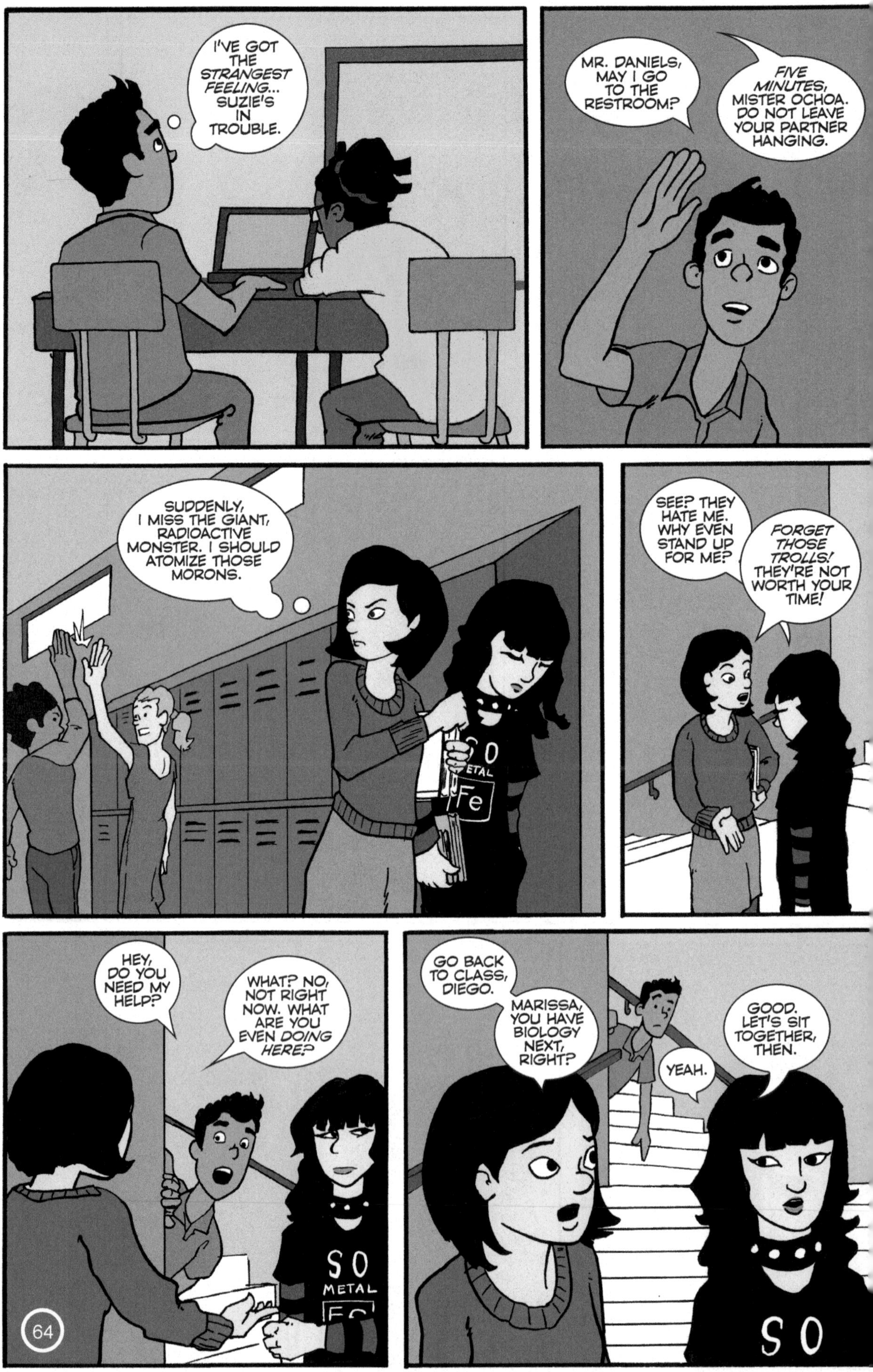
I'VE GOT THE *STRANGEST FEELING*... SUZIE'S IN TROUBLE.
MR. DANIELS, MAY I GO TO THE RESTROOM?
FIVE MINUTES, MISTER OCHOA. DO NOT LEAVE YOUR PARTNER HANGING.
SUDDENLY, I MISS THE GIANT, RADIOACTIVE MONSTER. I SHOULD ATOMIZE THOSE MORONS.
SO METAL Fe
SEE? THEY HATE ME. WHY EVEN STAND UP FOR ME?
FORGET THOSE TROLLS! THEY'RE NOT WORTH YOUR TIME!
HEY, DO YOU NEED MY HELP?
WHAT? NO, NOT RIGHT NOW. WHAT ARE YOU EVEN *DOING HERE?*
GO BACK TO CLASS, DIEGO.
MARISSA, YOU HAVE BIOLOGY NEXT, RIGHT?
YEAH.
GOOD. LET'S SIT TOGETHER, THEN.

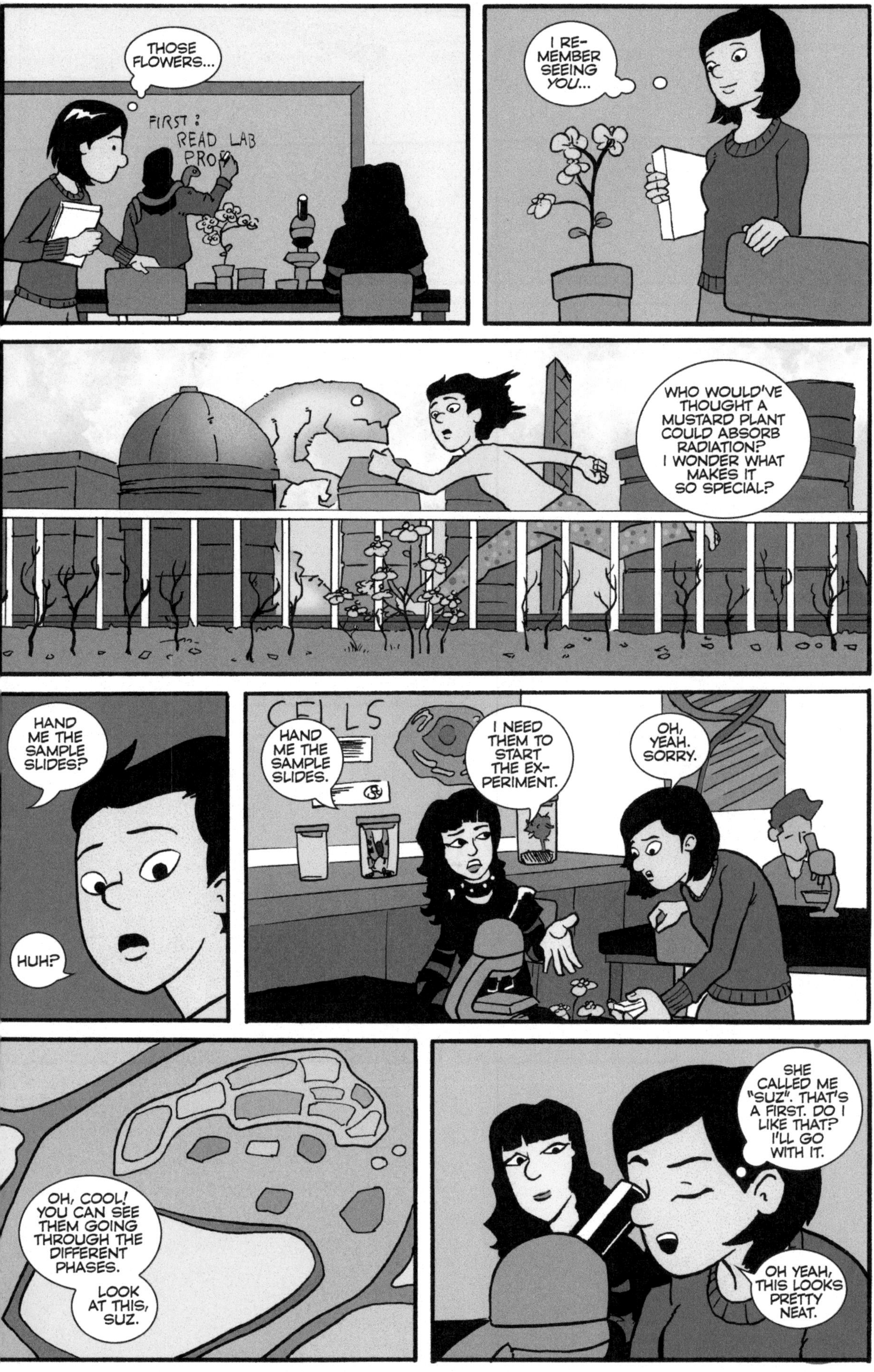
THOSE FLOWERS...
FIRST : READ LAB PRO
I RE-MEMBER SEEING YOU...
WHO WOULD'VE THOUGHT A MUSTARD PLANT COULD ABSORB RADIATION? I WONDER WHAT MAKES IT SO SPECIAL?
HAND ME THE SAMPLE SLIDES?
HUH?
CELLS
HAND ME THE SAMPLE SLIDES.
I NEED THEM TO START THE EX-PERIMENT.
OH, YEAH. SORRY.
OH, COOL! YOU CAN SEE THEM GOING THROUGH THE DIFFERENT PHASES.
LOOK AT THIS, SUZ.
SHE CALLED ME "SUZ". THAT'S A FIRST. DO I LIKE THAT? I'LL GO WITH IT.
OH YEAH, THIS LOOKS PRETTY NEAT.

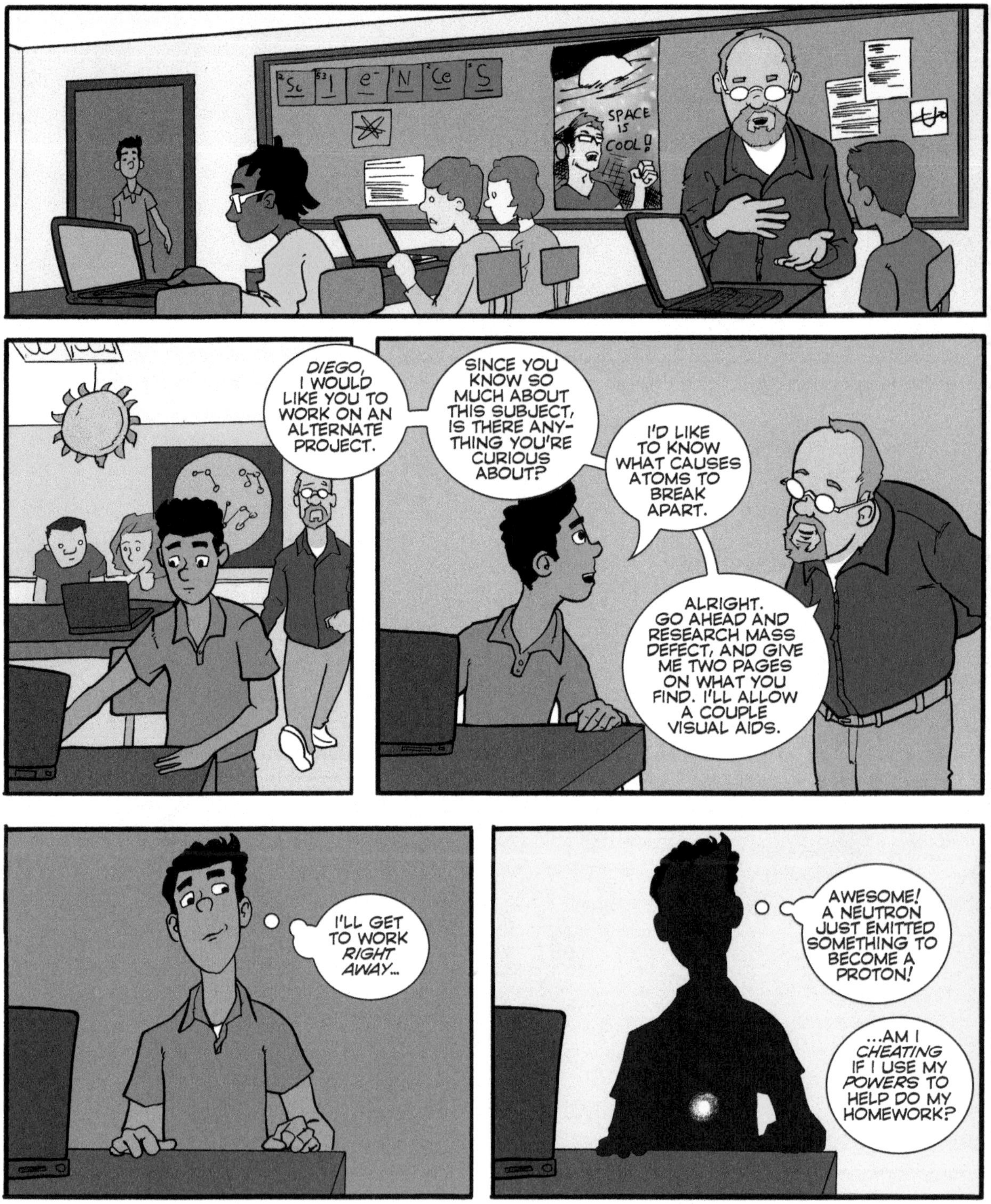
SPACE IS COOL!
DIEGO, I WOULD LIKE YOU TO WORK ON AN ALTERNATE PROJECT.
SINCE YOU KNOW SO MUCH ABOUT THIS SUBJECT, IS THERE ANYTHING YOU'RE CURIOUS ABOUT?
I'D LIKE TO KNOW WHAT CAUSES ATOMS TO BREAK APART.
ALRIGHT. GO AHEAD AND RESEARCH MASS DEFECT, AND GIVE ME TWO PAGES ON WHAT YOU FIND. I'LL ALLOW A COUPLE VISUAL AIDS.
I'LL GET TO WORK *RIGHT AWAY*...
AWESOME! A NEUTRON JUST EMITTED SOMETHING TO BECOME A PROTON!
...AM I *CHEATING* IF I USE MY *POWERS* TO HELP DO MY HOMEWORK?

$$^{40}_{19}K \longrightarrow \, ^{40}_{20}Ca + e^-$$

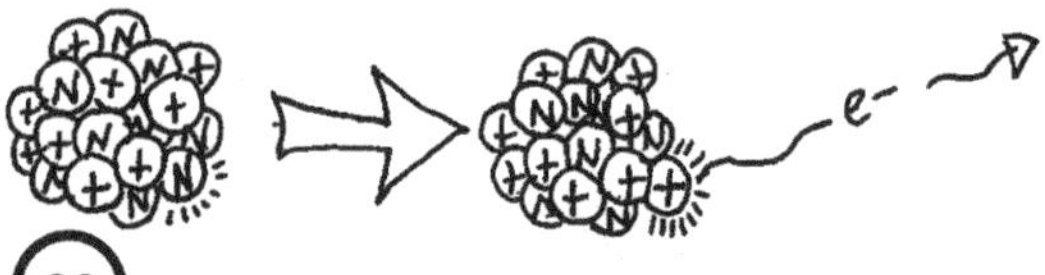
e-

Beta decay happens when a neutron emits an electron and becomes a proton, which makes it a new element considering it has a different number of protons after the decay

THIS THING IS *BLOODY NUTS!*

SELLAFIELD, TWO WEEK'S AGO.

YOU CAN SAY *THAT* AGAIN.

HOW ARE WE SUPPOSED TO *BEAT* THIS THING?

LET'S TRY A BLAST OF...

FREE ELECTRONS!

SHHKRSSSH

DID HE... JUST *ABSORB* MY FREE ELECTRONS?

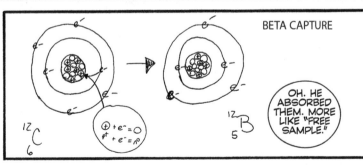

BETA CAPTURE

$^{12}_{6}C$

$\oplus + e^- = \bigcirc$
$p^+ + e^- = n^0$

$^{12}_{5}B$

OH. HE ABSORBED THEM. MORE LIKE "FREE SAMPLE."

IT JUST BETA CAPTURED ALL THOSE ELECTRONS! NOW IT'S EVEN MORE RADIOACTIVE... I DON'T THINK I HAVE ENOUGH ENERGY IN ME FOR ANOTHER SHOT. *I'M TAPPED.*

IT'S A WALKING NUCLEAR REACTOR...

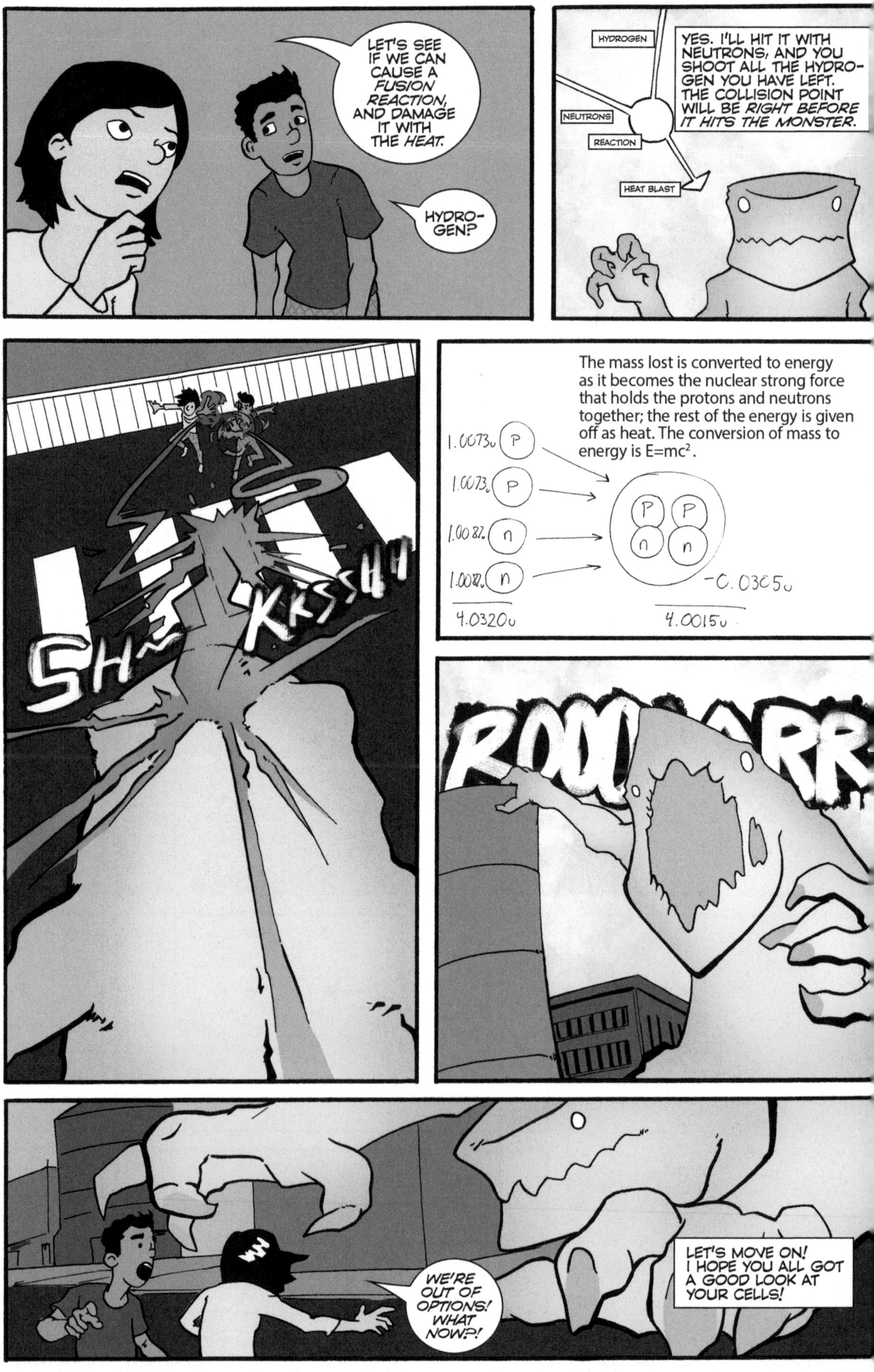

LET'S SEE IF WE CAN CAUSE A *FUSION REACTION,* AND DAMAGE IT WITH THE *HEAT.*
HYDROGEN?
HYDROGEN
NEUTRONS
REACTION
HEAT BLAST
YES. I'LL HIT IT WITH NEUTRONS, AND YOU SHOOT ALL THE HYDROGEN YOU HAVE LEFT. THE COLLISION POINT WILL BE *RIGHT BEFORE IT HITS THE MONSTER.*
SH~
KKSSHH
The mass lost is converted to energy as it becomes the nuclear strong force that holds the protons and neutrons together; the rest of the energy is given off as heat. The conversion of mass to energy is $E=mc^2$.
1.0073u P
1.0073u P
1.0087u n
1.0087u n
4.0320u
P P n n
-0.0305u
4.0015u
ROOOARR
WE'RE OUT OF OPTIONS! WHAT NOW?!
LET'S MOVE ON! I HOPE YOU ALL GOT A GOOD LOOK AT YOUR CELLS!

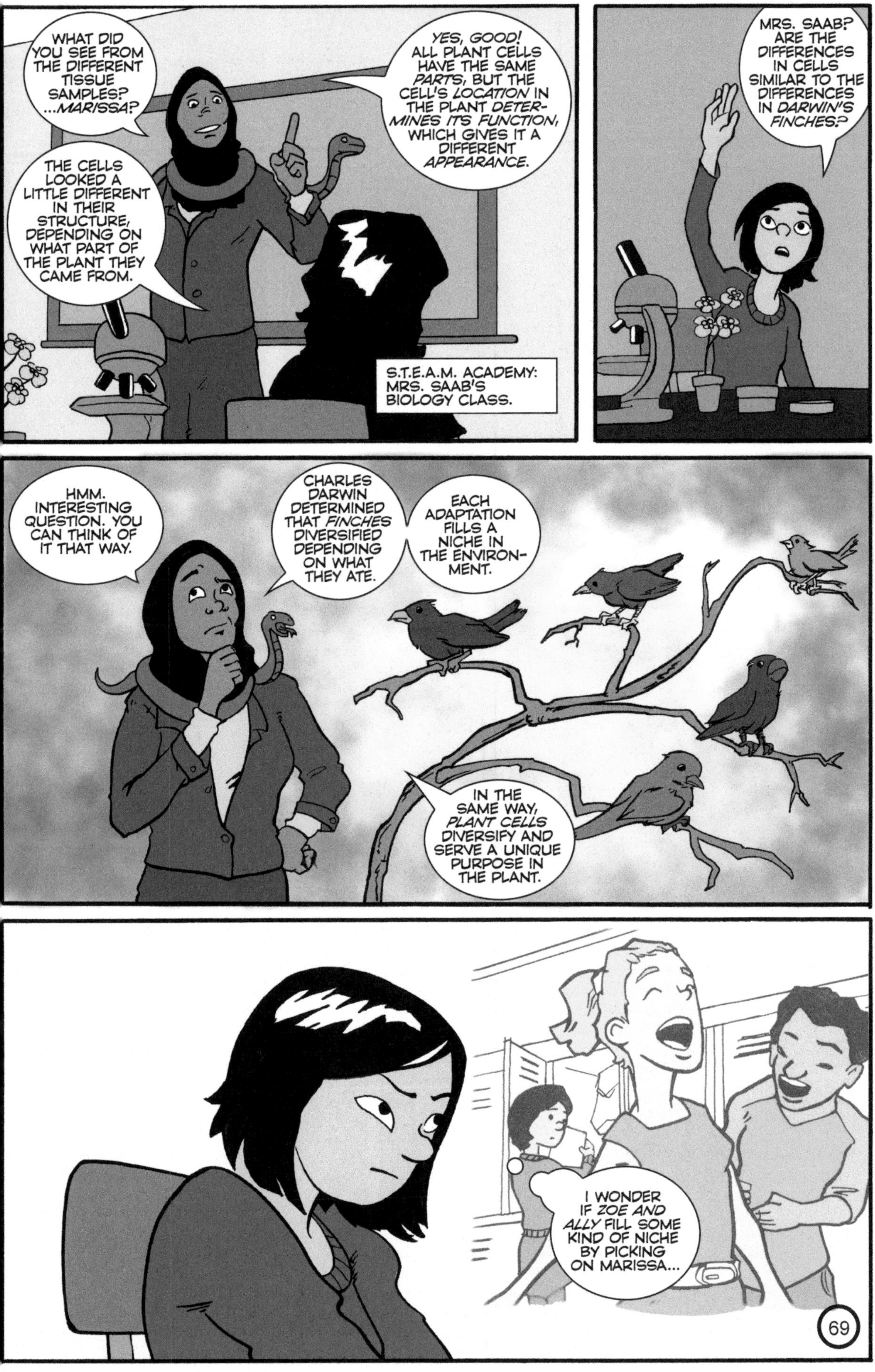
WHAT DID YOU SEE FROM THE DIFFERENT TISSUE SAMPLES? ...MARISSA?
THE CELLS LOOKED A LITTLE DIFFERENT IN THEIR STRUCTURE, DEPENDING ON WHAT PART OF THE PLANT THEY CAME FROM.
YES, GOOD! ALL PLANT CELLS HAVE THE SAME PARTS, BUT THE CELL'S LOCATION IN THE PLANT DETERMINES ITS FUNCTION, WHICH GIVES IT A DIFFERENT APPEARANCE.
S.T.E.A.M. ACADEMY: MRS. SAAB'S BIOLOGY CLASS.
MRS. SAAB? ARE THE DIFFERENCES IN CELLS SIMILAR TO THE DIFFERENCES IN DARWIN'S FINCHES?
HMM. INTERESTING QUESTION. YOU CAN THINK OF IT THAT WAY.
CHARLES DARWIN DETERMINED THAT FINCHES DIVERSIFIED DEPENDING ON WHAT THEY ATE.
EACH ADAPTATION FILLS A NICHE IN THE ENVIRONMENT.
IN THE SAME WAY, PLANT CELLS DIVERSIFY AND SERVE A UNIQUE PURPOSE IN THE PLANT.
I WONDER IF ZOE AND ALLY FILL SOME KIND OF NICHE BY PICKING ON MARISSA...

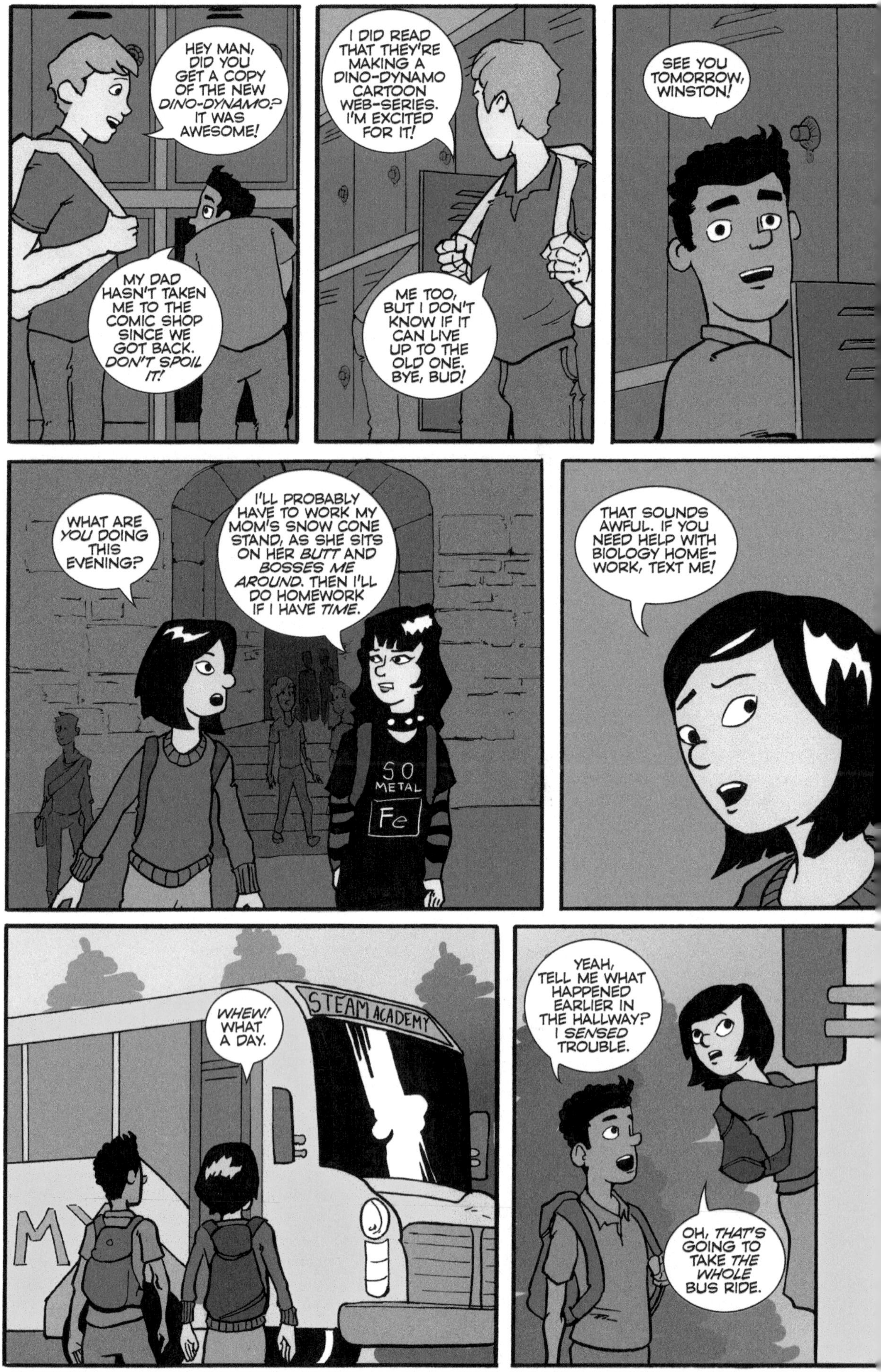
HEY MAN, DID YOU GET A COPY OF THE NEW *DINO-DYNAMO?* IT WAS AWESOME!
MY DAD HASN'T TAKEN ME TO THE COMIC SHOP SINCE WE GOT BACK. *DON'T SPOIL IT!*
I DID READ THAT THEY'RE MAKING A DINO-DYNAMO CARTOON WEB-SERIES. I'M EXCITED FOR IT!
ME TOO, BUT I *DON'T* KNOW IF IT CAN LIVE UP TO THE OLD ONE. BYE, BUD!
SEE YOU TOMORROW, WINSTON!
WHAT ARE *YOU* DOING THIS EVENING?
I'LL PROBABLY HAVE TO WORK MY MOM'S SNOW CONE STAND, AS SHE SITS ON HER *BUTT* AND *BOSSES ME AROUND*. THEN I'LL DO HOMEWORK IF I HAVE *TIME*.
SO METAL
Fe
THAT SOUNDS AWFUL. IF YOU NEED HELP WITH BIOLOGY HOME-WORK, TEXT ME!
STEAM ACADEMY
WHEW! WHAT A DAY.
YEAH, TELL ME WHAT HAPPENED EARLIER IN THE HALLWAY? I *SENSED* TROUBLE.
OH, *THAT'S* GOING TO TAKE *THE WHOLE* BUS RIDE.

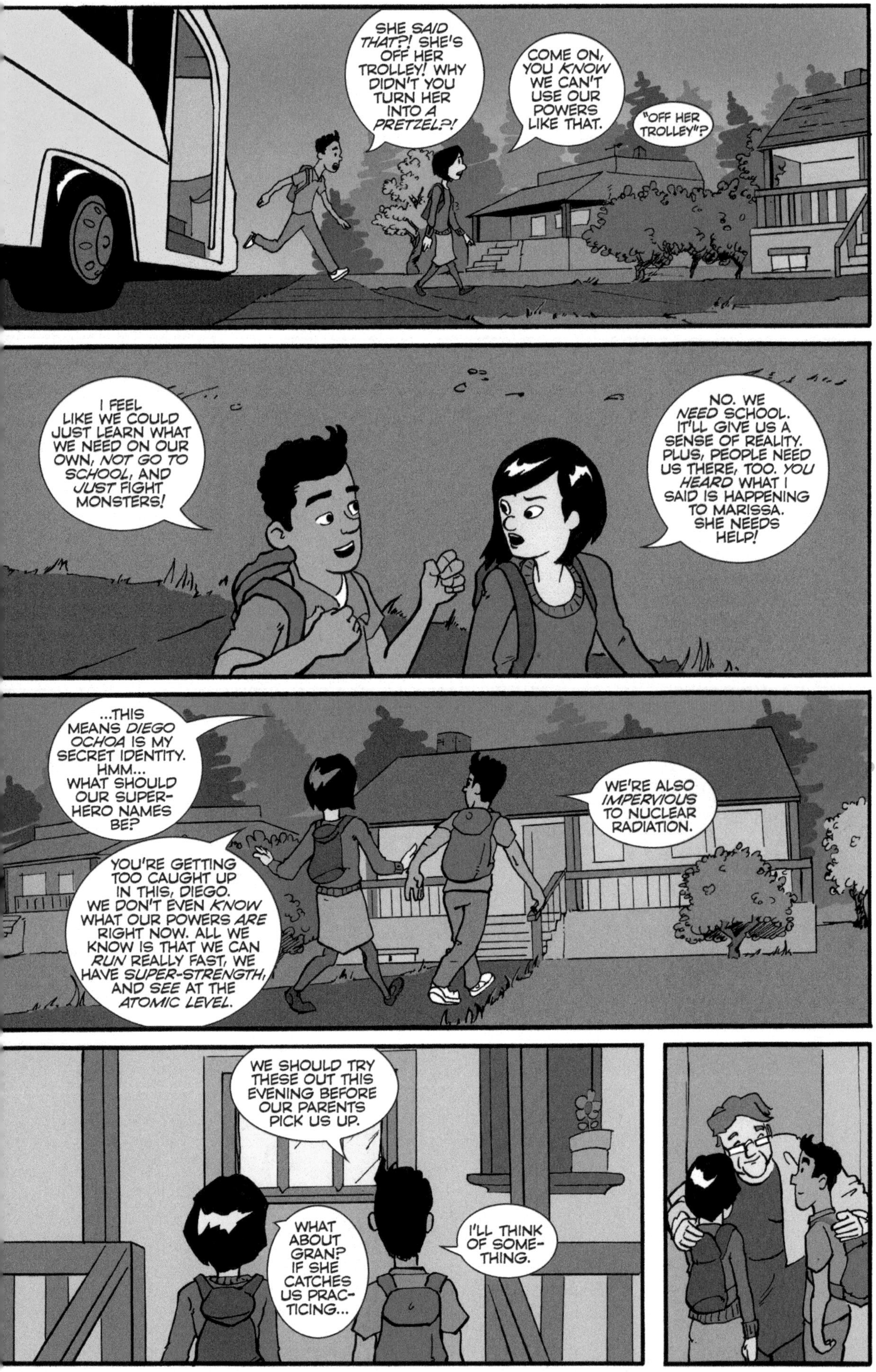
SHE SAID THAT?! SHE'S OFF HER TROLLEY! WHY DIDN'T YOU TURN HER INTO A PRETZEL?!
COME ON, YOU KNOW WE CAN'T USE OUR POWERS LIKE THAT.
"OFF HER TROLLEY"?
I FEEL LIKE WE COULD JUST LEARN WHAT WE NEED ON OUR OWN, NOT GO TO SCHOOL, AND JUST FIGHT MONSTERS!
NO. WE NEED SCHOOL. IT'LL GIVE US A SENSE OF REALITY. PLUS, PEOPLE NEED US THERE, TOO. YOU HEARD WHAT I SAID IS HAPPENING TO MARISSA. SHE NEEDS HELP!
...THIS MEANS DIEGO OCHOA IS MY SECRET IDENTITY. HMM... WHAT SHOULD OUR SUPER-HERO NAMES BE?
YOU'RE GETTING TOO CAUGHT UP IN THIS, DIEGO. WE DON'T EVEN KNOW WHAT OUR POWERS ARE RIGHT NOW. ALL WE KNOW IS THAT WE CAN RUN REALLY FAST, WE HAVE SUPER-STRENGTH, AND SEE AT THE ATOMIC LEVEL.
WE'RE ALSO IMPERVIOUS TO NUCLEAR RADIATION.
WE SHOULD TRY THESE OUT THIS EVENING BEFORE OUR PARENTS PICK US UP.
WHAT ABOUT GRAN? IF SHE CATCHES US PRAC-TICING...
I'LL THINK OF SOME-THING.

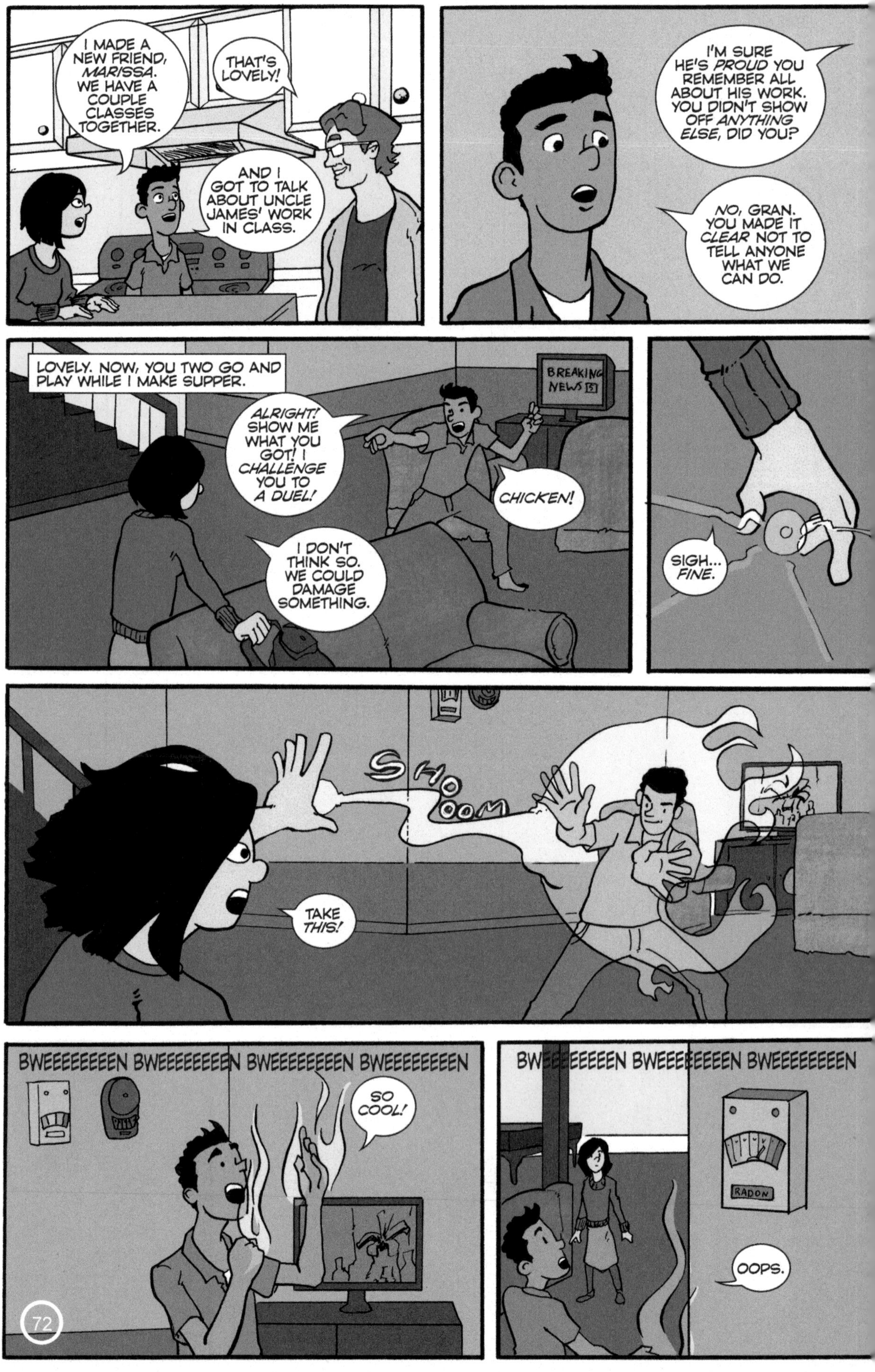
I MADE A NEW FRIEND, *MARISSA*. WE HAVE A COUPLE CLASSES TOGETHER.
THAT'S LOVELY!
AND I GOT TO TALK ABOUT UNCLE JAMES' WORK IN CLASS.
I'M SURE HE'S *PROUD* YOU REMEMBER ALL ABOUT HIS WORK. YOU DIDN'T SHOW OFF *ANYTHING ELSE*, DID YOU?
NO, GRAN. YOU MADE IT *CLEAR* NOT TO TELL ANYONE WHAT WE CAN DO.
LOVELY. NOW, YOU TWO GO AND PLAY WHILE I MAKE SUPPER.
BREAKING NEWS 5
ALRIGHT! SHOW ME WHAT YOU *GOT!* I *CHALLENGE* YOU TO *A DUEL!*
I DON'T THINK SO. WE COULD DAMAGE SOMETHING.
CHICKEN!
SIGH... *FINE*.
SHOOOOM
TAKE *THIS!*
BWEEEEEEEEN BWEEEEEEEEN BWEEEEEEEEN BWEEEEEEEEN
SO *COOL!*
BWEEEEEEEEN BWEEEEEEEEN BWEEEEEEEEN
RADON
OOPS.

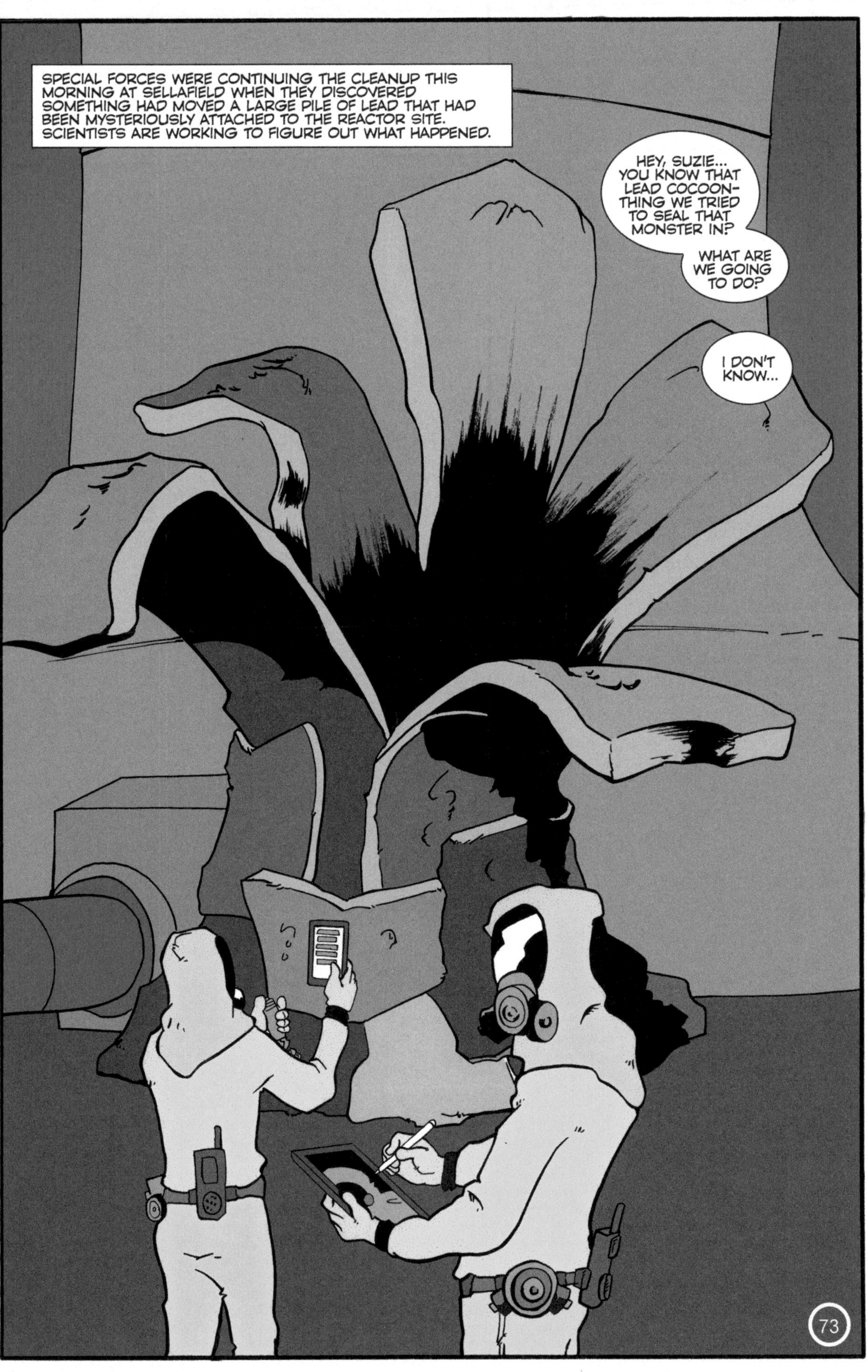
SPECIAL FORCES WERE CONTINUING THE CLEANUP THIS MORNING AT SELLAFIELD WHEN THEY DISCOVERED SOMETHING HAD MOVED A LARGE PILE OF LEAD THAT HAD BEEN MYSTERIOUSLY ATTACHED TO THE REACTOR SITE. SCIENTISTS ARE WORKING TO FIGURE OUT WHAT HAPPENED.
HEY, SUZIE... YOU KNOW THAT LEAD COCOON-THING WE TRIED TO SEAL THAT MONSTER IN?
WHAT ARE WE GOING TO DO?
I DON'T KNOW...

Chapter 4

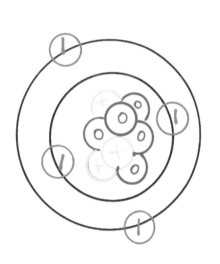

Be

9.012 amu

Beryllium emits many distinct lines
of color (purple, red, green, blue,
and more) when heated, but it
looks white to our eyes.

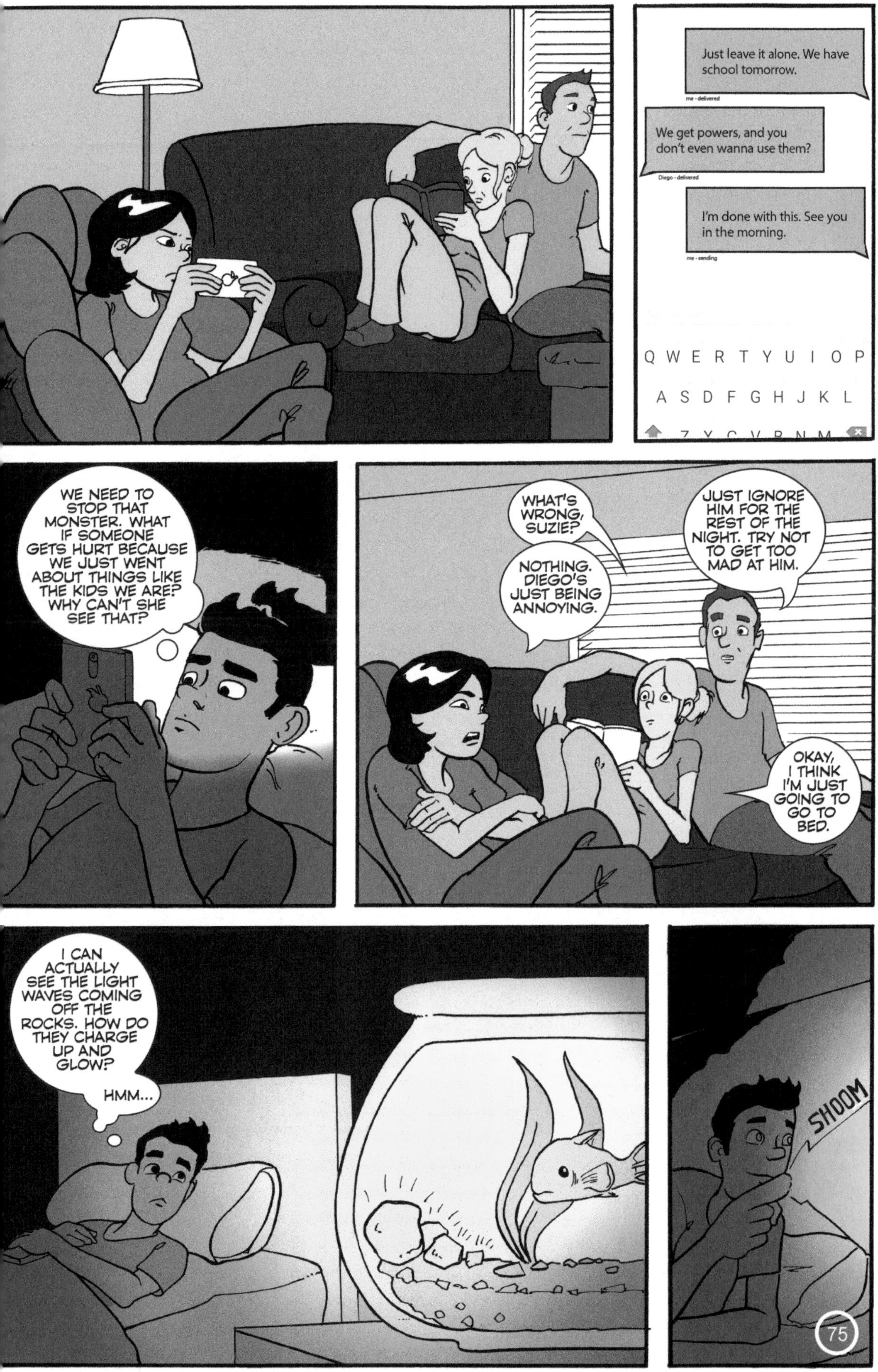
Just leave it alone. We have school tomorrow.
me - delivered
We get powers, and you don't even wanna use them?
Diego - delivered
I'm done with this. See you in the morning.
me - sending
Q W E R T Y U I O P
A S D F G H J K L
WE NEED TO STOP THAT MONSTER. WHAT IF SOMEONE GETS HURT BECAUSE WE JUST WENT ABOUT THINGS LIKE THE KIDS WE ARE? WHY CAN'T SHE SEE THAT?
WHAT'S WRONG, SUZIE?
NOTHING. DIEGO'S JUST BEING ANNOYING.
JUST IGNORE HIM FOR THE REST OF THE NIGHT. TRY NOT TO GET TOO MAD AT HIM.
OKAY, I THINK I'M JUST GOING TO GO TO BED.
I CAN ACTUALLY SEE THE LIGHT WAVES COMING OFF THE ROCKS. HOW DO THEY CHARGE UP AND GLOW?
HMM...
SHOOM

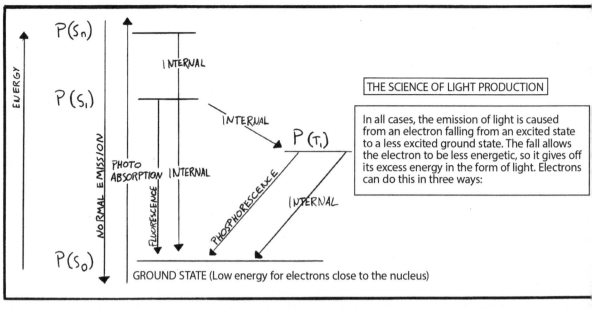

ENERGY
P(Sn)
P(S1)
P(S0)
NORMAL EMISSION
PHOTO ABSORPTION
INTERNAL
INTERNAL
INTERNAL
FLUORESCENCE
P(T1)
PHOSPHORESCENCE
INTERNAL
GROUND STATE (Low energy for electrons close to the nucleus)
THE SCIENCE OF LIGHT PRODUCTION
In all cases, the emission of light is caused from an electron falling from an excited state to a less excited ground state. The fall allows the electron to be less energetic, so it gives off its excess energy in the form of light. Electrons can do this in three ways:
1. NORMAL LIGHT PRODUCTION
Normally, the electron will fall straight down.
2. FLUORESCENCE
Sometimes, electrons will take a small step down. Energy is released as heat, and in a bigger step later, it releases light.
3. PHOSPHORESCENCE
In special circumstances, electrons will take a small step down, flip their spin, then take a big step down. This flipping of the electron's spin takes more time, which allows the material undergoing phosphorescence to glow in the dark well after it has absorbed the energy to excite its electrons.
I WONDER IF I CAN MAKE BIG UGLY LIGHT UP LIKE THAT?
MEANWHILE...

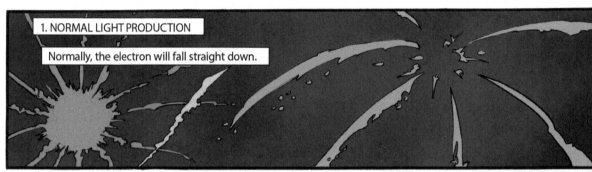

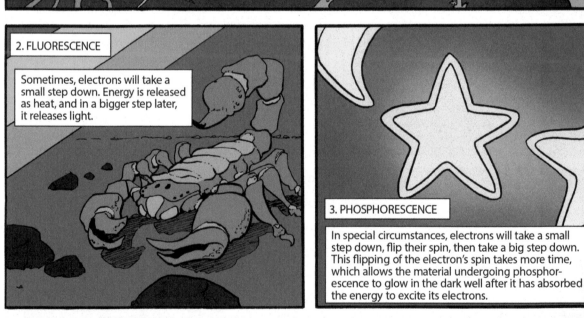

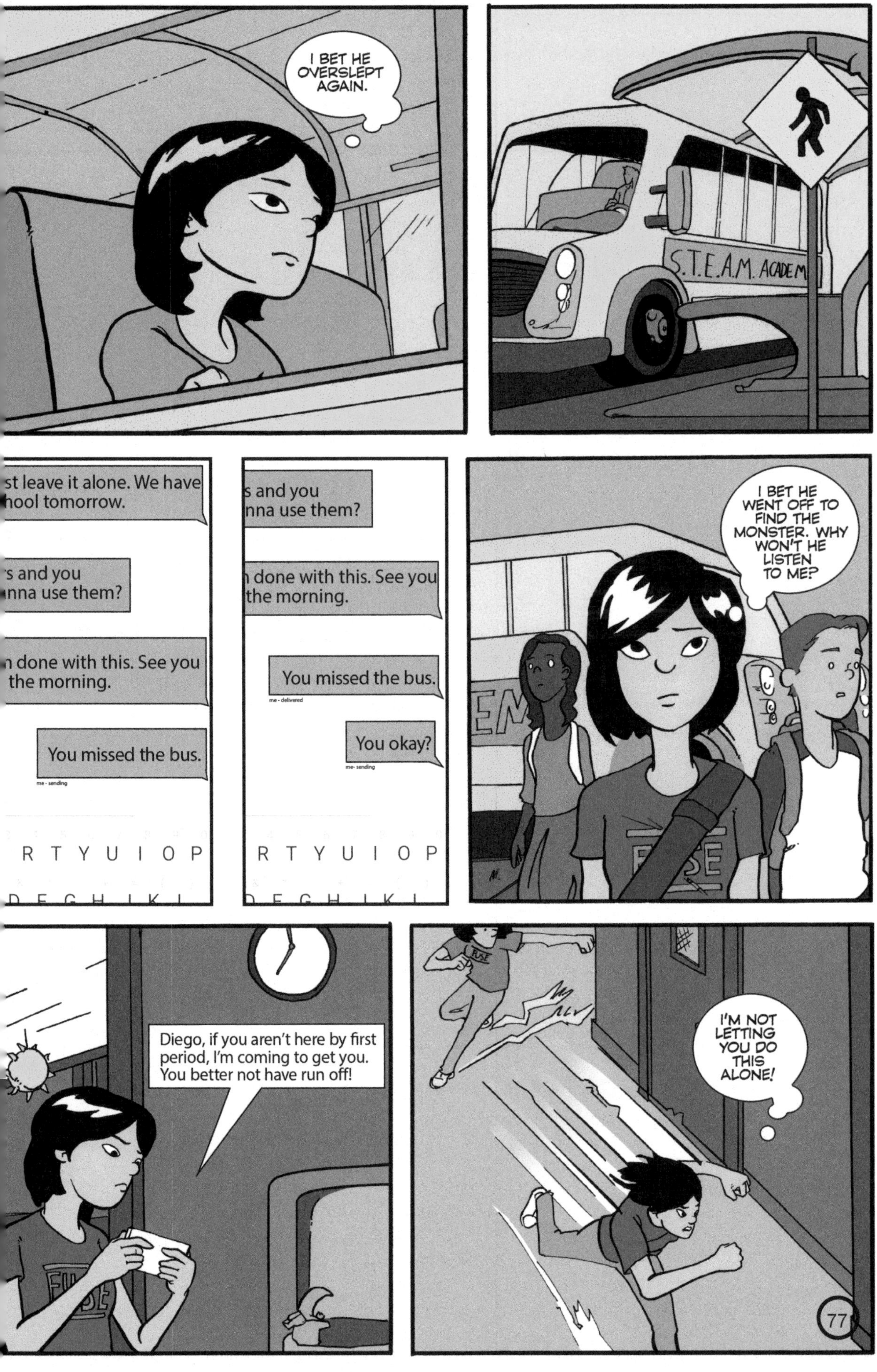
I BET HE OVERSLEPT AGAIN.
S.T.E.A.M. ACADEM
st leave it alone. We have
hool tomorrow.
s and you
nna use them?
n done with this. See you
the morning.
You missed the bus.
me - sending
R T Y U I O P
s and you
nna use them?
n done with this. See you
the morning.
You missed the bus.
me - delivered
You okay?
me- sending
R T Y U I O P
I BET HE WENT OFF TO FIND THE MONSTER. WHY WON'T HE LISTEN TO ME?
Diego, if you aren't here by first period, I'm coming to get you. You better not have run off!
I'M NOT LETTING YOU DO THIS ALONE!

THE ATLANTIC OCEAN.

WELL, IT TURNS OUT I DIDN'T NEED THE SNORKEL AFTER ALL!

THIS IS SO *ACE!*

BEING ABLE TO RUN ON WATER IS *NEVER GOING* TO GET OLD!

THE NIGHTMARE IS CONFIRMED. NOW, HOW DO I FIND THAT BUGGER?

NOTHING. THIS PLACE IS SO RADIO-ACTIVE THAT I CAN'T GET A SENSE OF WHERE THE THING WENT.

GAMMA RAYS   RADIO WAVES   MICRO WAVES   INFRARED   X-RAYS   ULTRA-VIOLET

HE CAN'T HAVE JUST EVAPORATED, CAN HE?

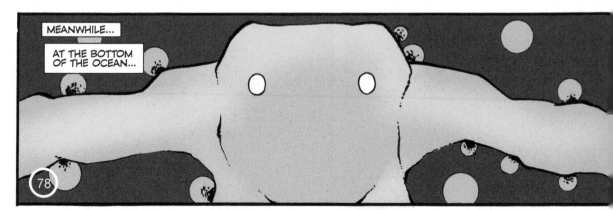

MEANWHILE...

AT THE BOTTOM OF THE OCEAN...

78

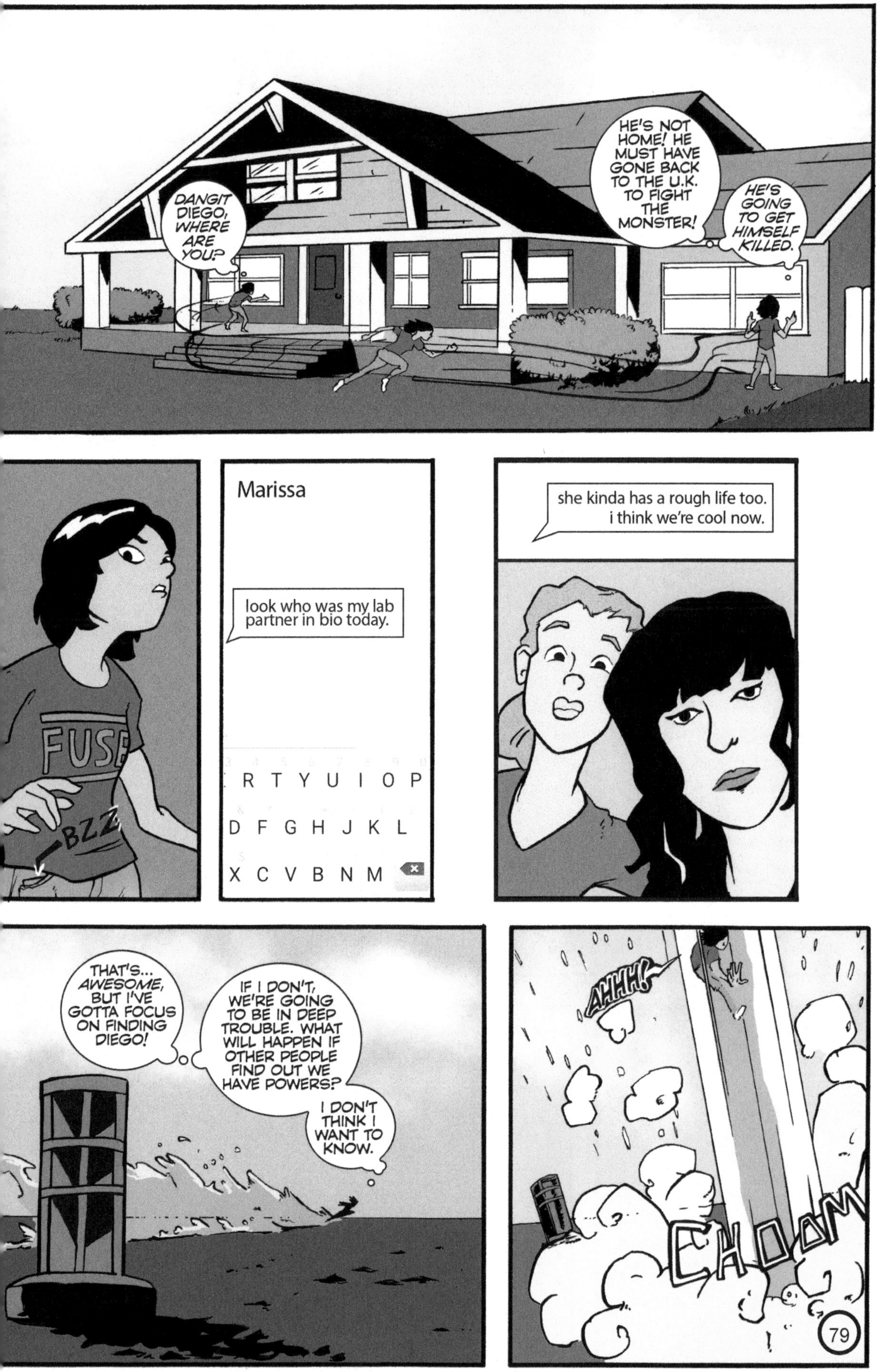
DANGIT DIEGO, WHERE ARE YOU?
HE'S NOT HOME! HE MUST HAVE GONE BACK TO THE U.K. TO FIGHT THE MONSTER!
HE'S GOING TO GET HIMSELF KILLED.
BZZ
FUSE
Marissa
look who was my lab partner in bio today.
R T Y U I O P
D F G H J K L
X C V B N M
she kinda has a rough life too. i think we're cool now.
THAT'S... AWESOME, BUT I'VE GOTTA FOCUS ON FINDING DIEGO!
IF I DON'T, WE'RE GOING TO BE IN DEEP TROUBLE. WHAT WILL HAPPEN IF OTHER PEOPLE FIND OUT WE HAVE POWERS?
I DON'T THINK I WANT TO KNOW.
AHHH!
CHOOM

WE LIVED BY THE REACTOR THAT BLEW UP LAST WEEK, AND WE CAN'T GO BACK TO OUR HOMES.

THE GOVERNMENT CAN'T DO ANYTHING YET, SO THE WEALTHY LAD WHO OWNS THE HOUSE UP THERE IS LETTING US SQUAT HERE UNTIL THEN.

WHAT CAN I DO TO HELP?

WHAT, A KID LIKE YOU?

UNLESS YOU'VE BROUGHT ME A NEW HOUSE FROM... *WHEREVER YOU'RE FROM,* OR YOU'VE GOT A *MAGIC WAND* TO CLEAR AWAY *ALL* THE RADIATION... *NOTHING.*

WELL, I— *WHOA!*

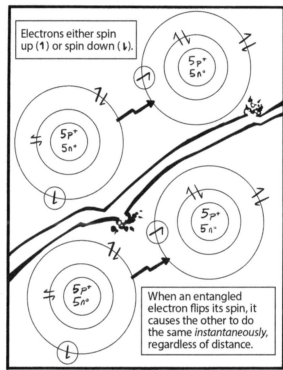

Electrons either spin up (↑) or spin down (↓).

$5p^+$ $5n^o$

$5p^+$ $5n^o$

$5p^+$ $5n^o$

$5p^+$ $5n^o$

When an entangled electron flips its spin, it causes the other to do the same *instantaneously,* regardless of distance.

SUZIE'S *DEFINITELY* IN DEEP TROUBLE.

I'M UHH... I *SHOULD* GO.

HEY THERE! NICE OF YOU TO DROP BY! NEED A LIFT?

OH MY GOSH I'M SO GLAD IT'S *YOU!* WHAT HIT ME?

LOOKS LIKE YOU FOUND THE MONSTER BEFORE I COULD!

80

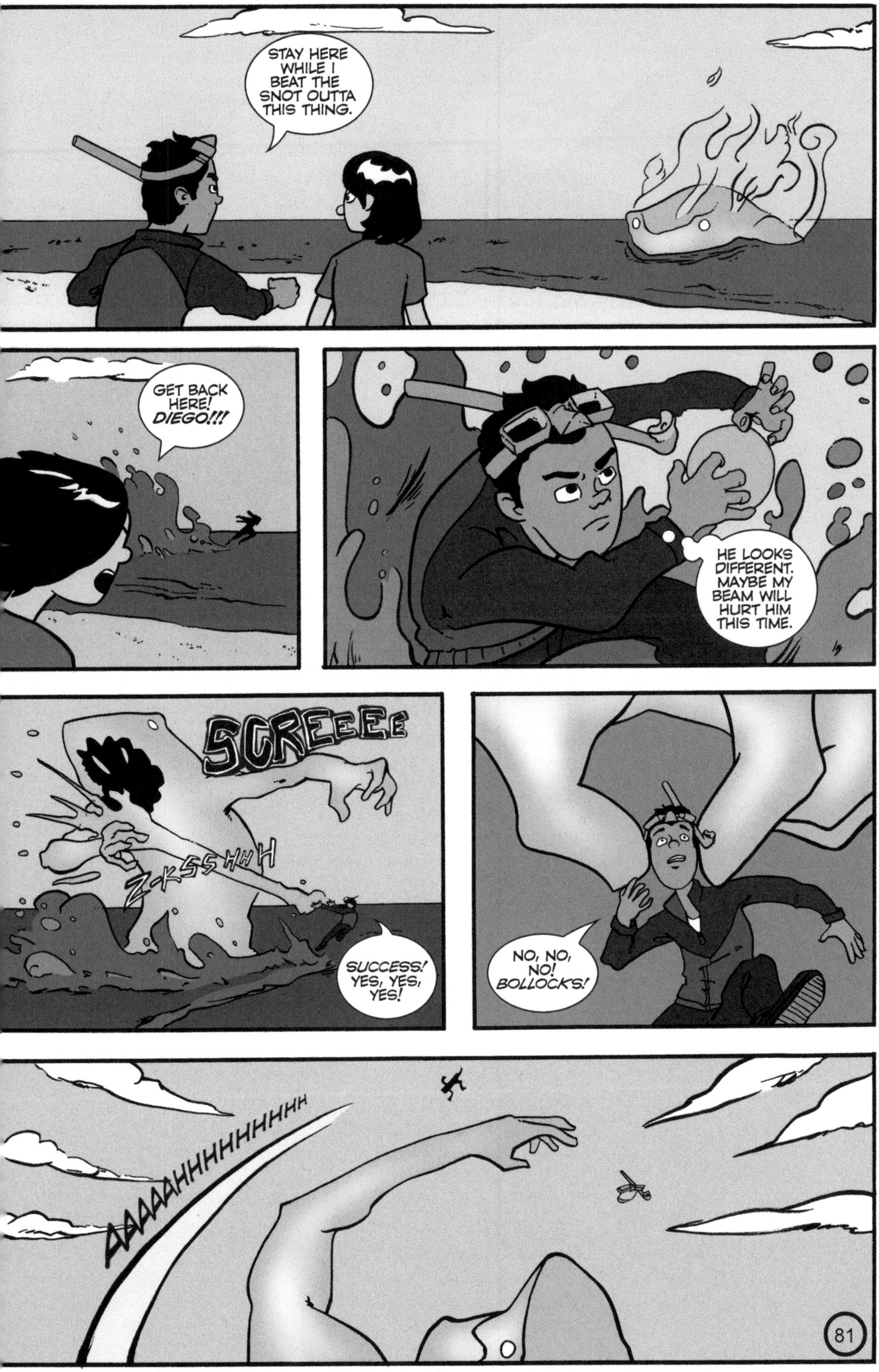
STAY HERE WHILE I BEAT THE SNOT OUTTA THIS THING.
GET BACK HERE! DIEGO!!!
HE LOOKS DIFFERENT. MAYBE MY BEAM WILL HURT HIM THIS TIME.
SCREEEEE
Z-KSSHHH
SUCCESS! YES, YES, YES!
NO, NO, NO! BOLLOCKS!
AAAAAHHHHHHHHH

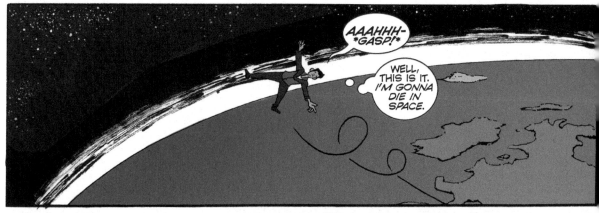

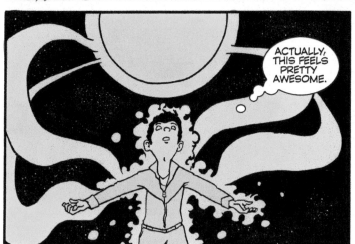

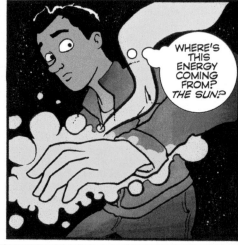

AAAHHH- *GASP!*
WELL, THIS IS IT. I'M GONNA DIE IN SPACE.
ACTUALLY, THIS FEELS PRETTY AWESOME.
WHERE'S THIS ENERGY COMING FROM? THE SUN?
8p+ 8n°
Excited
8p+ 8n°
YEAH! LET'S POWER UP!
6p+ 6n°
Excited electron
6p+ 6n°
SCIENCE OF ELECTRONS AND ENERGY LEVELS
7p+ 7n°
Nucleus
Energy Level 1
Energy Level 2
Bohr's Atomic Model
electrons orbit the nucleus like planets around the Sun. These orbits are called Energy Levels.
7p+ 7n°
1s
2s
X
2px
2pz
Z
2py
Also, electrons occupy different areas within energy levels, called orbitals. These orbitals' shapes are based on the likelihood of finding an electron in that area.
2py
2px
2pz
p orbitals are petal-shaped and broken into 3 subshells (x, y, z)
2px 2py 2pz
Energy Level 2
2s
2s is a larger encapsulating sphere
Energy Level 1
1s
1s orbital is spherical in shape

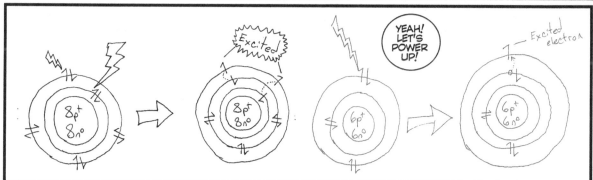

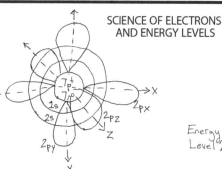

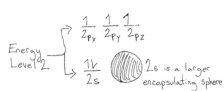

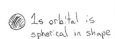

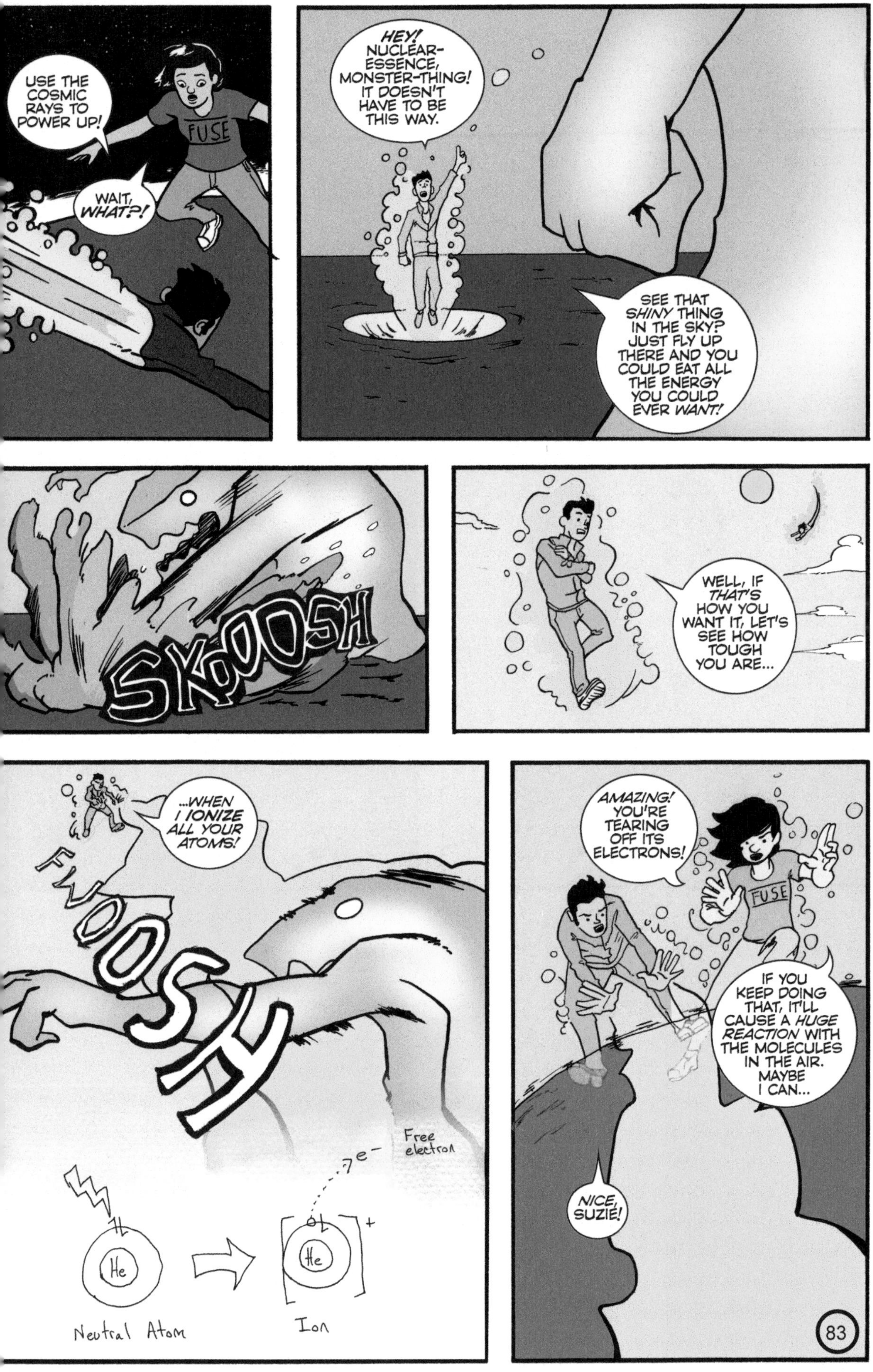
USE THE COSMIC RAYS TO POWER UP!
WAIT, WHAT?!
HEY! NUCLEAR-ESSENCE, MONSTER-THING! IT DOESN'T HAVE TO BE THIS WAY.
SEE THAT SHINY THING IN THE SKY? JUST FLY UP THERE AND YOU COULD EAT ALL THE ENERGY YOU COULD EVER WANT!
SKOOOSH
WELL, IF THAT'S HOW YOU WANT IT, LET'S SEE HOW TOUGH YOU ARE...
...WHEN I IONIZE ALL YOUR ATOMS!
FWOOSH
Free electron
e⁻
He
He
+
Neutral Atom
Ion
AMAZING! YOU'RE TEARING OFF ITS ELECTRONS!
IF YOU KEEP DOING THAT, IT'LL CAUSE A HUGE REACTION WITH THE MOLECULES IN THE AIR. MAYBE I CAN...
NICE, SUZIE!
FUSE
FUSE

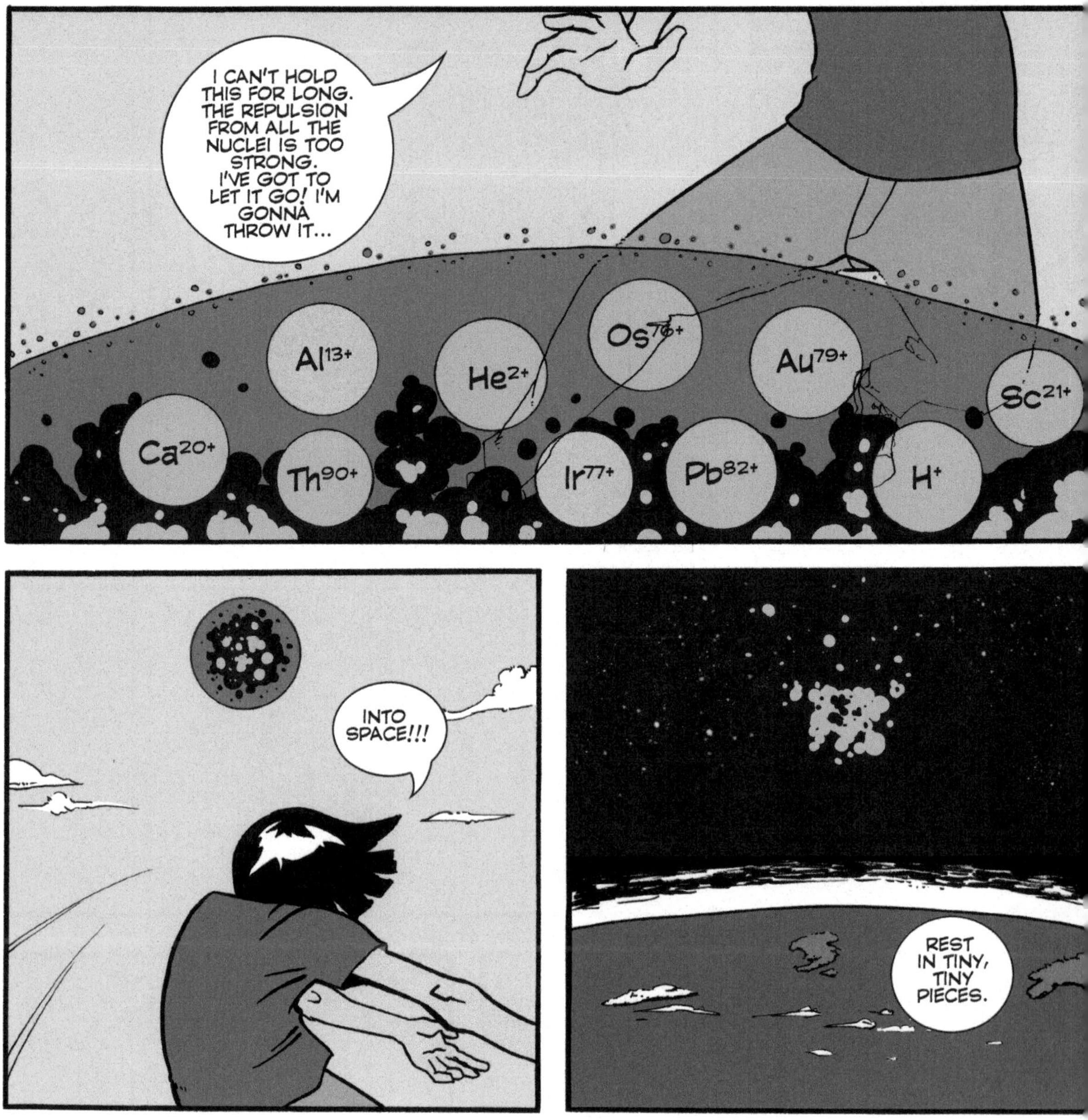
I CAN'T HOLD THIS FOR LONG. THE REPULSION FROM ALL THE NUCLEI IS TOO STRONG. I'VE GOT TO LET IT GO! I'M GONNA THROW IT...
Al13+
He2+
Os76+
Au79+
Sc21+
Ca20+
Th90+
Ir77+
Pb82+
H+
INTO SPACE!!!
REST IN TINY, TINY PIECES.

SCIENCE ON IONS

Atom	Ion	e⁻'s
H•	H^+	1 lost
Ca with 2 dots (:)	Ca^{2+}	2 lost
O with 6 dots	O with 8 dots, $2-$	2 gained
F with 7 dots	F with 8 dots, $1-$	1 gained

Atoms become ions by *gaining* or losing electrons.
Cations are *positive* ions, due to an atom *losing* electrons.
Anions are *negative* ions, due to an atom *gaining* electrons.

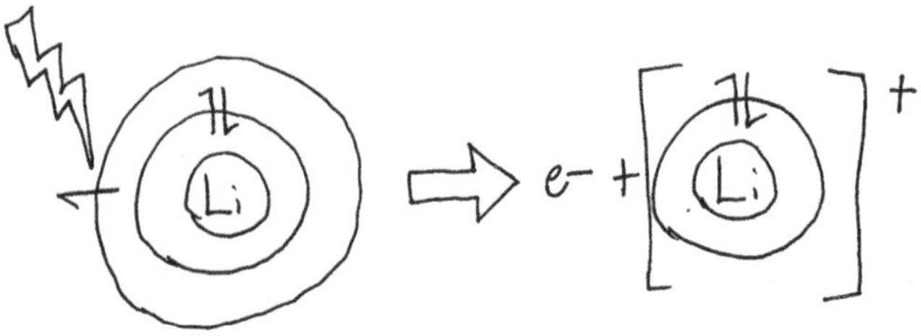
Li
e− +
Li
+

Electrons can absorb so much *energy* that they can escape from the nucleus and become free, making a cation. *(called ionization energy)*

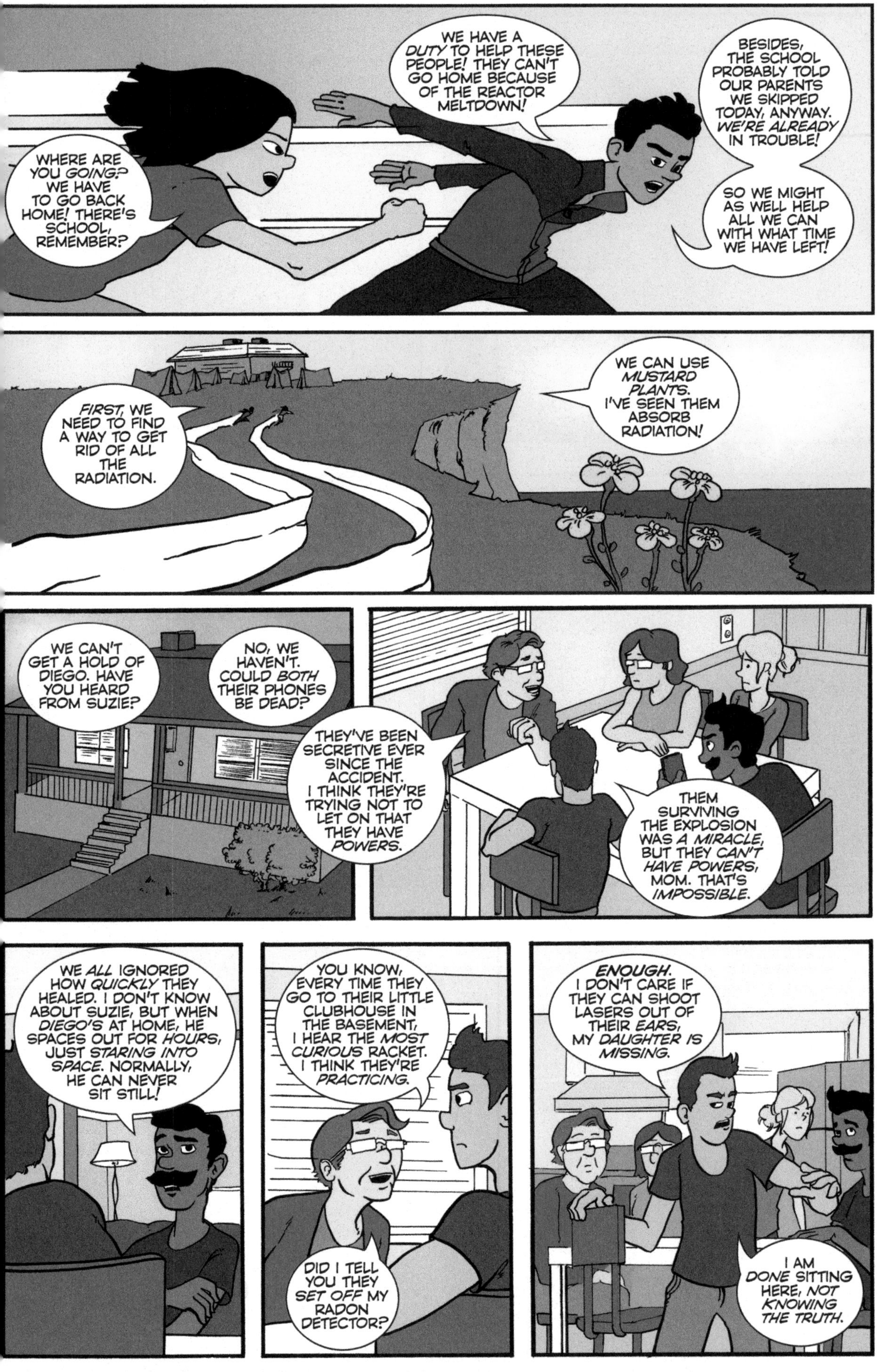
WHERE ARE YOU GOING? WE HAVE TO GO BACK HOME! THERE'S SCHOOL, REMEMBER?
WE HAVE A DUTY TO HELP THESE PEOPLE! THEY CAN'T GO HOME BECAUSE OF THE REACTOR MELTDOWN!
BESIDES, THE SCHOOL PROBABLY TOLD OUR PARENTS WE SKIPPED TODAY, ANYWAY. WE'RE ALREADY IN TROUBLE!
SO WE MIGHT AS WELL HELP ALL WE CAN WITH WHAT TIME WE HAVE LEFT!
FIRST, WE NEED TO FIND A WAY TO GET RID OF ALL THE RADIATION.
WE CAN USE MUSTARD PLANTS. I'VE SEEN THEM ABSORB RADIATION!
WE CAN'T GET A HOLD OF DIEGO. HAVE YOU HEARD FROM SUZIE?
NO, WE HAVEN'T. COULD BOTH THEIR PHONES BE DEAD?
THEY'VE BEEN SECRETIVE EVER SINCE THE ACCIDENT. I THINK THEY'RE TRYING NOT TO LET ON THAT THEY HAVE POWERS.
THEM SURVIVING THE EXPLOSION WAS A MIRACLE, BUT THEY CAN'T HAVE POWERS, MOM. THAT'S IMPOSSIBLE.
WE ALL IGNORED HOW QUICKLY THEY HEALED. I DON'T KNOW ABOUT SUZIE, BUT WHEN DIEGO'S AT HOME, HE SPACES OUT FOR HOURS, JUST STARING INTO SPACE. NORMALLY, HE CAN NEVER SIT STILL!
YOU KNOW, EVERY TIME THEY GO TO THEIR LITTLE CLUBHOUSE IN THE BASEMENT, I HEAR THE MOST CURIOUS RACKET. I THINK THEY'RE PRACTICING.
DID I TELL YOU THEY SET OFF MY RADON DETECTOR?
ENOUGH. I DON'T CARE IF THEY CAN SHOOT LASERS OUT OF THEIR EARS, MY DAUGHTER IS MISSING.
I AM DONE SITTING HERE, NOT KNOWING THE TRUTH.

THESE FLOWERS SHOULD AMPLIFY OUR ABILITY TO COLLECT RADIOACTIVE ATOMS.

AND WITH OUR SPEED, WE SHOULD HAVE THIS PLACE CLEANED UP IN NO TIME!

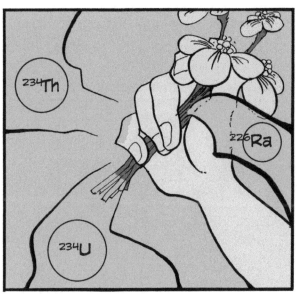

^{234}Th

^{226}Ra

^{234}U

^{210}Pb

^{210}Po

^{210}Bi

ALL DONE.

NOT QUITE. THEY WON'T HAVE ANY POWER TO THEIR HOMES. WE NEED TO BUILD A POWER SUPPLY FOR THEM.

SOLAR PANELS! ALL THE ROOFS SHOULD HAVE SOLAR PANELS!

OK, LET'S LOOK AT A *REAL* SOLAR PANEL BEFORE WE BUILD OUR OWN.

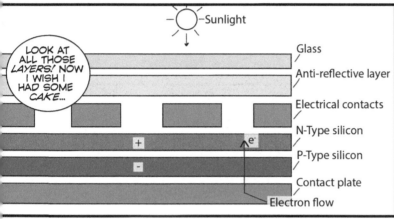

LOOK AT ALL THOSE *LAYERS!* NOW I WISH I HAD SOME *CAKE...*

Sunlight

Glass

Anti-reflective layer

Electrical contacts

N-Type silicon

P-Type silicon

Contact plate

Electron flow

$+$

$-$

e^-

WHAT? ALL THIS *MONSTER-FIGHTING* AND *CRISIS-SOLVING* MADE ME KINDA *HUNGRY.*

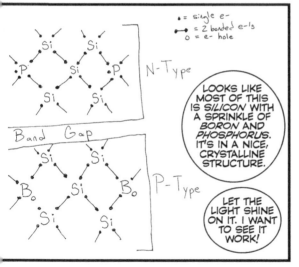

• = single e-
•—• = 2 bonded e-'s
o = e- hole

Si Si
P Si P
Si Si
N-Type

Band Gap

Si Si
Bₒ Si Bₒ
Si Si
P-Type

LOOKS LIKE MOST OF THIS IS *SILICON* WITH A SPRINKLE OF *BORON* AND *PHOSPHORUS.* IT'S IN A NICE, CRYSTALLINE STRUCTURE.

LET THE LIGHT SHINE ON IT. I WANT TO SEE IT WORK!

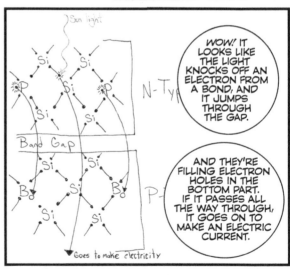

Sun light

Si Si
P Si P
Si Si
N-Typ

Band Gap

Si Si
Bₒ Si Bₒ
Si Si
P-

Goes to make electricity

WOW! IT LOOKS LIKE THE LIGHT KNOCKS OFF AN ELECTRON FROM A BOND, AND IT JUMPS THROUGH THE GAP.

AND THEY'RE FILLING ELECTRON HOLES IN THE BOTTOM PART. IF IT PASSES ALL THE WAY THROUGH, IT GOES ON TO MAKE AN ELECTRIC CURRENT.

WHERE ARE WE GOING TO *FIND* EVERYTHING WE NEED?

LET'S LOOK AT *THE BEACH.* I THINK WE CAN MAKE EVERYTHING FROM THE *SAND.*

I WAS RIGHT. EVERYTHING IS HERE. YOU SHOULD MAKE THE GLASS, AND COLLECT THE METAL FOR THE CONTACTS. I'LL MAKE THE SILICON LAYERS.

I'M ON IT!

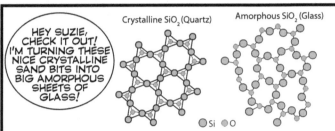

HEY SUZIE, CHECK IT OUT! I'M TURNING THESE NICE CRYSTALLINE SAND BITS INTO BIG AMORPHOUS SHEETS OF GLASS!

Crystalline SiO_2 (Quartz)

Amorphous SiO_2 (Glass)

Si   O

THAT'S NICE. THIS IS PRETTY TEDIOUS, TRYING TO PICK OUT A BUNCH OF BORON AND PHOSPHORUS.

SOME TIME LATER ...

LET'S GO PUT THESE ON ROOFS.

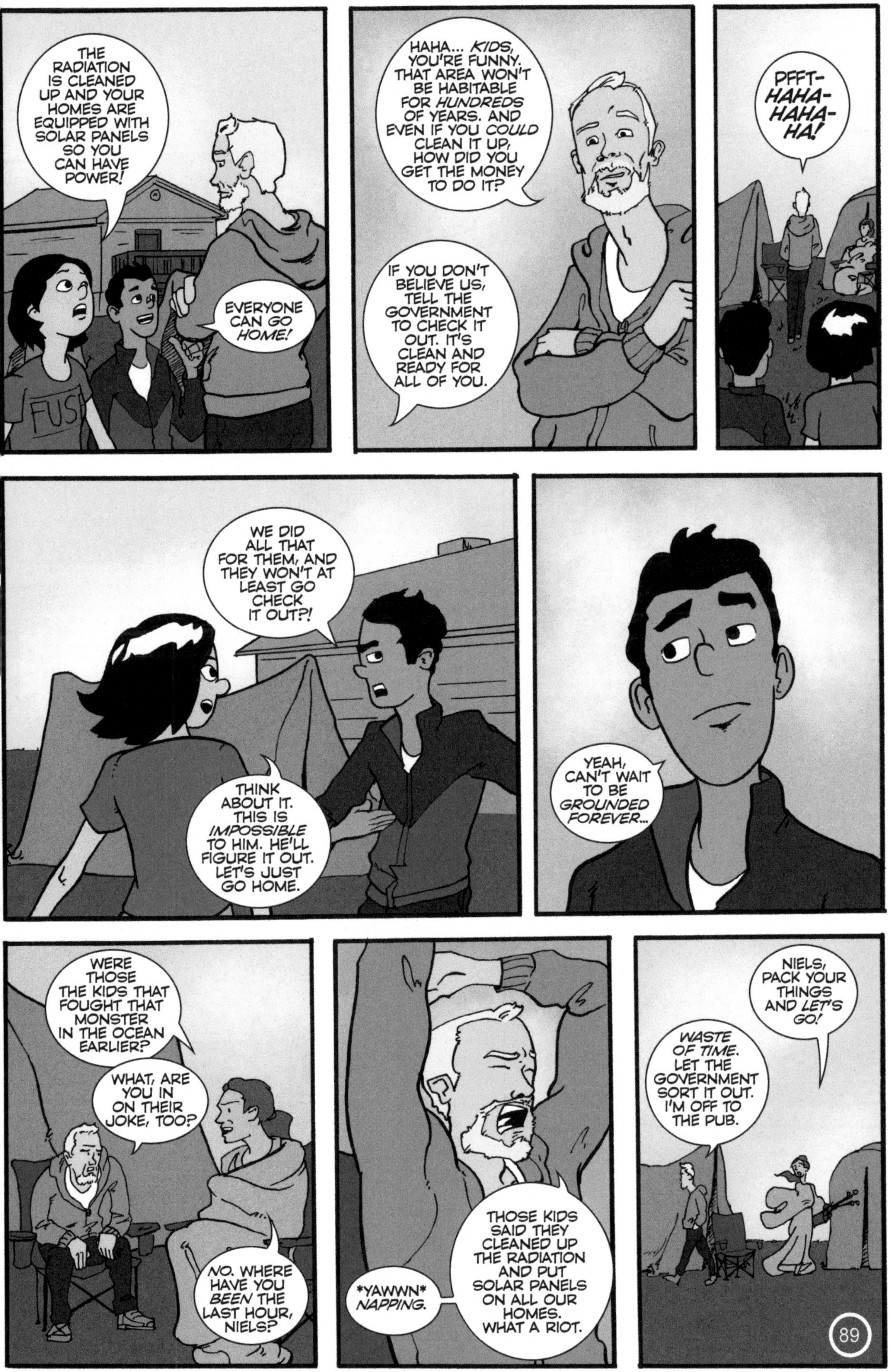
THE RADIATION IS CLEANED UP AND YOUR HOMES ARE EQUIPPED WITH SOLAR PANELS SO YOU CAN HAVE POWER!
EVERYONE CAN GO HOME!
FUSI
HAHA... KIDS, YOU'RE FUNNY. THAT AREA WON'T BE HABITABLE FOR HUNDREDS OF YEARS. AND EVEN IF YOU COULD CLEAN IT UP, HOW DID YOU GET THE MONEY TO DO IT?
IF YOU DON'T BELIEVE US, TELL THE GOVERNMENT TO CHECK IT OUT. IT'S CLEAN AND READY FOR ALL OF YOU.
PFFT-HAHA-HAHA-HA!
WE DID ALL THAT FOR THEM, AND THEY WON'T AT LEAST GO CHECK IT OUT?!
THINK ABOUT IT. THIS IS IMPOSSIBLE TO HIM. HE'LL FIGURE IT OUT. LET'S JUST GO HOME.
YEAH, CAN'T WAIT TO BE GROUNDED FOREVER...
WERE THOSE THE KIDS THAT FOUGHT THAT MONSTER IN THE OCEAN EARLIER?
WHAT, ARE YOU IN ON THEIR JOKE, TOO?
NO. WHERE HAVE YOU BEEN THE LAST HOUR, NIELS?
YAWWN NAPPING.
THOSE KIDS SAID THEY CLEANED UP THE RADIATION AND PUT SOLAR PANELS ON ALL OUR HOMES. WHAT A RIOT.
NIELS, PACK YOUR THINGS AND LET'S GO!
WASTE OF TIME. LET THE GOVERNMENT SORT IT OUT. I'M OFF TO THE PUB.

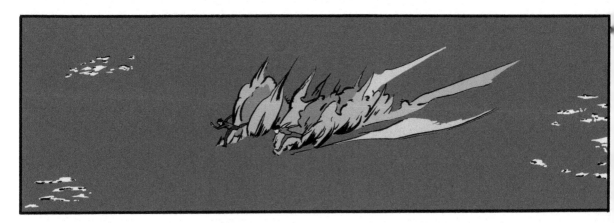

REMEMBER, WE TELL THEM THE TRUTH. THEY *WILL* KILL US, BUT WE *HAVE TO* TELL THEM.

I'LL BE 30 BEFORE THEY LET ME OUT OF THE HOUSE AGAIN. CAN'T WE JUST USE OUR *POWERS* TO *MAKE THEM* HAPPY ABOUT WHAT WE'RE DOING?

NO, *THAT WOULD BE WRONG.* PLUS, HOW WOULD WE EVEN DO THAT? WE MANIPULATE *ATOMS,* NOT *MINDS.*

WHERE HAVE YOU BEEN?!

YOU HAD US ALL WORRIED SICK! ARE YOU OKAY?

DIEGO AND SUZIE JUST SHOWED UP. THEY ARE OKAY. GET OVER HERE!

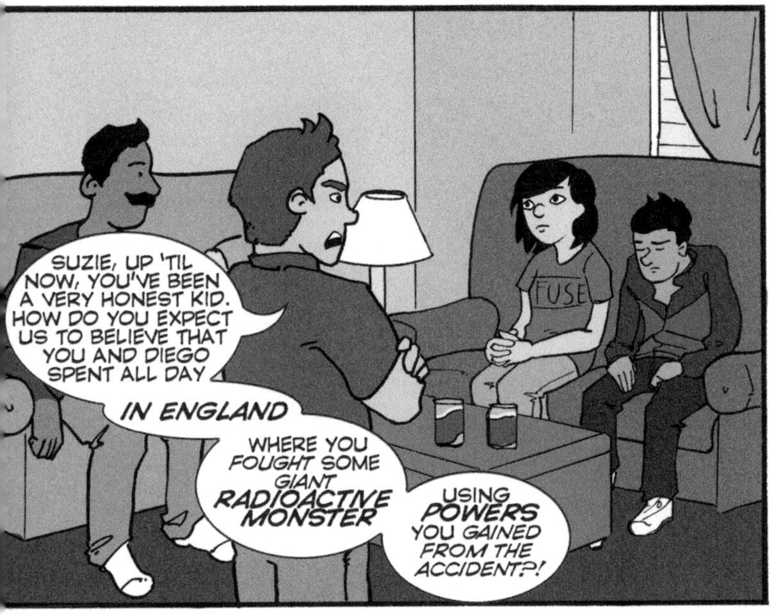
SUZIE, UP 'TIL NOW, YOU'VE BEEN A VERY HONEST KID. HOW DO YOU EXPECT US TO BELIEVE THAT YOU AND DIEGO SPENT ALL DAY
IN ENGLAND
WHERE YOU FOUGHT SOME GIANT RADIOACTIVE MONSTER
USING POWERS YOU GAINED FROM THE ACCIDENT?!
FUSE

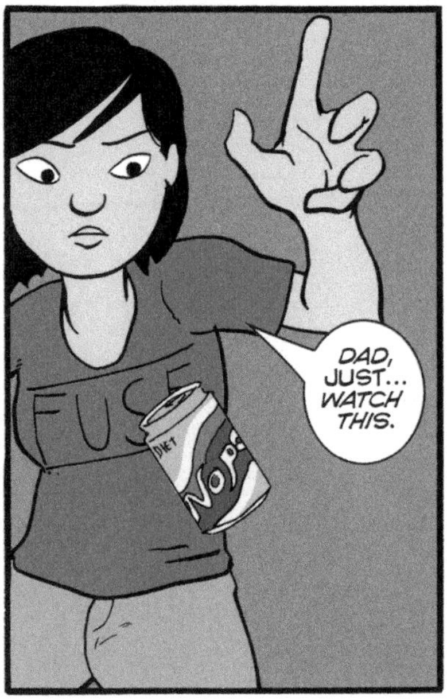
DAD, JUST... WATCH THIS.
FUSE

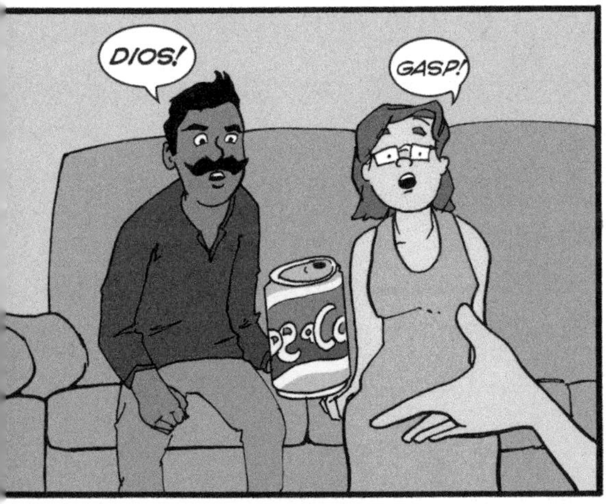
DIOS!
GASP!

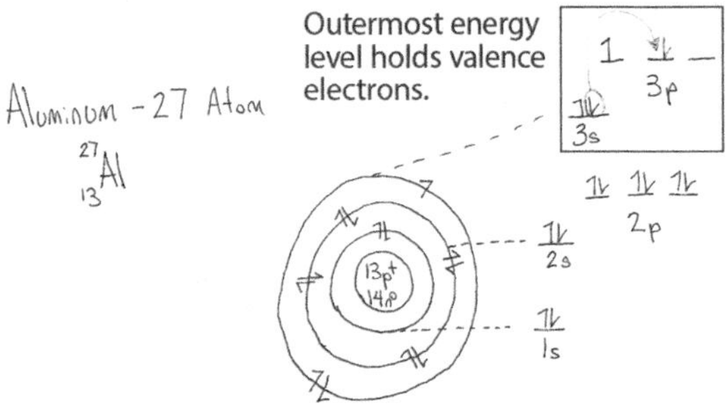
Aluminum -27 Atom
$^{27}_{13}Al$
Outermost energy level holds valence electrons.
3p
3s
2p
2s
1s
13p+
14n

The more unpaired electrons there are in the outermost energy level, the more magnetic an atom will be. *Aluminum is usually not magnetically active.* Suzie has caused an electron to flip its spin, giving the atom three unpaired electrons, thus making it more magnetically active.

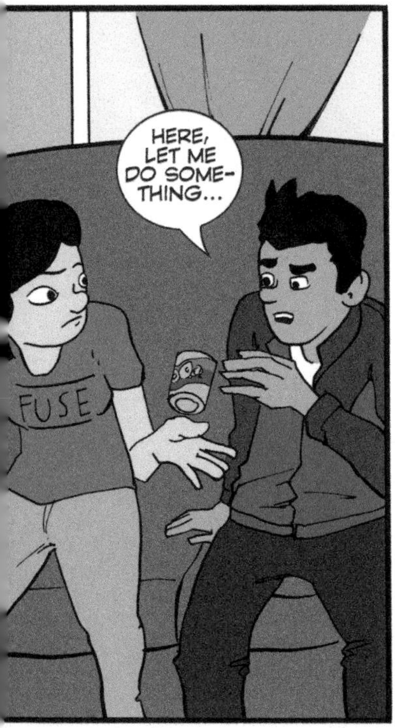
HERE, LET ME DO SOME-THING...
FUSE

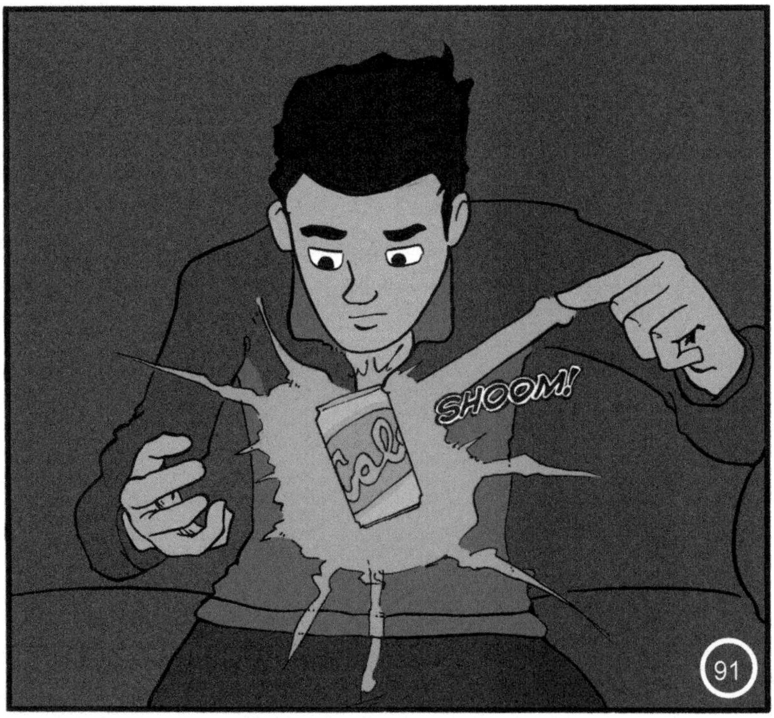
SHOOM!

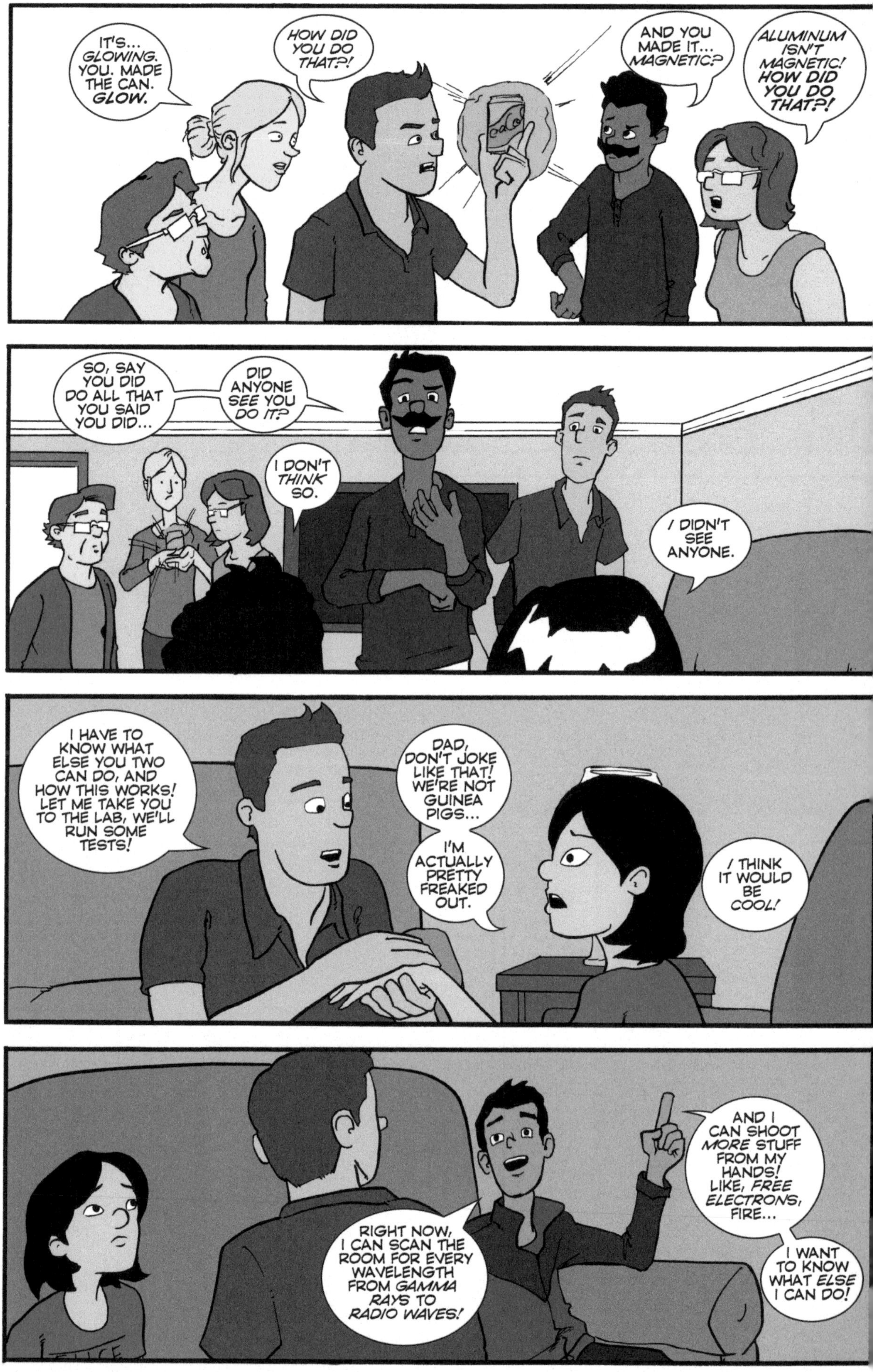

IT'S... GLOWING. YOU. MADE THE CAN. GLOW.
HOW DID YOU DO THAT?!
AND YOU MADE IT... MAGNETIC?
ALUMINUM ISN'T MAGNETIC! HOW DID YOU DO THAT?!
SO, SAY YOU DID DO ALL THAT YOU SAID YOU DID...
DID ANYONE SEE YOU DO IT?
I DON'T THINK SO.
I DIDN'T SEE ANYONE.
I HAVE TO KNOW WHAT ELSE YOU TWO CAN DO, AND HOW THIS WORKS! LET ME TAKE YOU TO THE LAB, WE'LL RUN SOME TESTS!
DAD, DON'T JOKE LIKE THAT! WE'RE NOT GUINEA PIGS...
I'M ACTUALLY PRETTY FREAKED OUT.
I THINK IT WOULD BE COOL!
RIGHT NOW, I CAN SCAN THE ROOM FOR EVERY WAVELENGTH FROM GAMMA RAYS TO RADIO WAVES!
AND I CAN SHOOT MORE STUFF FROM MY HANDS! LIKE, FREE ELECTRONS, FIRE...
I WANT TO KNOW WHAT ELSE I CAN DO!

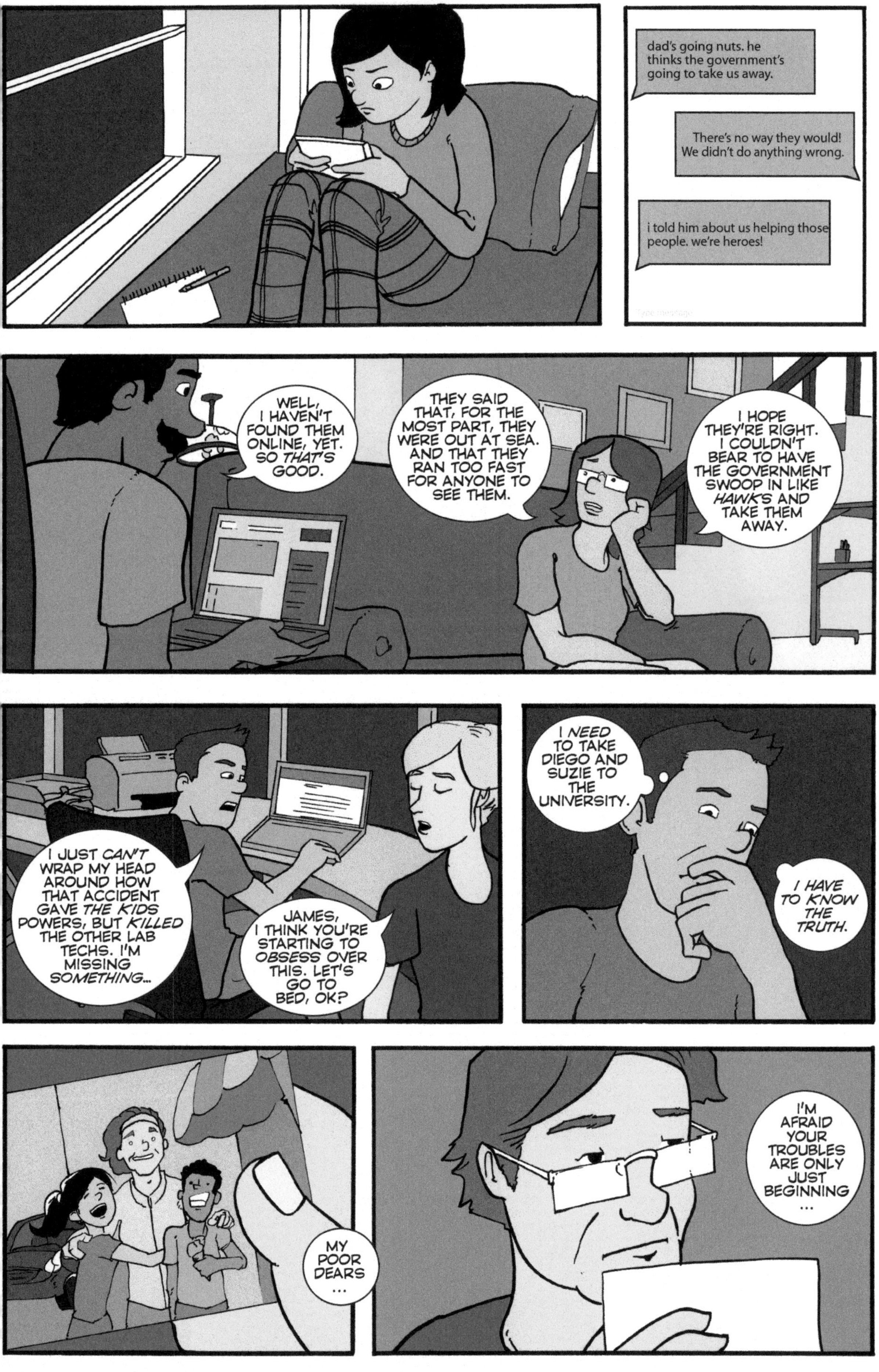
dad's going nuts. he thinks the government's going to take us away.
There's no way they would! We didn't do anything wrong.
i told him about us helping those people. we're heroes!
WELL, I HAVEN'T FOUND THEM ONLINE, YET. SO *THAT'S* GOOD.
THEY SAID THAT, FOR THE MOST PART, THEY WERE OUT AT SEA. AND THAT THEY RAN TOO FAST FOR ANYONE TO SEE THEM.
I HOPE THEY'RE RIGHT. I COULDN'T BEAR TO HAVE THE GOVERNMENT SWOOP IN LIKE *HAWKS* AND TAKE THEM AWAY.
I JUST *CAN'T* WRAP MY HEAD AROUND HOW THAT ACCIDENT GAVE *THE KIDS* POWERS, BUT *KILLED* THE OTHER LAB TECHS. I'M MISSING *SOMETHING*...
JAMES, I THINK YOU'RE STARTING TO *OBSESS* OVER THIS. LET'S GO TO BED, OK?
I *NEED* TO TAKE DIEGO AND SUZIE TO THE UNIVERSITY.
I HAVE TO KNOW THE TRUTH.
MY POOR DEARS ...
I'M AFRAID YOUR TROUBLES ARE ONLY JUST BEGINNING ...

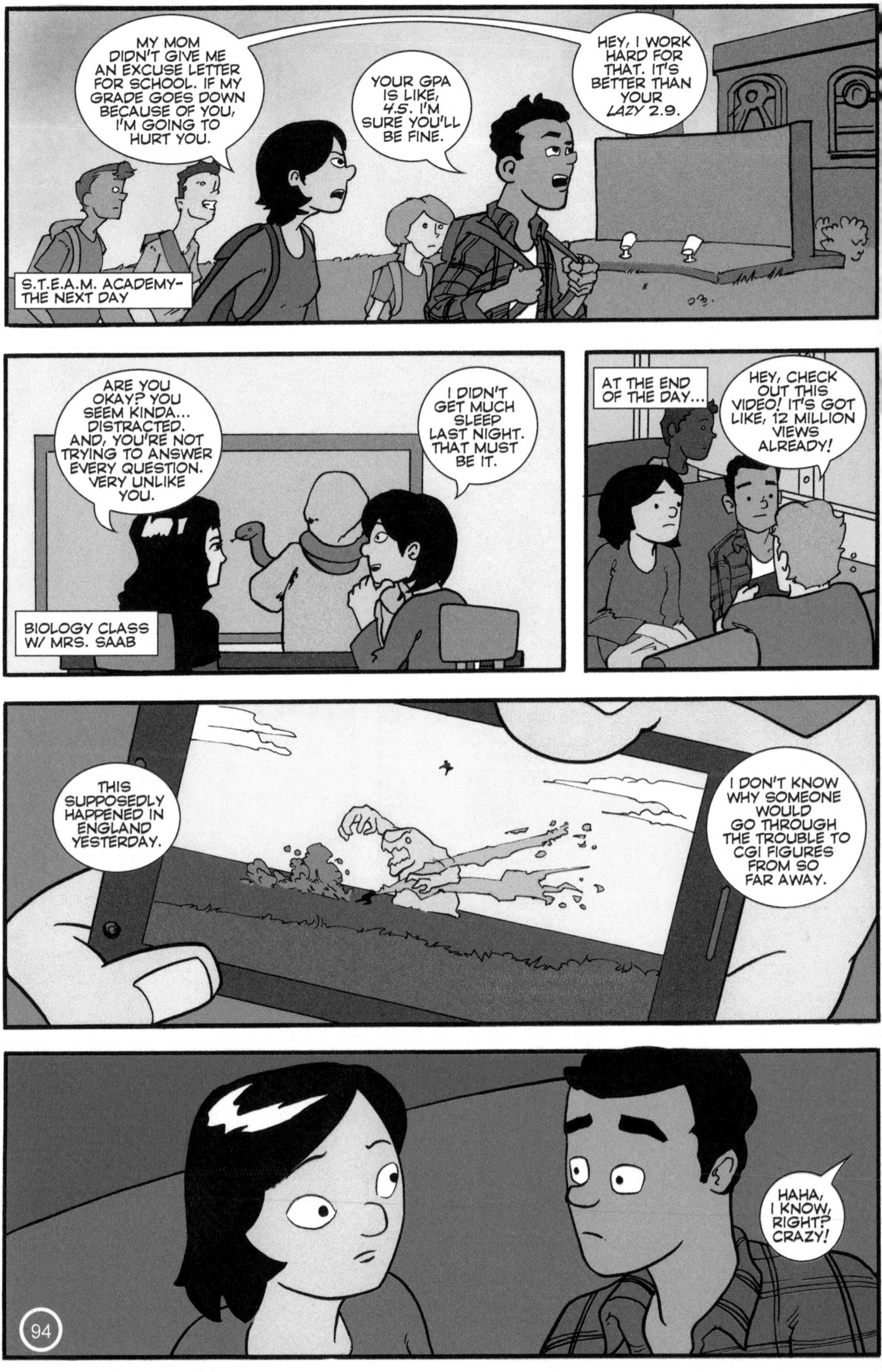
S.T.E.A.M. ACADEMY- THE NEXT DAY
MY MOM DIDN'T GIVE ME AN EXCUSE LETTER FOR SCHOOL. IF MY GRADE GOES DOWN BECAUSE OF YOU, I'M GOING TO HURT YOU.
YOUR GPA IS LIKE, *4.5*. I'M SURE YOU'LL BE FINE.
HEY, I WORK HARD FOR THAT. IT'S BETTER THAN YOUR *LAZY* 2.9.
BIOLOGY CLASS W/ MRS. SAAB
ARE YOU OKAY? YOU SEEM KINDA... DISTRACTED. AND, YOU'RE NOT TRYING TO ANSWER EVERY QUESTION. VERY UNLIKE YOU.
I DIDN'T GET MUCH SLEEP LAST NIGHT. THAT MUST BE IT.
AT THE END OF THE DAY...
HEY, CHECK OUT THIS VIDEO! IT'S GOT LIKE, 12 MILLION VIEWS ALREADY!
THIS SUPPOSEDLY HAPPENED IN ENGLAND YESTERDAY.
I DON'T KNOW WHY SOMEONE WOULD GO THROUGH THE TROUBLE TO CGI FIGURES FROM SO FAR AWAY.
HAHA, I KNOW, RIGHT? CRAZY!

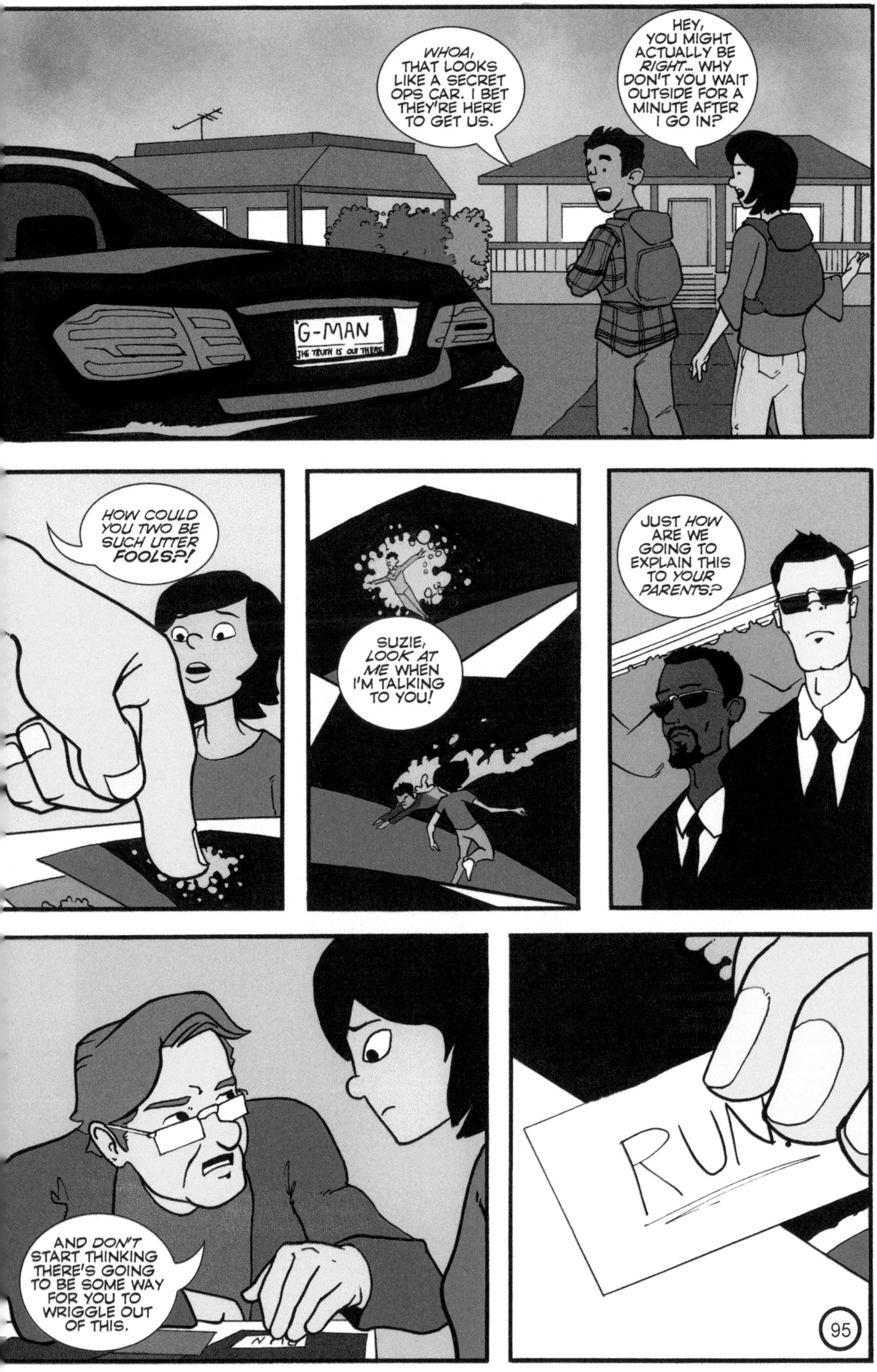
WHOA, THAT LOOKS LIKE A SECRET OPS CAR. I BET THEY'RE HERE TO GET US.
HEY, YOU MIGHT ACTUALLY BE RIGHT... WHY DON'T YOU WAIT OUTSIDE FOR A MINUTE AFTER I GO IN?
G-MAN
THE TRUTH IS OUT THERE
HOW COULD YOU TWO BE SUCH UTTER FOOLS?!
SUZIE, LOOK AT ME WHEN I'M TALKING TO YOU!
JUST HOW ARE WE GOING TO EXPLAIN THIS TO YOUR PARENTS?
AND DON'T START THINKING THERE'S GOING TO BE SOME WAY FOR YOU TO WRIGGLE OUT OF THIS.
RUN

Lab Reports

There's even more science to be found behind the story of Suzie and Diego's adventures. Teachers and curious readers, read on for lab reports with more science specifics that explain certain events in *CheMystery.*

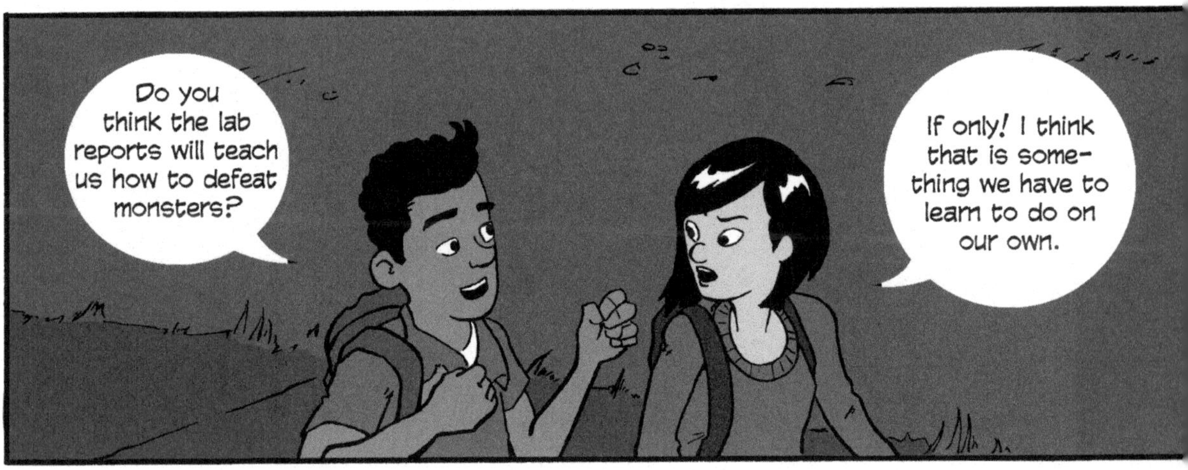
Do you think the lab reports will teach us how to defeat monsters?
If only! I think that is some-thing we have to learn to do on our own.

CHE[M⁺]YSTERY LAB REPORTS
"A Matter of Facts"

PAGE 8

Paraffin wax is a substance used in many different products.

They are made of long carbon chains, around 24 atoms long, bonded together saturated with the rest of its bonds to hydrogen atoms, which in short is called an alkane molecule.

These are wonderful hydrophobic molecules that can come from petroleum or can be made synthetically in high purity.

$$CH_3-(CH_2)_{24}-CH_3$$

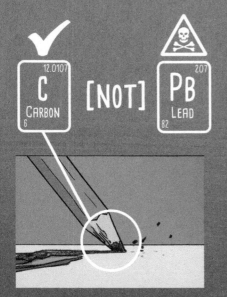

$^{12.0107}$ C CARBON 6 **[NOT]** ^{207} PB LEAD 82

PAGE 10

That lead in your pencil is not lead.

If it were you would not be allowed to use it for fear of poisoning.

It is really graphite, which is a pure carbon molecule.

Interestingly, diamond is made of pure carbon molecules, called an allotrope, and the only difference is the angle in which the atoms bond.

PAGE 11

There are multiple ways to create oil paints, which can produce different textures, colors and longevity.

If you're interested in making your own paint I encourage you to play around with the process to discover how each component impacts the final product.

REFINED LINSEED OIL

DRY PIGMENTS

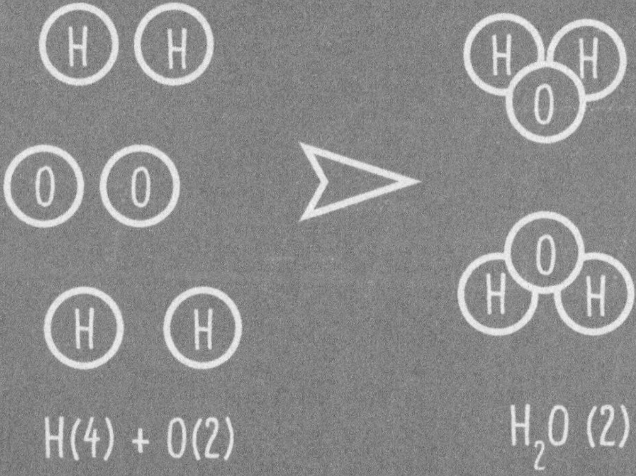

$H(4) + O(2)$

$H_2O (2)$

PAGE 12

Chemical reactions are when two atoms or compounds chemically combine by sharing or transferring electrons to become a new compound, which has completely different properties.

A polymerization reaction is a type of reaction used to link molecules together.

PAGE 14

How doesn't enjoy a good fart joke? What, is it just me?

PAGE 16-24

EDTA is short for Ethylenediaminetetraacetic acid, which is named using organic nomenclature that is different from the nomenclature for non-organic covalent compounds or ionic compounds. EDTA works as a chelating agent, which means it will bond several times to a metal ion. This ability makes the molecule ideal for capturing free metal ions in the body making them inactive and harmless to the body. The acetic acid group lose a hydrogen making the oxygen negative and attractive to positive metal ions that can be poisonous.

ETHYLENE-DI AMINE-TETRA ACETIC ACID

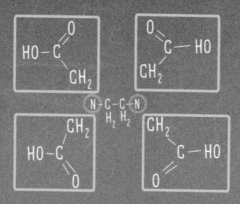

HO—C
O
CH2
C—HO
N-C-C-N
H2 H2

DI = 2
TETRA = 4

H
H
EDTA
M+

LD_{50} VALUES OF VARIOUS CHEMICALS

SUBSTANCE	LD_{50} (MG/KG)
CADMIUM (CD)	1.3+
SELENIUM (SE)	1.3+
ARSENIC (AS)	6+
TABLE SALT (NACL)	3,000=
SUGAR ($C_{12}H_{22}O_{11}$)	30,000=

Everything is poisonous in certain amounts, even water! Sure, cadmium, lead, arsenic and selenium are significantly more poisonous. Toxicologists study how all substances affect us and label materials with an LD 50 , which is the amount of a substance someone would have to consume to kill 50% of the population. Because our bodies are complex entities not all of us will die by consuming the same amount of a substance.

There is a tremendous amount of science that goes into baking, some of which was covered in these pages.

I strongly suggest watching Alton Brown's TV series Good Eats, especially season 2, episode 22 for the science behind making a pound cake.

He is truly a culinary scientist.

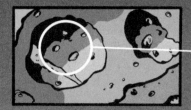

SMALL POCKETS ARE LEFT BEHIND AS THE WATER LEAVES THE CAKE

HEAT CHANGES THE STATE OF H_2O FROM A LIQUID TO A GAS

A MATTER OF FACTS

CLASSIFYING MATTER

Pure Substance- A substance that is the same throughout. (All of one type of atom, compound or molecule).

Element- The simplest form of matter, the simplest of which is Hydrogen and all are found on the table, periodically.

Compound- A substance made of two or more atoms chemically bonded together.

Mixture- A substance made of 2 or more different elements or compounds.

Heterogeneous Mixture- A type of mixture that does not have the same composition throughout.

Homogeneous Mixture- A type of mixture that looks the same throughout its composition.

PROPERTIES & CHANGES

Physical Property- A property that can be measured without altering the chemical composition.

Intensive- Does not depend on the amount of a substance.

Extensive- Does depend on the amount of a substance.

Chemical Property- A property that is indicative of its ability to react.

Physical Change- A change in a substance that does not alter the chemical composition.

Chemical Change- A change in a substance that does alter the chemical composition.

GO EVEN DEEPER WITH THE AWESOME RESOURCES AT ATOMICUNIVERSE.ORG!

CHE[M⁺]YSTERY LAB REPORTS
"Atomic Insight"

PAGE 31

Democritus (born around 460 BC and died around 370 BC) is widely credited for the first concept of the atom but he studied under Leucippus, who may have also contributed to this concept. He was alive during the time of Aristotle. Unfortunately, his concept of the elements (earth, wind, fire, water and aether) was not widely accepted for hundreds of years.

JAMMIN' OUT WITH THE ELEMENTS!

PAGE 33-34

Melanin is a polymer made by our bodies to protect us from harmful sunlight. Eumelanin, which is depicted on page 34, is better at blocking UV light than the lighter melanin, pheomelanin. Both are made from amino acids.

Aloe Vera can help the skin in many ways; in this instance the major component would be through the antioxidant properties of its metallothionein protein.

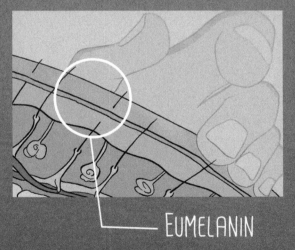

EUMELANIN

(EWWWWW- MELANIN)

PAGE 35-37:

The beginning of the twentieth century saw an explosion of discoveries about the atom. Thomson's lab in England was the working space as many of the most famous scientists in human history practiced there. Even Bohr worked in Thomson's lab but only for a brief while, as there were difficulties, before he joined Rutherford's lab to compose his masterful work. James Chadwick is a brilliant scientist, often not given his due, for discovering neutrons. Neutrons were very difficult for scientists to discover since they have no charge.

ATOMI-WOW!

PAGE 42

Protons and neutrons go together like peanut butter and jelly, one held together by the strong force and the other by bread. Just like there's a perfect ratio of peanut butter to jelly for you there's also a perfect ratio of protons to neutrons; the ratio varies for each element just as it does for each person. When the proton to neutron ratio is askew it causes the atom to be radioactive. Releasing radioactive decay is how the nucleus rids itself of extra protons or neutrons to reach the sweet spot.

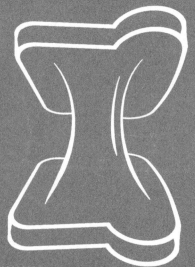

PAGE 43

Radiation can fundamentally alter your DNA. If radioactive decay with the right amount of energy hits an atom in the DNA strand it can alter that element, eventually leading to nothing or cancer. If the energy is intense it can just burn the cells and the more cells it destroys the more serious the burn. Radiation is nothing to play with. Doctors can use it in targeted applications to help us in some instances but overall, radiation is bad.

PAGE 45-48

This is getting into a bit of quantum theory. Electrons behave like both particles and waves. The famous double slit experiment exemplifies this. Shoot electrons at a single slit and it will behave like particles and make a single line but shoot them at a double slit and they will behave like waves. How electrons behave depends on your method of observation! Confused? No worries, it's wacky stuff and we are still trying to understand it.

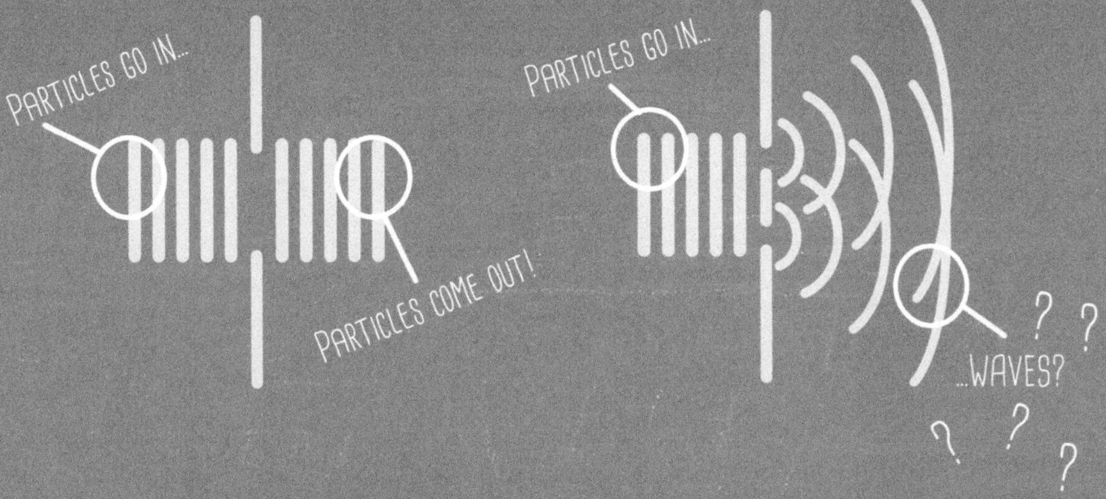

PARTICLES GO IN...
PARTICLES COME OUT!
PARTICLES GO IN...
...WAVES?

MY FAVORITE COLOR IS ULTRA-VIOLET...

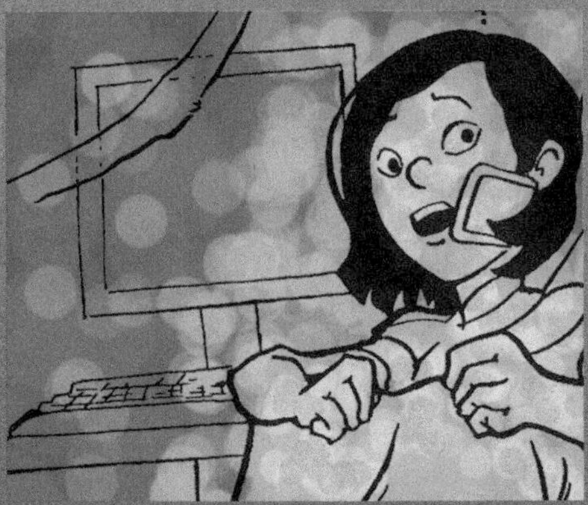

...BUT YOU'VE PROBABLY NEVER SEEN IT!

The electromagnetic spectrum (EMS) is huge. The visible spectrum, which we see in, is only a small portion of it. These waves can be longer or shorter which can put them in a range we cannot see. Suzie and Diego have gained ability to select which part of the EMS that they see. For those of us without super powers, we have night vision goggles to be able to see infrared waves (which shows heat) and we wear sunglasses to keep the ultraviolet (UV) waves out.

Diego is able to see deeper and deeper into materials, so the scale becomes increasingly smaller, from a piece of wood all the way to its atoms. Each scale is almost like it's own world. Think about how different life would be if you were a chemical in a cell or an atom in a sea of other atoms instead of a person in this macro-world.

As Diego zooms in he sees a certain isotope of carbon: carbon-14. This isotope of carbon is used to date how old a material is. If this tree died yesterday or 100 years ago it will have a different amount of C-14. A living thing intakes a certain amount of C-14 but when it dies it stops and existing C-14 undergoes radioactive decay.

Suzie sees ozone form. Ozone is very important to our environment. If it is in our air it can be a dangerous oxidant, which is why smog is dangerous to breathe. However, ozone is a good thing in the upper atmosphere to block some of the harmful rays from the sun.

PROTON: A POSITIVELY CHARGED SUBATOMIC PARTICLE. WEIGHS APPROXIMATELY 1 AMU (ATOMIC MASS UNIT). LOCATED IN A NUCLEUS.

NEUTRON: A NEUTRAL SUBATOMIC PARTICLE WEIGHS APPROXIMATELY 1 AMU. LOCATED IN A NUCLEUS.

NUCLEUS: A VERY SMALL, HIGH-DENSITY PART OF AN ATOM LOCATED IN THE CENTER. IT CONTAINS PROTONS AND NEUTRONS AND THUS CONTAINS THE MAJORITY OF THE MASS OF AN ATOM.

ELECTRON: A NEGATIVELY CHARGED SUBATOMIC PARTICLE. WEIGHS TWO THOUSAND TIMES LESS THAN A NEUTRON. LOCATED IN AN ELECTRON CLOUD.

ELECTRON CLOUD: LOW-DENSITY AREA OF THE ATOM OCCUPIED BY ELECTRONS AND TAKES UP MAJORITY OF THE SPACE OF AN ATOM.

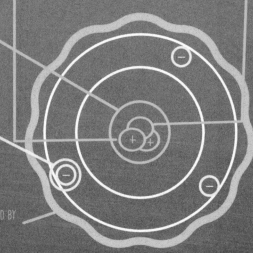

GO EVEN DEEPER WITH THE AWESOME RESOURCES AT ATOMICUNIVERSE.ORG!

CHE[M+]YSTERY LAB REPORTS

"Nuclear Knowledge"

PAGE 54-59

Nuclear Equations are used to explain what happens in a specific nuclear reaction.

Example: A Helium-4 atom merges with a Nitrogen-14 atom to produce a Hydrogen-1 atom and an Oxygen-16 atom.

URANIUM-238 SPLITS TO PRODUCE THORIUM-234 AND HELIUM-4

$$^{238}_{92}U \rightarrow ^{234}_{90}TH + ^{4}_{2}HE$$

Fission and Fusion
Fission is when an atom's nucleus splits into multiple atoms. This is currently the process we use to generate nuclear power.

Fusion is when two or more atoms come together to form one atom. This type of reaction is what powers the sun.

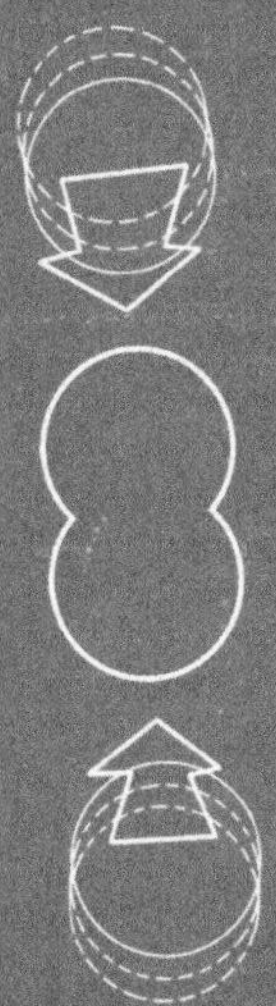

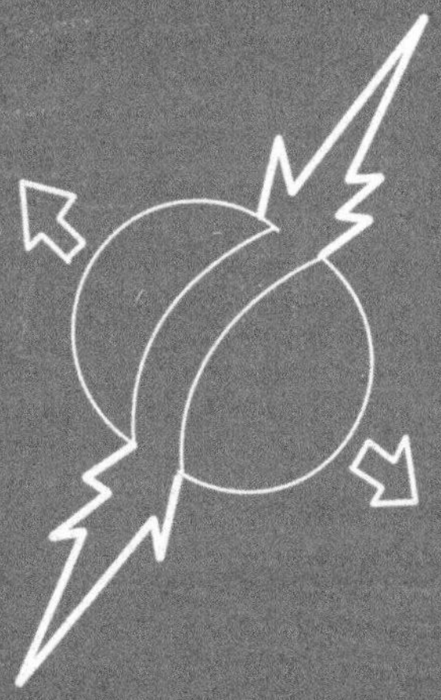

Types of radiation:
There are 3 main types discussed: alpha, beta and gamma.

Alpha radiation has a helium nucleus and can be stopped by paper.

Beta radiation has an electron and can go through paper but can be stopped by aluminum.

Gamma radiation is pure energy and can go through paper and aluminum but can be stopped by thick lead.

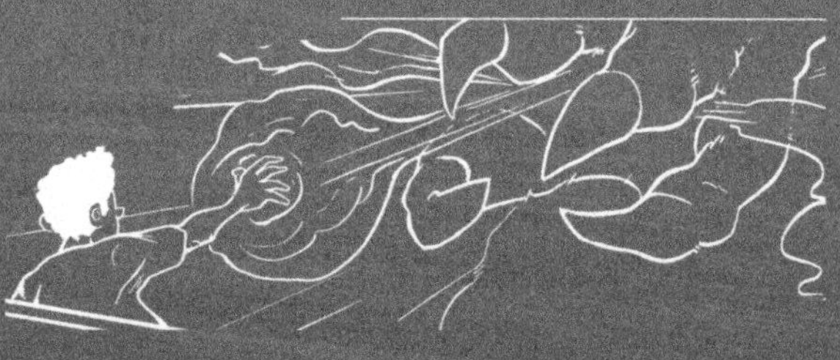

CHEMISTRY, BIOLOGY, YOU SHOULD NEVER BE LATE FOR CLASS!

FIRST?
READ LAB
PROC

PAGE 65

How did biology end up in here? Well, biology is just applied chemistry. (I do not recommend telling your biology teacher that).

LESS MASS

PAGE 67-68

$E=mc^2$ look familiar? It's Einstein's famous equation. This equation shows us how mass is converted to energy and vice versa.
Energy (E) = mass (m) x speed of light squared (c^2)
In fusion there's mass lost when forming the nucleus and this mass is converted into energy. Since fusion is what powers our sun you can imagine the amount of power that is given off.

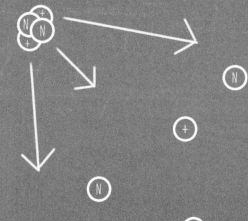

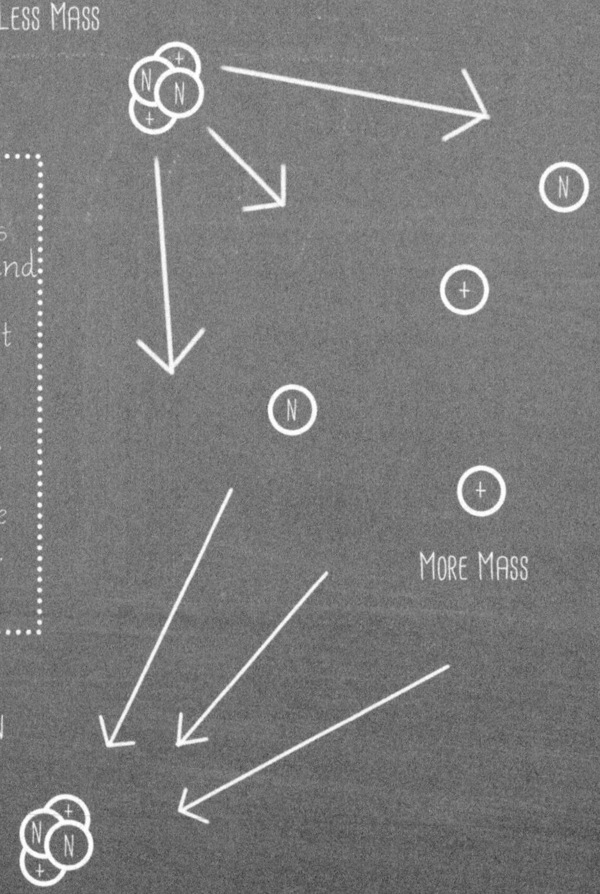

MORE MASS

LESS MASS AGAIN

GO EVEN DEEPER WITH THE AWESOME RESOURCES AT ATOMICUNIVERSE.ORG!

CHE[M⁺]YSTERY LAB REPORTS

"Quantum Boogaloo"

PAGE 82

Electron Cloud- when looking at an atom with all the orbitals, it looks like a cloud.

Ion- charged particle.
Cation- positively charged particle.
Anion- negatively charged particle.

Isotope- an atom with a certain mass. Not all atoms of a certain element have the same mass, as they can have differing numbers of neutrons.

Electromagnetic Radiation- where electric and magnetic fields vary simultaneously like visible light, x-rays and radio waves.

Bohr Model vs. Quantum Mechanical Model- the Bohr model puts electrons inhabiting energy levels whereas the quantum mechanical model puts them in orbitals.

Quantum- the amount of energy required to move an electron from one energy level to another.

Ground State- an electron at its lowest possible energy level.

Excited State- an electron that is at a high energy level, then the lowest available.

Electron Cloud

Al^{13+}
He^{2+}
Os^{76+}
Au^{79+}
Sc^{21+}
Ca^{20+}
Th^{90+}
Ir^{77+}
Pb^{82+}
H^{+}

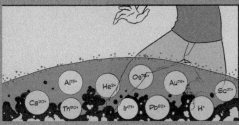

EVEN SUZIE CAN'T REPEL CHARGES OF THIS MAGNITUDE!

BOHR MODEL

VS

QUANTUM MECHANIC MODEL

CHEMISTRY IS ANYTHING BUT BOHR-ING!

SHOOM!

DONT TRY THIS AT HOME KIDS!

Visible Spectrum (ROY G BIV)- the visible part of the electromagnetic spectrum (red, orange, yellow, green, blue, indigo, violet).

Continuous Spectra- a continuation from color to color, like a rainbow.

Line Spectra (Atomic Emission Spectra)- when a single atom is excited it gives off specific colors of light and the few colors that are given off create lines, thus line spectra.

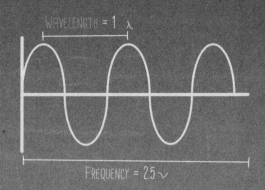

WAVELENGTH = 1 λ

FREQUENCY = 2.5 ν

WAVELENGTH THE LENGTH OF A WAVE TROUGH TO TROUGH OR CREST TO CREST.

FREQUENCY: THE NUMBER OF WAVES THAT TRAVEL THROUGH IN ONE SECOND.

TALK ABOUT SOAKING UP THE SUN!

Wavelength/Frequency Calculations. $c = \lambda \nu$ this equation shows the relationship between the speed of light, wavelength and frequency. The speed of light is constant, in a vacuum, and by changing the frequency it will alter the wavelength and vice versa.

Energy Calculations. $E = h\nu$ this equation shows the relationship between energy, frequency and Plank's constant. Plank's constant does not change so when the energy changes the frequency will change and vice versa.

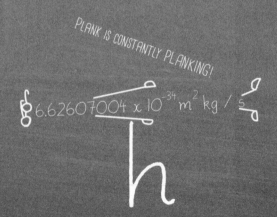

PLANK IS CONSTANTLY PLANKING!

$6.62607004 \times 10^{-34}$ m^2 kg / s

h

About the Illustrator

I hate writing about myself, so I'll tell you about some of my experience making this comic. When I was in high school, I moved to a different state, and wound up taking biology twice. So, to me, the territory we cover in this book is incredibly technical. Luckily, Chris is a good teacher. I can only imagine how interesting his chemistry classes are.

We only have models of what atoms look like because no one's actually seen one. This presented an interesting design challenge for me. When I was coming up with the look for the kids' atomic-level vision quests, I drew inspiration from some paintings by Lora Zombie. (My wife and I have a couple of her paintings up right now.) I wanted the space within atoms to look like, well, space.

Josh Reynolds comes from a military household, and has seen almost every corner of the U.S. He started drawing at the age of six, made his first comics at the age of thirteen, and at twenty-two, earned his BFA in Sequential Art from the Savannah College of Art and Design.

See more of my work here: behance.net/JoshReynolds
And here: instagram.com/josh_reynolds_draws/

About the Author

C. A. Preece is a high school chemistry teacher in central Kentucky and a graduate student at the University of Kentucky studying S.T.E.M. education, where he aims to research the effects of learning chemistry through comics.

C. A. grew up on Meathouse Road in Martin County, Kentucky for most of his childhood. He later attended Morehead State University (MSU) for a B.S. in chemistry, the University of Kentucky for chemistry graduate school, and returned to MSU for a M.A. in teaching. C. A. has been teaching high school since 2010.

Comics have always been a passion for C. A. as he bought his first for a dime from his uncle Dan at the age of 4. His love of comics and science have merged in his website atomicuniverse.org, panels at comic conventions on science in comics, and science consulting on a couple comic series (*Solar: Man of the Atom* by Frank Barbiere and *Lazarus* by Greg Ruka).

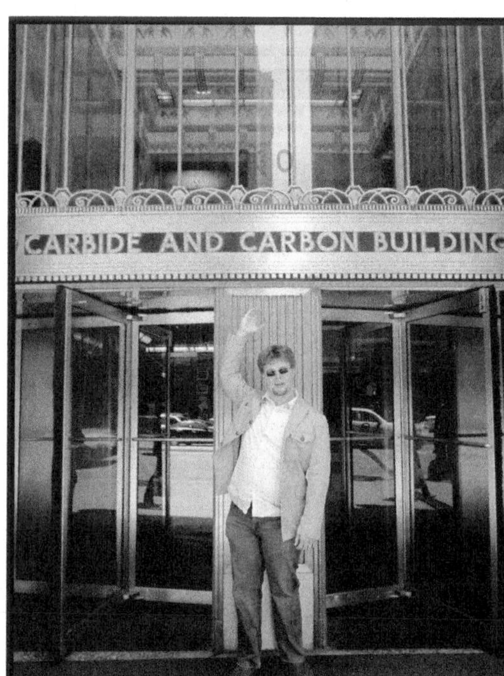
CARBIDE AND CARBON BUILDIN

Acknowledgements

Oh, my! It's here... in your hands I mean. What a remarkable journey it has been for this to be in your hands. I had an idea of creating an engaging narrative using the comic medium to help my students learn chemistry and about two years later that product is released to the public and now in your hands. This is amazing to me. As much work and love as I put into this I would not have been able to complete it without amazing people continuing to love and inspire me. My friends Keil Williams, Sara Perkins, Drew Needham, Amanda Hamilton, Liz Prather, Charlotte Heycraft, and Christine Gutierrez who all helped me by proof reading, listening to me yammer on or helped me keep going by lending a supportive hand. My family who have always loved and supported me through all my crazy ideas: Nina (grandma), Ricky (dad), Mary (step mom), Melania (aunt), Carrie (aunt), my beloved late grandpa (Bill) and late uncle (Jim). Most of all, I have to tip my hat to the man who started and continues to foster my love of comics, my uncle Dan.

Now, of course I must thank all those who have worked on this one-of-a-kind chemistry comic: Hannah for editing and being amazingly supportive, Kyle and Brandi for doing great work on the science sections, Josh and Rachel for working so hard to make every page you see beautiful, and finally Rachel and Robert who took a chance on my crazy idea!

- C.A. Preece -

CPSIA information can be obtained
at www.ICGtesting.com
Printed in the USA
FSOW04n0156280517
34557FS

9 781634 110082